Recipes from Historic

CALIFORNIA

Other Books by the Authors

Recipes from Historic America

Recipes from Historic Colorado

Recipes from Historic Louisiana

Recipes from Historic Texas

The Great American Sampler Cookbook

At Ease in the White House

The New American Sampler Cookbook

The American Sampler Cookbook

How to Sell to the United States Government

The Homeschool Handbook

Recipes from Historic

CALIFORNIA

A Restaurant Guide and Cookbook

LINDA & STEVE BAUER

Taylor Trade Publishing
Lanham • New York • Boulder • Toronto • Plymouth, UK

If you would like to share comments about the book, ask the authors to lecture for your group, or you desire autographed copies, please contact us at bauerbooks@gmail.com

Published by Taylor Trade Publishing
An imprint of The Rowman & Littlefield Publishing Group, Inc.
4501 Forbes Boulevard, Suite 200, Lanham, Maryland 20706
www.rlpgtrade.com

Distributed by NATIONAL BOOK NETWORK

Library of Congress Cataloging-in-Publication Data
Bauer, Linda.
 Recipes from historic California : a restaurant guide and cookbook / Linda and Steve Bauer.
    p. cm.
 ISBN-13: 978-1-58979-348-4 (cloth : alk. paper)
 ISBN-10: 1-58979-348-X (cloth : alk. paper)
 eISBN-13: 978-1-58979-400-9
 eISBN-10: 1-58979-400-1
 1. Cookery, American—California style. 2. Restaurants—California—Guidebooks. 3. Historic buildings—California—Guidebooks. I. Bauer, Steve, 1943– II. Title.
 TX715.2.C34B38 2008
 641.59794—dc22   2008014862

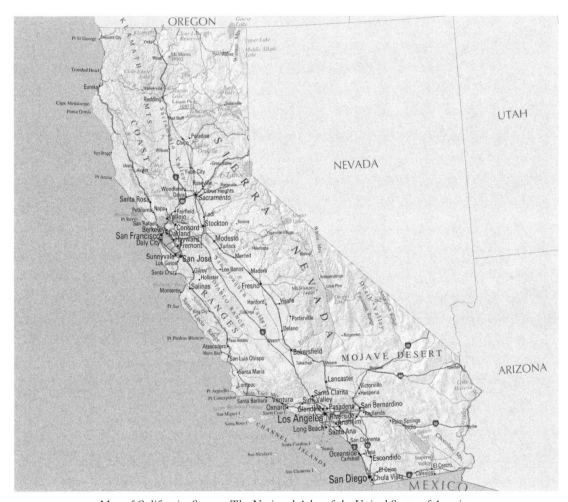

Map of California. Source: The National Atlas of the United States of America.

CONTENTS

INTRODUCTION

Enchantment lingers whenever the mention of California appears. It is the number-one destination for travel and tourism in the entire United States. More than $75 billion of direct travel spending occurs in California. More than 65 percent of the total travel dollars comes from Californians themselves, while they are simply enjoying and exploring the multifaceted environs of their vast state.

Friendly and carefree Californians enjoy a greater number of climates, landforms, and geographical regions than residents in any other state in the United States. The many varied types of terrain range from mountains, beaches, forests, and huge cities to rolling hills, lakes, and deserts. Historian Kevin Starr described the climates along the coasts and valley as the "American Mediterranean." The California coastline stretches for 1,264 miles from Oregon to Mexico with some of the most breathtaking scenery in all of America. More than half of the people reside in the coastal area and most of those live in San Diego Bay, the Los Angeles Basin, and the San Francisco Bay Area.

The semiarid or steppe climate covers areas of the San Joaquin Valley and the edge of the Mojave Desert. Much of this region is the reason for including the state in the Sunbelt. The Central Valley is located between the Coastal Ranges and the Sierra Nevada, more than 400 miles long and about 50 miles wide. It is the most fertile and productive agricultural area in the state, and arguably one of the most fertile and productive areas in the world.

The desert climate resides in the southeastern third of the state and the alpine is located in the highest elevations of the Klamath Mountains, Sierra Nevada, and the Modoc Plateau. Mt. Whitney, the highest point in the United States outside of Alaska, rises 14,495 feet above sea level in the Sequoia National Park. Residents love to indulge in the accompanying sports, history, and varieties of fresh food. Whether it is mixed greens on the golf course or in the salad bowl, California is known for plenty of excellent outdoor activities and fresh and lively foods.

California boasts countless travel and tourism destinations with food, entertainment, and sports for all ages and interest. The state is a paradise for travelers, especially history buffs, to enjoy the vast array of sites from missions to hotels, seascapes, bridges, and forested parks.

Only California has the quail as the state bird, the grizzly bear as the state animal, the California coast redwood or Sequoia as the official tree, and the golden poppy as the state flower. The beauty of the state is further depicted with the state marine mammal as the gray whale. The golden trout is the state fish and the desert tortoise is the state reptile. Furthermore, gold is the official mineral of the Golden State and is treasured due to its beauty and scarcity. Gold has played a large part in the history of the state seen through the mists of time. The discovery at Sutter's Mill on January 24, 1848, made news throughout the world and ushered in a wave of both immigration and statehood.

California has been blessed with a rich history of more than thirty different ethnic groups. Indians, Anglos, Africans, Mexicans, and Asians have all added to the life of California. They have worked together to form a variety of cuisines using the freshest ingredients. California cooking is world famous. No wonder the state motto, "Eureka, I have found it!," which referred to the gold discovery, is sometimes used to describe the perfect meal.

In our more than twenty years of writing international food and travel columns, we have been amazed at the way an excellent restaurant with a special atmosphere enhances any dining experience or vacation. The combination of a historic venue combined with interesting cuisine, whether it is Southwest, California, Oriental, classic, or family style, is a dining adventure. It is exciting to enjoy a great meal at a former cruise ship, a bank, historic hotel, or an old stagecoach stop.

Simply choose one of the regions and decide which historic restaurants to visit. The restaurant is described with a page or more of history. The location and way to contact the restaurant is offered along with several recipes, which are served on the menu.

After a visit, the diner may wish to recreate the dish at home. Our experience has shown that many people love to read cookbooks and travel guides. This book aims to please both and allows singles, couples, and families to learn a great deal of information about California history and enjoy the bounty of fresh produce, livestock, and excellent chefs.

Most of the restaurants are in the moderate range, but they do vary. We attempted to include all ranges. If cost is a factor, please phone for the price.

Remember—many of the restaurants in *Recipes from Historic California* are very popular and it is important to *call ahead for reservations*!

Bon Appétit!

Northern California

—

In the High Sierra, the Cordillera splits California in half with two different views of the state. Whitewater rivers, charming towns, and national parks dot the west. Ski resorts, western towns, and deep blue lakes are sprinkled across the east. This is often referred to as California's Recreational Playground.

The San Francisco Bay Area is often called California's Casablanca. This area is comprised of vineyards, the fantastic Golden Gate Bridge, and many distinctly different communities. Fresh seafood, cable cars, Coit Tower, Lombard Street, Haight-Ashbury, and the colorful Victorian houses known as the Painted Ladies all make for a thoroughly interesting city.

Tall trees, succulent wine grapes, and rolling hills are part of the beauty of the north coast. Stately elk, magnificent Sequoias, and remote lighthouses draw visitors from all over the world. Delicious oysters thrive in chilly Humboldt Bay and grace the menus of many restaurants. Historic parks and railroads offer a chance to relive the past.

The Gold Country is the most historic area of the state because in 1848 gold was discovered in the area of Sutter's Mill. It was also a strategic stop on the Pony Express route and it is where Mark Twain penned his famous story "The Celebrated Jumping Frog of Calaveras County." Petroglyphs and artifacts of Native Americans are located at Grinding Rock State Park. Jamestown was the backdrop for *Butch Cassidy and the Sundance Kid*.

The Shasta Cascade, comprised of lakes, volcanoes, and mountains, along with the famous Mount Shasta, thrills outdoor adventurers. Theodore Roosevelt once proclaimed Burney Falls the eighth wonder of the world. Near Red Bluff, the William B. Ide Adobe State Historic Park is believed to be the home of the only California Republic President.

"The ultimate [travel destination] for me would be one perfect day in San Francisco. It's a perfect 72 degrees, clear, the sky bright blue. I'd start down at Fisherman's Wharf with someone I really like and end with a romantic dinner and a ride over the Golden Gate Bridge. There's no city like it anywhere. And, if I could be there with the 'girl of my dreams,' that would be the ultimate!"

—Larry King, talk show host

BOUCHON

The history of Yountville is offered in some detail under The French Laundry. Named after George Calvert Yount, who was the first white settler in the area, Yountville has a very storied past.

Yount not only started the grape-growing industry of the Napa Valley right here in the town named for him, but also has an unusual connection to the history of the Old West. Yount is credited with having a part in the rescue of the well-known Donner Party. With the group moving slowly through the mountains in their quest to enter California, one of the leaders, James Frazier Reed, left the main group with a small party to seek a shortcut. The other leaders, brothers George and Jacob Donner, took the rest of the party on a different route, became stranded in the mountains, and were eventually missed at the destination.

Reed did not know what route they had taken but a vivid dream by Yount revealed many precise details. Yount convinced everyone that he knew where the Donner Party was stranded. Reed gathered some supplies and set out with a rescue party to the site described by Yount in his dreams. They found the Donner Party exactly where Yount said they would be. Despite the treacherous winter weather, 48 of the original 87 men, women, and children in that wagon train survived.

Bouchon is a French word that describes a particular style of cafe from the province of Lyon. The restaurant Bouchon opened in 1998 in a historic Wells Fargo stagecoach stop built in the late 1800s. Located in downtown Yountville, Bouchon offers authentic French bistro fare. The restaurant's interior features a unique mosaic floor, burgundy velvet banquettes, antique light fixtures, and an expansive hand-painted mural by the noted French artist Paulin Paris. If you have never seen a French zinc bar, you must visit Bouchon just for the opportunity to admire one.

Summer months in Yountville are perfect for a great French meal or just an appetizer and cocktail on the outdoor patio.

Bouchon
6534 Washington Street
Yountville, California 94599
(707) 944-8037

1 ounce (2 tablespoons) Cirac
vodka

½ ounce (1 tablespoon) Lillet

½ ounce (1 tablespoon) Crème de
Pêche

Ice

Lemon twist

Orange twist

Bouchon Martini

Mix the vodka, Lillet, and Crème de Pêches with ice
and strain into a cold martini glass. Garnish with the
lemon and orange twists.

YIELD
1 drink

Day Boat Scallops with Parsnip Puree and Cider Beurre Blanc

PARSNIP PUREE

In a medium pot, bring the parsnips, milk, and butter almost to a boil, then lower the heat and simmer gently until very tender. Drain, reserving the cooking liquid. Puree the parsnips in a food processor until smooth. Season to taste. Transfer to a clean pot and set aside, covered, to keep warm.

BEURRE BLANC

While the parsnips are cooking, combine the cider, shallots, peppercorns, and bay leaves in a heavy stainless steel pot. Bring to a boil and then lower the heat to a strong simmer. Cook until the cider is reduced to about 2 cups syrup. Remove from the heat.

Whisk in the butter piece by piece, until it is all incorporated and the liquid is satiny. Strain through a fine mesh strainer into a small pot. Keep warm.

APPLES

Combine 1 cup of water, the wine, sugar, bay leaf, cloves, and star anise in a heavy stainless steel pot. Bring to a boil and stir until the sugar dissolves. Lower the heat so the liquid just barely simmers. Add the apples and poach until just tender.

Drain the apples and dry them thoroughly with paper towels. Melt butter in a heavy skillet over medium-high heat. When the butter is bubbling, add the apples

PARSNIP PUREE

2 pounds parsnips, peeled and roughly chopped

1 quart whole milk

¼ pound (1 stick) butter

Salt and freshly ground pepper

BEURRE BLANC

1 quart apple cider

2 shallots, sliced

6 whole black peppercorns

2 bay leaves

½ pound (2 sticks) cold butter, cut into cubes

APPLES

1 cup water

3 cups white wine

1 cup sugar

1 bay leaf

2 whole cloves

1 piece star anise

2 flavorful apples, preferably organic, peeled, halved, and cored

1 tablespoon unsalted butter

(continued on next page)

6

SCALLOPS

16 large dayboat scallops

Salt and freshly ground pepper

Clarified butter

GARNISH

¼ cup skinned hazelnuts, toasted
and lightly crushed

cut-side down. Sauté until golden, then turn over and reduce the heat to low to keep them warm.

SCALLOPS

Dry the scallops thoroughly with paper towels. Season lightly with salt and pepper. Over high heat, melt just enough clarified butter in a large heavy skillet to film the bottom; pour out any excess. (If you don't have a skillet large enough to hold the scallops in one layer, cook them in batches.) When the butter is very hot but not smoking, place a layer of scallops in the pan. Let them cook undisturbed for about 2 minutes, until golden on the bottom. Quickly turn them over with tongs and sear the other side until golden. (If you are cooking the scallops in two batches, remove the first batch from the pan and set them aside on a plate, loosely covered with foil to keep warm. Wipe out the pan, add more clarified butter, and when it is hot, cook the remaining scallops.)

To serve, reheat the parsnip puree if necessary, adding a little of the cooking liquid if it seems too thick. Plate up! Drizzle four plates with beurre blanc (white butter). Divide the parsnip puree among the plates, top each with an apple half, cut side up, and arrange the scallops around the apple. Fill the center of the apple with more sauce, and sprinkle hazelnuts over everything.

YIELD

Serves 4

CALISTOGA INN

Construction of the Calistoga Inn was completed in 1882 by an entrepreneurial family from Italy. They were attracted to the area after the pioneer Sam Brannan bought the hot sulphur springs property nearby to build the "Saratoga of the Pacific." The area would eventually become present-day Calistoga.

The inn grew in popularity and, by the 1930s, its reputation had reached all the way to Southern California. Hollywood stars Carol Lombard and Charles Laughton filmed a movie at the Calistoga Inn about an Italian grape-grower from Napa (which is actually 25 miles away) and his mail-order bride.

Five major wars, the Depression, and periods of neglect have certainly challenged the inn, but it survived and even thrived. Contrary to all the neighbors who were busily expanding their wine operations, the inn gave birth to Calistoga Beer and the Napa Valley Brewing Company in 1987. For the first time in more than half a century, beer was brewed commercially in Napa County. Within two years, the brewery had hired a full-time, dedicated brewmaster and was regularly producing its four principal beers, Calistoga Wheat Ale, Calistoga Pilsner, Calistoga Red Ale, and Calistoga Porter.

A mother-and-son team runs the business. Susan "Rosie" Dunsford was the founder and principle owner of the popular Rosie's Café at Lake Tahoe. She now oversees the food operations with Executive Chef Jon Roscher. Son Michael Dunsford Jr. studied the principles of wine-making and brewing in college. He now manages the hotel, restaurant, and brewery.

Today, the inn offers patio dining on the banks of the Napa River, as well as indoor dining in a room reminiscent of the early days of Calistoga. An authentic 18-room, turn-of-the-century inn and a modern microbrewery, nestled in the original water tower, complete the property.

Calistoga Inn Restaurant and Brewery
1250 Lincoln Avenue
Calistoga, California 94515
(707) 942-4101

3 cups good-quality mayonnaise

2 to 3 tablespoons curry powder
(to taste)

1 teaspoon dry mustard

1 teaspoon kosher or sea salt

½ teaspoon coarsely ground black
pepper

3 dashes Tabasco sauce

⅓ cup grated red onion (about 1
small onion)

Curry Dip

This is really good with roasted asparagus or vegetable crudités.

Mix all the ingredients in a small bowl, cover, and chill.

Note: It is important to grate the onion, not chop it.

YIELD

About 3½ cups

Lake County Pear Cake

This cake is also delicious made with apples instead of pears.

Preheat the oven to 325 degrees. Butter a 10-inch tube or Bundt pan. Sprinkle it lightly with breadcrumbs and shake to distribute them all over the inside. Knock out any extra. (This cake likes to stick to a pan that is only buttered. Dry breadcrumbs will release a cake better than butter and flour would.)

With a spoon or electric mixer, cream the butter and sugar. Beat in the eggs one at a time.

Sift the flour, then sift it again with the soda, salt, cinnamon, and mace or nutmeg.

Gradually stir the dry ingredients into the butter-sugar-egg mixture with a spoon. When all of the flour mixture has been added, briefly mix with an electric mixer to ensure that the ingredients are well combined.

Using a large spoon or spatula, fold in the pears and walnuts. Pour the batter into the prepared pan.

Bake for 1 to 1¼ hours, until a tester in the middle of the cake comes out clean. Cool slightly in the pan, then turn out onto a wire rack to cool completely. If some of the cake has stuck to the pan, remove the pieces from

½ pound (2 sticks) butter at room temperature, plus extra for the pan

Very fine dry breadcrumbs

2 cups sugar

3 large eggs

3 cups all-purpose flour

1½ teaspoons baking soda

½ teaspoon salt

1 teaspoon ground cinnamon

1 teaspoon ground mace or grated nutmeg

3 cups chopped peeled ripe pears

2 cups chopped walnuts

Lime-Ginger Cream (recipe follows)

LIME–GINGER CREAM

½ cup heavy cream

1 cup sour cream

⅓ cup chopped candied ginger

2 tablespoons sugar

1½ teaspoons grated lime zest

the pan and patch the cake while it is warm; it will cool to perfection.

Serve with dollops of Lime-Ginger Cream.

LIME–GINGER CREAM

Whip the heavy cream to soft peaks. Fold in the sour cream, ginger, sugar, and lime zest.

YIELD

One 10-inch cake

THE CLAREMONT RESORT & SPA

"One of the few hotels in the world with warmth, character, and charm."

—Frank Lloyd Wright, architect

The gold rush of 1849 brought thousands of people to California, all hoping to get rich—though only some did. Bill Thornburg, a Kansas farmer, was one of the lucky ones. He brought his wife and daughter with him, and their dreams of living in a castle became a reality when Bill struck it rich.

He used his new wealth to purchase 13,000 acres of the old Peralta and Vicente Spanish land grants. This was the site for his "castle" which included several stables and facilities for raising foxes. Thornburg went so far as to hire British grooms to care for the horses, supervise the fox population, and organize foxhunts in the California countryside. The estate served the family well for several years.

When the daughter grew up, she married a British Lord and moved with him to England. Shortly thereafter, Bill's wife died and he sold the property to the Ballard family. In July of 1901, while the Ballards were out on the estate, a fire erupted. Fueled by a dry and windy day, the "castle," built of wood rather than stone, burned to the ground. The winds even carried the flames across the hills and destroyed a number of other homes before it was contained.

Except for the livery stables, barn, and some of the costly furnishings, the castle was virtually a total loss. It sat in ruins for several years until Frank Havens and his partner "Borax" Smith took control. They hoped to build a hotel so grand that it would have trains running directly in the lobby. Legend has it that the two men played a game of chance, either cards or checkers, and Havens won. He and his Claremont Hotel Company began construction in 1905, but the San Francisco earthquake of 1906 and the resulting economic uncertainty caused a substantial delay.

The new hotel finally was completed in 1915 as the sprawling Mediterranean hostelry seen today. With a lobby larger than almost any other hotel on the West Coast, an onsite private school, and radio station, The Claremont Hotel was one of the nation's grand transient and resident hotels. In 1937, Claude Gillum, an employee since 1926, purchased the property for $250,000 and virtually rebuilt it from the foundation up, completely renovating the interior.

A state law prohibited the sale of alcohol within a one-mile radius of the University of California. Because the hotel is situated on the borderline between Berkeley and Oakland, it was presumed

to be within the one-mile radius. Thus, not allowed to serve liquor, The Claremont was without a bar. An enterprising female student at the University became suspicious of everyone's assumptions. She and some friends measured the shortest route from the University to the front steps and found that The Claremont was a few feet outside the one-mile radius, meaning a bar could be opened. The Paragon Bar & Café rewarded the woman free drinks for the rest of her life.

The Claremont Resort & Spa
41 Tunnel Road
Berkeley, California 94705
(510) 843-3000

Oven-Roasted Wild Salmon
Spring Pea–Goat Cheese Ravioli
with Baby Artichoke, Roasted Chanterelles, and Barigoule Sauce

PREPARING ARTICHOKES

Place wine, olive oil, water, and mirepoix in a pot along with a bouquet garni, pinch of salt, and half a lemon. Clean the artichokes of needles and cut off tops and tough outer leaves. Place in pot and cook until tender but firm.

Let artichokes cool in broth, then strain and reserve liquid for Barigoule sauce. Pick out the artichokes, clean further if needed, and discard rest of ingredients.

PREPARING SPRING PEA–GOAT CHEESE RAVIOLI

Begin to bring a pot of water up to a boil. Meanwhile, mix goat cheese, blanched peas, 1 tablespoon of tarragon, and lemon zest. Season with a little salt and pepper and set aside. Next, lay down eight wonton wrappers on a cutting board. Divide the filling among the eight wonton skins in a neat little mound in the center. Use a little water or egg wash around the edge. Place another wrapper on top and gently mold around goat-cheese filling. They are ready to boil when fish is cooking.

FINAL STEPS AND PLATING

Coat chanterelles in olive oil and toss with salt and pepper and your choice of shallots and herbs. Place on roasting sheet and roast 5–7 minutes in 350-degree oven.

½ bottle good white wine

1 cup olive oil

1 cup water

Mirepoix (a combination of cut onions, carrots, and celery)

1 bouquet garni (your choice of bay leaf, parsley stems, peppercorns, and thyme sprigs in cheesecloth)

½ lemon

8 baby artichokes, cooked à la Barigoule

8 ounces goat cheese

½ cup fresh English peas, blanched

2 tablespoons tarragon, chopped, divided

1 teaspoon lemon zest

Salt and pepper

16 wonton skins/wrappers, round

Egg wash or water

Vegetable oil, scant for coating

1 pound chanterelles

2 tablespoons olive oil

Choice of chopped fresh herbs, optional

Shallots, chopped, optional

(continued on next page)

 *14*

8 6-ounce salmon fillets, such as
Copper River

1 pint teardrop or grape tomatoes
(3–4 per plate)

1 pint Barigoule sauce

2–3 tablespoons of sweet butter

1 cup micro greens or herb salad

Season salmon fillets with salt, pepper, and remaining tarragon if you want. Sauté in a pan with oil for 3 minutes on each side over medium-high heat. While the fish is cooking, warm the artichokes in about 8 ounces of the cooking liquid.

Meanwhile, drop your raviolis into soft boiling water with salt for 1–2 minutes. When done, remove from water and place in a bowl with a little olive oil and season. Keep warm. Re-warm your chanterelles in pan until hot and add tomatoes. Cook for one minute more. Check seasoning and add herbs if desired.

In dinner bowls, place the artichokes, chanterelles, and tomatoes attractively on bottom. Place the salmon neatly on top.

Next, place the ravioli on the salmon. Take the Barigoule sauce (reduce if necessary) and add 2–3 tablespoons of sweet butter. Incorporate and neatly nap around the fish and vegetables. Garnish with micro greens or herb salad and serve.

Pineapple-Orange Bavarian
Fresh Berries and Raspberry Coulis

Soften gelatin in warm water (soften over heat, if necessary) and keep warm. Bring pineapple and orange juice to a boil, remove from heat and add gelatin, lemon juice, sugar, and salt. Mix thoroughly and cool until slightly thickened. Gently mix in stiffly whipped evaporated milk. Next, pour into either individual molds or one larger one and portion at the table.

PLATING

Unmold Bavarian onto the center of your favorite plate. Drizzle with raspberry sauce around mold. Garnish with seasonal berries, place a mint sprig on the top of mousse, and dust with powdered sugar.

BAVARIAN

2 teaspoons gelatin, granulated

½ cup warm water

1 cup crushed pineapple

1 cup orange juice

1 tablespoon lemon juice

½ cup sugar

Pinch salt

1 cup evaporated milk

GARNISH

1 cup raspberry sauce

1 pint fresh berries

8 mint sprigs

Powdered sugar

POACHING LIQUID

2 cups grenadine

1 cup water

¼ cup honey

3 sticks cinnamon

5 star anise

4 bay leaves

6 whole cloves

RHUBARB

8 settings of rhubarb sticks (2 per setting)

8 3-ounce slices foie gras

8 sticks cinnamon for garnish

8 star anise for garnish

¼ cup ginger, julienned very thin & fried lightly

8 sprigs chervil for garnish

Seared Artisan Foie Gras with Poached Rhubarb, Fried Ginger and Spiced Gastrique

Bring poaching ingredients to a boil and shut off. Place trimmed rhubarb in pan and pour poaching syrup over rhubarb and let gently steep until tender but firm. If rhubarb becomes soft, remove and let liquid cool then pour back over rhubarb. This can be done the day before.

PLATING

Gently warm rhubarb in the poaching liquid and keep warm. Next, season foie gras slices and sear on medium-high in sauté pan for 1–2 minutes on each side. On a square plate (optional), neatly crisscross two pieces of rhubarb in the upper middle of plate, and lean a piece of foie gras against the rhubarb. Drizzle some of the poaching liquid around the foie gras/rhubarb (reduce if necessary) and garnish with a cinnamon stick and star anise. Attractively place a small fried ginger piece on top of the foie gras and garnish with chervil sprig.

YIELD

Serves 8

CLIFF HOUSE

As Mexico and Alta California gained independence from Spain in 1821, the door was opened for immigrants and settlers from around the world. They came in relatively small numbers, until 1848 when gold was discovered at Sutter's Mill. The flood of Forty-Niners the following year precipitated statehood in 1850. Miners and entrepreneurs added to the population boom.

One of these businessmen was C. C. Butler, who recognized a distinction in that customers might want some things but had to have others. Butler gathered some partners and opened the Lone Mountain Cemetery in 1854, certain that business would follow. They expected that there was room there to bury all of the dead of San Francisco for the next fifty years.

In 1863, Butler teamed with John P. Buckley in another business that the public had to have. They built the first Cliff House restaurant overlooking the beautiful shore of the Pacific Ocean. Designed to attract the wealthy members of San Francisco's society, it also enjoyed the attention of Mark Twain and Presidents Grant, Hayes, and Harrison.

Elsewhere, Adolph Sutro, who would later become the San Francisco mayor, arrived in San Francisco in 1850 aboard the steamship *California*. Already possessing some wealth, he went into business offering services to the miners. His fortunes improved dramatically when the silver boom hit in 1859. He established a mill for the separation of silver from the mine tailings, and he invented the Sutro tunnel to make mining more efficient and profitable.

Sutro used his wealth to buy major portions of the land in San Francisco, eventually becoming the largest landowner. In 1881, Sutro bought the Cliff House, then had a railroad built to allow easier access to it by the public.

On Christmas Day, 1894, the original Cliff House burned to the ground. Sutro turned the tragedy into opportunity by rebuilding the Cliff House in the grand style of a French chateau. His vision produced a restaurant with eight levels, spires, and an observation tower that rose 200 feet above sea level. He enjoyed the renewed Cliff House for only two years, and passed away in 1898 after a long illness. He did not live to greet Buffalo Bill or Presidents McKinley and Teddy Roosevelt when they came to see this renowned attraction.

Surprisingly, this enormous structure survived the Great Earthquake and fires of 1906, but once again burned to the ground in 1907. Not everyone thought the French chateau style Cliff House was attractive. At the time of its second demise, the local paper said it had been ". . . a thing of complicated and amazing ugliness."

Sutro's daughter carried on the family tradition and rebuilt the third Cliff House in 1909. This version was a neoclassical design, which continued the luxurious dining that wealthy patrons had come to expect.

The Cliff House remained in the Sutro family until 1952 when it passed to George Whitney, a wealthy local developer. The restaurant was remodeled several times before it was purchased by the National Park Service in 1977. More recent renovations have expanded the facility, adding the new two-story Sutro Wing, which is now the main dining room. The original 1909 structure is now the Bistro, which features an elegant zinc bar and a private dining room that can seat 140.

The Cliff House offers diners breathtaking views of the Pacific Ocean and exceptional meals, with emphasis on seafood and organically grown products. Much of its history is evident in the hundreds of autographed pictures of the rich and famous on display.

Cliff House
1090 Point Lobos Avenue
San Francisco, California 94121
(415) 386-3330

Alaskan Halibut with Parmesan Crust

Mix together the flour, breadcrumbs, and Parmesan cheese in a small mixing bowl. Set aside.

In a second bowl, mix the egg and milk to make an egg wash. Season the halibut filets with salt and pepper. Dredge the halibut filets in the egg wash and then press the filet into the breadcrumb mixture.

Using an oven-safe pan, sear halibut on both sides until golden brown. Place pan in preheated 350-degree oven for 6 minutes or until halibut is cooked through.

LEMON CAPER SAUCE

In a sauté pan, add the wine and the capers. Over high heat, reduce by half. Add fresh lemon juice to taste. Adjust seasoning with salt and white pepper. To finish, add butter, stirring constantly. Pour finished sauce over cooked fish and serve.

YIELD
Serves 4

"Part of the secret of success in life is to eat what you like, and let the food fight it out inside."

—Mark Twain

---

2 tablespoons flour

1 cup Japanese breadcrumbs (panko)

½ cup Parmesan cheese, grated

1 egg

1 cup milk

4 6-ounce halibut filets

LEMON CAPER SAUCE

½ cup white wine

1 tablespoon capers

Splash of lemon juice

Salt

White pepper

2 tablespoons butter

The "Ben Butler" Dungeness Crab Sandwich

½ bunch green onions, chopped fine

3 ounces roasted red peppers, diced (pimentos may be substituted)

½ cup mayonnaise

½ teaspoon Tabasco sauce

1 tablespoon Worcestershire sauce

1 tablespoon dry mustard

1 pound crabmeat, drained

Rye bread

Cheddar cheese, sliced

In 1862, Major General Benjamin Butler commanded Union troops occupying New Orleans. He hanged a man for desecrating the Union flag and the local ladies of the evening who were still loyal to the South reacted. As Union troops patrolled the streets, they emptied their toilets over the balconies onto them, misleading history into thinking they threw toilet seats. How could these events possibly relate to the Cliff House? Seal Rock under the restaurant was dominated by a large male seal who somehow managed to get a real toilet seat lodged around his neck. The locals named him Ben Butler and the Cliff House named a sandwich after him.

Mix the first six ingredients together well. Add the crabmeat and mix until all of the crab is coated.

On each piece of rye bread, spread 2 ounces of mixture. Use two pieces of rye per serving. Place under broiler or salamander until heated through. Add cheddar cheese and heat until melted.

Serve immediately; a small salad makes a nice accompaniment.

World Famous Cliff House Popovers

Combine eggs, salt, and sugar in a mixing bowl. Blend well on medium speed. Add milk and mix well. Lower the speed and add in the flour, about a cup at a time. Mix thoroughly and scrape down sides of bowl if needed. Add the oil and mix for approximately 20 seconds. Chill batter up to two days ahead. This allows the batter to rest and ensures a better product. Batter will appear to have a foam on top when you use it. Simply rewhip the batter with a hand whip before using.

Pour mixture into well-greased and oiled popover pan (see note below on preparing the pan), filling each cup ⅔ full with batter. Bake at 350 degrees for 40–45 minutes. If you have a convection oven, lower the heat by 25 degrees and cook for 35 minutes. Popovers are done when the egg-yellow color of the batter turns to an even brown. If you take the popovers out too early, they will collapse quickly.

Note: To season a muffin pan for popovers, preheat the pan in a hot oven. When you are ready to cook the popovers, simply brush the inside of the cups using a pastry brush with a mixture of ¼ cup flour and ¼ cup cottonseed oil. Thoroughly coat the surface of the pans and drain off any excess oil. Now you are ready to put

10 eggs

1 teaspoon salt

1½ tablespoons sugar

1 quart milk

1 quart flour

¼ cup salad oil

batter in each cup. The oiling of the pan with flour and oil helps the popover to rise evenly.

"Leaving San Francisco is like saying goodbye to an old sweetheart. You want to linger as long as possible."

—Walter Cronkite, newscaster

THE CULINARY INSTITUTE OF AMERICA AT GREYSTONE

When New Spain achieved independence in 1821, Alta California was under the control of the new government in Mexico. General Mariano Vallejo commanded the military troops stationed north of San Francisco, but he was sympathetic to the wishes of many Californios to be free, even from the new administration.

After the Mexican-American War of 1846–1848, Vallejo supported the new government and had title to a vast land grant, which encompassed much of the current Napa Valley. The City of St. Helena is located in the center of Vallejo's land grant.

From its beginning, the fertile valley has been an agricultural center. Noting the wild grapes growing in the region, French varieties were eventually imported, giving rise to the largest and most prolific wine region in the Americas. St. Helena has since become an important business and banking center for the wine industry.

Food and wine go together, and The Culinary Institute of America at Greystone is one of the best places to experience that commingling. The CIA at Greystone was originally built to serve as Greystone Cellars. When it was completed in 1889, Greystone was the largest stone winery in the world. A cooperative winery serving Upper Napa Valley grape-growers, it had a planned capacity of 2 million gallons. The 117,000-square-foot structure, with 22-inch thick walls of locally quarried tufa stone, was designed by Hammond McIntyre, who also designed Trefethen, Inglenook (now Rubicom Estates), and Far Niente.

The phylloxera epidemic in the Napa vineyards at the close of the nineteenth century lasted through the Prohibition era, and drastic decline in wine production rendered Greystone virtually dormant. In 1950, the Christian Brothers, a Catholic lay teaching order, purchased the property to increase production of their well-known brands of wines, brandies, and ports under the direction of Brother Timothy, whose world-famous corkscrew collection of more than 1,000 items is displayed on the first floor of Greystone.

The Greystone facility and the exclusive marketing rights to the Christian Brothers' brands were acquired in 1990 by Heublein, Inc., an international food and beverage distributor. The

acquisition was concluded just after the 1989 Loma Prieta earthquake, which severely damaged the northern portion of the building. Heublein generously sold the building and a nearby 15-acre merlot vineyard to the Culinary Institute of America for about 10 percent of its $14 million value in 1993.

The CIA completed a major renovation of the building and opened for classes in 1995. Some of the unique features preserved during the renovation include the stars on the outside walls (an early attempt at seismic management); the huge redwood entrance doors, complete with carvings of salamanders and grape clusters; the gold-leaf Christian Brothers signature; the 2,000-gallon redwood casks (filled with water to prevent them from drying out); and the original Christian Brothers' barrel-making display. During the renovation, they also preserved some of the brandy-producing stills and equipment, as well as entrances to several caves dug into the back hillside. These may someday be used for classrooms, private dining rooms, or storage.

The Greystone Cellars building, the heart of the campus, houses teaching kitchens and bake-shops, Ecolab Theatre, De Baun Theater for public cooking exhibitions, De Baun Café, a market-place, and a restaurant.

Greystone hosts numerous cooking demonstrations, special events, seminars, and travel programs. Visitors to the campus can dine at the school's Wine Spectator Restaurant and shop at the Spice Islands Marketplace for cookware, bakeware, culinary tools, and specialty food products. It's a great place to visit for food and wine lovers alike.

The Culinary Institute of America at Greystone
2555 Main Street
St. Helena, California 94574
(707) 967-1010

Salmon Tartare with Potato Croquette

A crispy potato cup provides the perfect balance for the lush flavors of this elegant, raw salmon preparation. And it looks spectacular, too.

TARTARE

Mix all ingredients, except lemon juice. Season with salt and pepper. Keep in the refrigerator until just before serving, and then add lemon juice to taste. (Can be prepared up to 8 hours before serving.)

CROQUETTES

Bake potatoes until tender. Using an oven mitt and large spoon, remove potato flesh from skin while still warm. Run potatoes through food mill or potato ricer one at a time into a large bowl.

Thoroughly mix in butter, egg yolks, and crème fraiche. Season with salt and pepper. Let it cool.

When completely cooled, use a small scoop or your hand to make 1-inch balls of the potato dough. Make a small indentation on the top with your thumb. Dip each ball in the flour, then the beaten egg, then the panko breadcrumbs. Place on a cookie sheet lined with waxed paper, cover loosely and chill. (Recipe can be prepared to this point up to 24 hours before cooking.)

SALMON TARTARE

½ pound fresh salmon fillet, minced very fine

2 shallots, minced

2 teaspoons lemon zest

½ teaspoon Dijon mustard

1 tablespoon capers, rinsed and chopped

½ bunch chives, chopped

½ cup extra virgin olive oil

Fresh lemon juice to taste

POTATO CROQUETTES

4 Idaho potatoes

1 tablespoon unsalted butter, diced

2 egg yolks

2 tablespoons crème fraiche or sour cream

Kosher salt and freshly ground white pepper

¾ cup all-purpose flour

2 whole eggs, beaten

¾ cup panko or other finely ground breadcrumbs (panko can be found in Asian markets)

GARNISH

¼ cup crème fraiche (or sour cream) mixed with 1 teaspoon lemon juice

Sprigs of chervil, chives, or parsley

Bake at 350 degrees for 12–15 minutes, or until golden and crisp. For the garnish, serve the croquettes with a spoon of Salmon Tartare in the indentation, topped with a little lemon crème fraiche and sprig of chervil.

❧ YIELD ❧

40 croquettes

Steamed Hong Kong Dumplings

These mild dumplings are delicately steamed to create a texture that melts in your mouth.

Place halibut in bowl of food processor with metal blade. Pulse until fish is ground to a paste.

Mix fish and all other dumpling ingredients in a large bowl until well combined. Use moistened hands to shape into 1-inch balls.

Line a basket steamer with tinfoil and brush the foil with butter. Place the dumplings on the foil and put the basket over a pot of water. Cover, bring water to a boil (being careful that the water doesn't touch the basket) and steam over a gentle simmer for 8 to 10 minutes until dumplings are firm.

DIPPING SAUCE

Combine soy sauce, sugar, sesame oil, rice wine vinegar, and orange juice in a saucepan. In a small bowl, whisk cornstarch into cold water until completely dissolved (a slurry). Bring the sauce to a simmer and whisk in cornstarch slurry. Cook for several minutes until sauce begins to thicken.

Serve dumplings warm, glazed with the dipping sauce, and sprinkled with scallions.

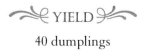
YIELD

40 dumplings

DUMPLINGS

3 cups finely ground halibut or tilapia filet

¼ cup scallion, minced

¼ cup peeled and minced fresh ginger

1 cup shiitake mushrooms, minced

½ cup prosciutto, minced

¼ cup dry sherry

¼ cup soy sauce

1½ tablespoons sugar

¼ cup cornstarch

DIPPING SAUCE

1 cup soy sauce

¼ cup sugar

1 tablespoon dark sesame oil

½ cup rice wine vinegar

1 cup fresh orange juice

2 tablespoons cornstarch

2 tablespoons cold water

1 cup finely sliced scallions

Crispy Chicken Wings with Sweet and Sour Sauce

2 pounds chicken wings, without drumette

SAUCE

2 tablespoons dark sesame oil

1 tablespoon chopped, fresh ginger

1 tablespoon chopped garlic

¼ cup orange juice concentrate

¾ cup rice vinegar

¼ cup dry sherry wine

1 pint chicken stock (reserved from wings)

1 tablespoon cornstarch

1 tablespoon cold water

GARNISH

1 tablespoon black sesame seeds

½ cup minced scallions

CHICKEN WINGS

In a stockpot, place chicken wings and enough water to barely cover. Simmer over low heat until tender, about 1 hour.

When cooked, let the wings cool in the liquid. Drain off the resulting stock to a large bowl and remove any fat that rises to the top. Strain stock through a fine sieve and reserve for the sweet and sour sauce.

Trim away the wing tip, excess skin, and cartilage from either end of the wing to expose and loosen the bone. Carefully remove all of the bone for a completely boneless chicken wing.

SAUCE

Heat a large saucepan over medium heat. Add sesame oil and warm. Then add all ingredients through chicken stock and bring to a boil.

Whisk cornstarch into cold water, to make a slurry. Once the sauce comes to a boil, add the slurry, stirring constantly, and return to a boil. Remove from heat when thick enough to coat the back of a spoon. Adjust final consistency with additional stock as needed.

Fry or grill the braised chicken wings until the skin is crisp. Dip into sweet and sour sauce and serve while hot, sprinkled with sesame seeds and scallions.

⤚❧ YIELD ☙⤙

20–24 wings and 1 pint of sauce

DEPOT HOTEL

There is an abundance of water, good soil, and an excellent climate in Sonoma, which explains why it is one of the most prolific agricultural counties in America today. These exceptional attributes also explain why Native Americans settled in the area thousands of years ago. Tribes included the Pomo-Kashaya, Wapo, and Patwin, who were still here when the Spanish, Russian, and European settlers arrived in the sixteenth century seeking timber, fur, and farmland.

In 1823, Mission San Francisco Solano de Sonoma, the last and northernmost of twenty-one California missions, was established by Father Junípero Serra. It was the only California mission installed after Mexico achieved independence from Spain. According to the Native Americans, Sonoma translates to "valley of the moon" or "many moons." Their legends say this was the land where the moon nestled, giving rise to the names Sonoma Valley and The Valley of the Moon.

Sonoma was first recognized by Mexico as a city in 1835. General Mariano Guadalupe Vallejo, a prominent military leader sympathetic to a California free of Mexican control, led the transformation of Sonoma into a thriving Mexican pueblo. He directed the construction of the 8-acre central plaza, which is still the largest in California. Vallejo also laid out the street grid and the 110-foot-wide Broadway. Closely tied to political power, he was named military governor of Alta California in 1838.

In 1846, California underwent a revolt against Mexican control similar to the 1835–1836 Texas-style rebellion. Sonoma was declared the capital of the "Bear Flag Republic" on June 14, and Vallejo was captured and imprisoned by the rebels. The town's status as the capital of California lasted only 25 days, ending when California was annexed by the United States. Two years later, Vallejo eventually supported the Americans when Mexico ceded all of California along with much of the rest of the Southwest to the United States following the end of the Mexican-American War.

Vallejo went on to become a California state senator, but due to the appropriation of many land holdings by the new government, he still lost almost all of his real estate, which at one point amounted to seven million acres. When he died in 1890, in Sonoma, he was leading a very modest life. Vallejo's support of the Americans in California against his native Mexican heritage is a testament to what it means to become a citizen of a country.

Sonoma was also quickly populated by prospectors and settlers during the California Gold Rush. It became one of California's original counties, created at the time of statehood in 1850. The lush valley would grow quickly.

Development in Sonoma brought the railroad, and the railroad brought passengers. The Depot Hotel was built some time in the late 1800s for these passengers arriving from San Francisco. Located only one block away from the historic Sonoma Plaza, the Depot Hotel is a beautifully restored plumstone building. The original owners opened the hotel's restaurant to serve both the local townspeople and visitors. Today, this historic building no longer offers rooms to rent. It houses an excellent restaurant serving food in a casual and charming country-inn style.

One of the most well-known Italian restaurants in the Sonoma Valley, the Depot Hotel is one of the landmarks of the Sonoma Valley wine country. The glass-enclosed Garden Room in back opens onto a beautiful private garden with shady decks and brick terraces surrounding a reflecting pool and Roman fountain. A favorite spot with locals, the Depot Hotel Restaurant takes pride in extending Sonoma hospitality to visitors and sharing the cuisine and wines of Sonoma Valley.

In 1989, Chef Ghilarducci received the prestigious national award Master Chef of America. This honor, extended to only 5 percent of the chefs in America, is particularly valued as it is awarded by professional chefs in recognition of the talents of a few of their colleagues. The restaurant has also been consistently awarded three stars by the Mobil Travel Guide.

Sonoma Valley wines can be served by the glass at the cozy wine bar and at the fireside tables in the parlor. Wine service is also available in the Garden Room and outside spaces. The chef also teaches cooking classes in French and Italian cuisine.

Depot Hotel
241 First Street West
Sonoma, California 95476
(707) 938-2980

7 ounces cannellini beans

1¼ pounds of raw prawns, shelled

2 ripe summer tomatoes, peeled, seeded, and diced small

6 fresh basil leaves, chopped

½ cup extra virgin olive oil

Salt and pepper to taste

Gamberonie Fagioli

Tuscan style prawns and cannellini beans

Cook the beans for 1 hour in plain water. Let it sit for one hour, covered. Pour off the water and then rinse the beans. Refill the pot with fresh salted water. Cook for another hour, until tender. Drain.

Bring a separate large pot of salted water to the boil and drop in the prawns. Cook 5 minutes and then cool just enough to handle.

Peel the prawns. Combine the peeled prawns with the beans, tomatoes, basil, and olive oil. Add salt and pepper to taste. Serve warm.

YIELD
Serves 4 as an appetizer

Gnocchi Di Spinaci (Malfatti)

Spinach and ricotta dumplings

Put the spinach in a sauté pan and cook with just a small amount of water, covered. Season to taste with salt, pepper, and nutmeg. When tender, drain well and squeeze dry. Chop very finely and then beat together with the ricotta and butter. (A food processor works very well for this.)

Next, beat in the flour and eggs, and then adjust seasoning to taste. Bring a large pot of salted water to the boil. Shape all of the spinach gnocchi mixture into walnut-sized dumplings. Cook in the boiling water a few at a time—scooping each out as it cooks and floats to the surface.

Drain all of the dumplings when they are done. Place in a buttered baking dish and sprinkle with Parmesan cheese. Bake for 10–15 minutes at 425 degrees.

YIELD

Serves 4

1 pound fresh spinach, very well washed

Salt and pepper

Nutmeg

8 ounces ricotta

2 tablespoons sweet butter, softened

⅔ cup flour

1 egg plus 1 egg yolk, well beaten

Melted butter, for dish

Fresh grated Parmesan cheese

2 3-pound chickens

Salt and pepper

1 tablespoon olive oil

1 medium zucchini, cut in
    wedges

8 large mushrooms, quartered

2 large fresh artichoke bottoms,
    blanched and quartered

Pinch of Italian herbs

Pinch of sage

1 teaspoon minced garlic

1 teaspoon minced shallots

1 cup dry white wine

½ cup veal demi-glace sauce

Pollo Alla Toscana

Tuscan-style chicken with zucchini, mushrooms, and artichokes

Bone and cut the chickens so that there is one large semi-boneless piece of breast and thigh per person. (Alternatively, purchase whole chicken breasts or whole leg/thigh pieces.)

Season the chicken with salt and pepper to taste. Heat the oil in a large oven-safe sauté pan and add the chicken, skin side down. Place the pan in a 400-degree oven and cook the chicken for 15–20 minutes.

Remove the pan from the oven, add the vegetables, and stir well. Turn the chicken pieces over on top of the vegetables, skin side up. Return to the oven and cook an additional 10 minutes.

Place the sauté pan on top of the stove and add the herbs, garlic, and shallots. Sauté for one minute and then add the white wine and veal demi-glace sauce. Remove the chicken to a service platter.

Cook the sauce for an additional 4 minutes, pour over the chicken and serve.

YIELD

Serves 4

THE FAIRMONT SAN FRANCISCO

The magnificent Fairmont San Francisco was originally intended to be a monument to James Graham Fair. "Bonanza Jim" was one of San Francisco's wealthiest citizens, having struck it rich in a Nevada silver mine. He left his great fortune to his daughters, Tessie and Virginia Fair when he died in 1894. They began construction of the hotel in 1902 but, as time passed, their dreams became a burden. The sisters sold the property in 1906 to Herbert and Hartland Law, in exchange for two existing office buildings at Mission and New Montgomery Streets.

The hotel was not yet open when the Laws took over, but the massive structure was completed and the interior furnishings had been delivered. The hotel was purchased on April 6, less than two weeks before the great San Francisco earthquake and fire was to all but level the city. Photographs show The Fairmont standing proudly at the top of the hill, while all around there was devastation and rubble. The elegant building escaped the earthquake damage but the fires, which burned uncontrollably, finally reached the top of Nob Hill 24 hours later.

The Laws took the burden of social responsibility seriously and went ahead with plans to repair, redecorate, and restore The Fairmont. Exactly one year after the earthquake, a grand banquet celebrating the opening was held, with 600 pounds of turtle, 13,000 oysters, and $5,000 worth of California and French wines. That evening, fireworks illuminated not only the beautiful new hotel, but also the 1,000 ships at anchor in the Bay and City Hall and all the buildings that had risen from the ashes of nature's wrath. San Francisco was alive and well again.

The Fairmont became the social hub of the City. Some wealthy families, displaced by the earthquake, took up residence there for many years. Meanwhile, the Law brothers hired the Palace Hotel Company to manage The Fairmont. Shortly thereafter, Tessie (Fair) Oelrichs returned to her beloved City after her husband passed away while on a transatlantic crossing. She once again became the owner and hostess par excellence of San Francisco's most famous hotel.

In 1917, D. M. Linnard, who owned a chain of hotels in California, took over the management, and in 1924, bought the controlling interest from the Oelrichs family. Linnard sold The Fairmont to George Smith in 1929. Smith, a mining engineer, had just completed the Mark Hopkins Hotel. He immediately undertook a major renovation, including adding an indoor pool, named the Fairmont Plunge.

36

Linnard repurchased the hotel in 1941, only to sell it again after the war to Benjamin Swig, an East Coast businessman. Once again, The Fairmont "rose from the ashes." Swig hired Dorothy Draper, the most famous decorator of the time, to give the hotel a badly needed facelift. Dorothy had just finished her remarkable redo of The Greenbrier in West Virginia. But she had a different vision for The Fairmont. She visualized the hotel as an enlarged copy of a Grand Venetian Palace but also wanted to capture the charm and romance of San Francisco. Her goal was to restore The Fairmont to its position as the center jewel in the crown of the Golden Age of San Francisco.

The "Draper touch" was a great success, attracting international attention. Its resurgence was confirmed when it hosted the International Conference that led to the birth of the United Nations. Once again, history was being made at The Fairmont. The plaque commemorating the drafting of the Charter for the United Nations is on display outside the Garden Room on the lobby level, while the flags of the original signatories fly proudly above the porte cochere.

Draper also turned the Venetian Room into San Francisco's premier Supper Club. Guests and locals dined and danced to big-name entertainment: Ella Fitzgerald, Nat King Cole, Marlene Dietrich, Joel Grey, Bobby Short, Vic Damone, and James Brown, to name a few. The Venetian Room is most famous as the place where Tony Bennett first sang "I Left My Heart in San Francisco."

The Fairmont Plunge was recreated as if guests were aboard the S.S. *Tonga*, which provided a "ship-shape" atmosphere, along with exotic drinks and Chinese food. A further facelift turned the "ship" into the Tonga Room, with its musical boat in the middle of the pool. Patrons sit under tiki huts while enjoying a refreshing mai tai and an exotic South Sea menu. The gleaming dance floor was originally the deck of the S.S. *Forrester*, one of the last of the tall ships to sail the route between San Francisco and the South Sea Islands.

The Fairmont stands tall in the city's history. Its Cirque Room was the first bar to open in San Francisco following Prohibition. San Francisco's first glass elevator carries people to the Crown Room at the top of the tower, offering a spectacular view of the city. The fabled Penthouse—The Fairmont's most exclusive accommodation at $12,500 per night—was constructed in 1926 as a residence for John S. Drum, president of the American Trust Company.

As in the novel *Hotel* by Arthur Hailey (which later became a TV series filmed at The Fairmont), Ben Swig eventually moved into the Penthouse, high above Nob Hill, with a bird's-eye view

of his beloved City by the Bay. His roomy abode was often home to many VIPs. Chief Justice Earl Warren, Governor Pat Brown, and General Omar Bradley were but a few to share his hospitality. Since Ben Swig passed away, the Penthouse has been used as a luxury accommodation for presidents, heads of state, celebrities, and other dignitaries.

As the San Francisco residence for every U.S. president since William Howard Taft, The Fairmont garnered a world-class reputation that grew into a collection of grand hotels bearing its name. In 1999, Fairmont Hotels merged with Canadian Pacific Hotels to form Fairmont Hotels & Resorts, the largest operator of luxury hotels and resorts in North America.

As the company's flagship property, The Fairmont San Francisco once again made history when it greeted the twenty-first century with an award-winning $85 million restoration. Central to the Financial District, Union Square, and Fisherman's Wharf, The Fairmont is located at the only spot in San Francisco where each of the city's cable car lines meet.

The Fairmont San Francisco
950 Mason Street
San Francisco, California 94108
(415) 772-5000

1 teaspoon cornstarch

1 teaspoon water

3 sheets nori seaweed, cut in
6 large triangles

6 Vietnamese rice paper wrappers

2 ounces wasabi powder

1 tablespoon water

¼ cup crème fraiche

1¼ pounds sushi-grade
#1 Ahi Tuna

¼ cup pickled pink ginger,
julienned

1 bunch shiso leaf (Japanese
mint), chopped

2 ounces sesame oil

12 ounces smoked salmon

1 package daikon sprouts

1 bunch chervil

Ahi Tuna Tartare and Smoked Salmon on Rice Paper with Ginger, Wasabi Crème Fraiche, and Crisp Nori

For the nori garnish, mix cornstarch with water and coat the nori just before frying. Fry in neutral oil at 375 degrees. Also fry the rice paper wrappers ahead of time. Try to shape into small cups. They will both keep for 2 days in covered dry container. Mix the wasabi powder with water to combine, then whisk into crème fraiche.

AHI TARTARE

Dice the tuna into ½-inch cubes, removing any white threads. Place in small metal bowl. Just before service, mix in ginger, shiso, sesame oil, and pinch of black pepper.

PLATING

Lay 2 ounces smoked salmon onto each plate. Drizzle with wasabi crème fraiche. Place rice wrapper cup on top and spoon in 3 ounces tuna tartare. Garnish each plate with daikon, chervil, and crispy nori.

"Everybody has a favorite city. I have two, London and San Francisco. . . . This fortuitous mating of marine grandeur and terrestrial snugness is what makes the place, to me, the most individual and engaging of American cities."

—Alistair Cooke, journalist

Sesame-Crusted Pan-Seared Salmon with Jasmine Rice, Citrus Beurre Blanc, Baby Bok Choy, and Tamari-Honey Glaze

Cut bell pepper and green onion in thin julienne strips and place in ice water to curl. Make beurre blanc by reducing citrus juices in saucepan by three-fourths and whisk in butter on low heat to emulsify.

To make soy honey glaze, simmer soy sauce and add honey. Thicken with cornstarch slurry.

Sear salmon on skin side in very hot oven-safe skillet until crisp, approx. 2 minutes. Turn over filet. Onto crisp skin side, spread tahini sauce on lightly and coat with sesame seeds. Place pan in 375-degree oven and cook 5–7 minutes.

Blanch bok choy in boiling water just before service, and place next to rice in large bowl. Surround with citrus sauce. Place salmon on top and drizzle with soy glaze. Garnish with bell pepper and onion pieces.

"You know what it is? (San Francisco) is a golden handcuff with the key thrown away."

—John Steinbeck, author

1 piece red bell pepper

3 pieces green onion

½ cup orange juice

Juice of 1 lemon

1 pound butter

6 ounces lite soy sauce

2 ounces honey

1 tablespoon cornstarch, dissolved in 1 tablespoon water

2½ pounds salmon filet, boned with skin on, king or local variety

3 tablespoons tahini sesame paste

2 ounces black & white sesame seeds, mixed.

6 pieces baby bok choy, cut in half lengthwise

3 cups jasmine rice, cooked

12 slices pancetta, thinly sliced

12 pieces large dry-pack fresh
    scallops (about 1½ pounds)

3 tablespoons olive oil

2 cups young watercress leaves
    with tender stems (discard
    woody stems)

Corn Cream (recipe follows)

Black pepper, freshly ground

Seared Scallops with Corn Cream

Preheat the broiler. Lay the pancetta in a single layer on a baking sheet and run under the hot broiler. Rotate so that the pancetta evenly cooks for 2–3 minutes. You want to just barely cook and firm it up. It should still remain pliable but will be opaque and not browned.

Gently unwind the pancetta and then wrap around the outside of each scallop, leaving the flat sides bare. Secure with a toothpick, if necessary.

Heat the oil in a large heavy-bottomed sauté pan over medium-high heat until very hot and just beginning to smoke. Using tongs, carefully place the scallops flat side down and cook until golden brown, about 2 minutes. Turn and cook the other side until browned, about 1 minute.

Arrange the watercress leaves in the center of warm plates and place the scallops on top. Spoon the Corn Cream around the outside and garnish with a grinding or two of black pepper. Serve immediately.

YIELD

Serves 6

Corn Cream

This is a good example of how vegetable purees can be turned into delicious sauces. You could use the same approach utilizing sweet peas, roasted butternut squash, carrots, etc.

Warm the butter in a deep saucepan over moderate heat. Add the onions and chile powder and sauté until onions are soft but not brown. Add the stock and the corn; cover and simmer until vegetables are very soft, about 10 minutes. Add cream and sherry and bring to a simmer. Off heat, carefully puree in a blender until very smooth. Strain through a fine mesh strainer, pressing down on the solids. Discard solids and return sauce to pan and keep warm. Season to your taste with salt and additional chile.

Sauce can be made a day or two ahead and stored covered and refrigerated.

YIELD
Yields about 2 cups

2 tablespoons butter or olive oil

1 cup chopped onion

½ teaspoon medium-hot chile powder, such as chimayo or chipolte

2 cups chicken or vegetable stock

1½ cups sweet corn kernels, fresh or frozen

⅔ cup heavy cream

2 teaspoon dry sherry (optional)

Salt

THE FAIRMONT SONOMA MISSION INN & SPA

The original Fairmont Hotel was the vision of San Francisco natives, Tessie and Virginia Fair. It had been planed as a monument to their father, who made a fortune mining silver in Nevada. The building process was so taxing on them, they decided to sell the original hotel property in San Francisco, just days before the great earthquake and resulting fires destroyed much of the city.

Returning to the property a few years later, after it had been rebuilt, they eventually sold it to Ben Swig, who retained the name. The tradition of elegant hospitality has continued for a full century now under the Fairmont name. Each Fairmont hotel works very hard to be the area's social hub for the rich and famous.

The Fairmont Sonoma Mission Inn & Spa location dates back to the Native Americans who discovered the natural underground hot mineral waters. They considered this site a sacred healing ground. Their "sweathouse" stood near the spring for generations. In 1840, an eccentric San Francisco physician, Dr. T. M. Leavenworth, was the first to develop the hot springs for commercial use.

Half a century later, Captain H. E. Boyes, an enterprising young Englishman who immigrated to the area, acquired the property and struck 112-degree water at a depth of 70 feet while drilling a well for drinking water. Within five years, the Boyes Hot Springs Hotel was constructed on the site of the current Mission Inn. It wasn't long before wealthy San Franciscans were arriving by boat and train to partake of the healing waters at the finest hot mineral water resort in California.

Disaster struck in 1923. A fire destroyed both the hotel and most of Boyes Hot Springs. The current inn rose from the ashes the following year as an architecturally accurate replica of a California mission. In a very short time, the inn was once again filled with guests, and the hotel was acknowledged as one of the finest in all of Northern California.

The Great Depression in 1929 plunged the resort into receivership. It remained closed until 1933, when it was purchased by Grass Valley hotelier Emily Long and restored to prosperity. As with many great hotel properties in America, the hotel fell under the control of the government during World War II. The Navy made it an "R&R" site for sailors and marines until 1945.

After the war, various sports teams used the inn as a training headquarters, and The Big 3 restaurant was established, quickly becoming a gathering place for locals and hotel guests alike. Pres-

ently the longest-running, continuously operated restaurant in Sonoma Valley, The Big 3 anchors the corner of Highway 12 and Boyes Boulevard at the entrance to the inn.

A major renovation in 1980 returned the inn to its 1920s grandeur, and the spa was added in 1981. Since then, the spa was expanded in 2000 with architecture and landscaping reminiscent of a true European spa.

The Fairmont Sonoma Mission Inn & Spa
100 Boyes Boulevard
Sonoma, California 95476
(707) 938-9000

STEW

1 free-range turkey,
12–14 pounds

1 onion, peeled,
studded with cloves

1 onion, peeled, cut in half

2 carrots, peeled

2 leeks, cleaned

3 celery sticks

2 bay leaves

½ ounce thyme

1 ounce parsley

White peppercorn and salt to taste

GARNISH

6 turned yellow turnips

6 turned turnips

1 acorn squash, cut in 6 pieces

12 turned potatoes

3 leeks, cleaned

12 turned sweet potatoes

12 turned carrots

20 large pearl onions

Free-Range Turkey "Pot-au-Feu" with Winter Vegetables

Pot-au-feu, *meaning "pot on fire" in French, refers to a dish of meat and vegetables slowly cooked in water. A first course of the rich broth is often served prior to the course with the meat and vegetables. In France, the tradition is to serve pot-au-feu with mustard, pickled gherkins (cornichons), and coarse salt.*

In a large cooking pot, place the turkey and the vegetables tied together by category and cover with water. Caramelize each half onion, tie parsley, bay leaves and thyme together, into a bouquet garni, place peppercorn in a cheese cloth and add to the preparation. Salt the pot-au-feu, to taste. Bring to a boil, skim well and continuously. Let simmer and cook for about 2½ hours.

Cook all of the garnishing vegetables separately in another cooking pot with some turkey broth. Present the turkey on a nice tray with all the turned vegetables and some cooking broth.

Note: With the leftover vegetables and broth you can make an excellent turkey vegetable soup. Also, if you can find whole winter black truffles, I recommend sliding a few thick slices of ⅛ inch under the skin of the breasts and thighs. It is delicious and adds a wonderful flavor to your turkey and broth. You can use as many slices as you like or can afford! Bon appetite!

YIELD

Serves 6

Court Bouillon Shrimp on Celery, Apple, Leek, and Black Truffle Remoulade with French Mache

Place all court-bouillon ingredients in a cooking pot, bring to a boil and cook for 20 minutes. Keep simmering until cooking the shrimps.

Cut the middle part of the leeks into nice wheels. Discard the part that is too green. Cut the white part into a thin julienne. Blanch the wheels and the julienne. Set aside.

Poach the shrimps in the court-bouillon, refresh (place in an ice bath to halt the cooking process), and reserve.

Peel and julienne the celery root and the apple. Blanch separately and refresh.

Mix the three juliennes with olive oil mayonnaise, black truffle oil, salt, and pepper. Place two jumbo shrimp into a 4-ounce mold (or aluminum cup), then fill up with the julienne mixture. Blend the truffle peelings with the truffle juice until nicely pureed.

Unmold the shrimp on a plate, place drops of truffle puree around, then add a few leek slices/wheels and French mâche on the top.

YIELD

Serves 4

COURT-BOUILLON

1 quart water

1 cup white wine

1 sliced lemon

1 sliced carrot

1 sliced stalk celery

½ sliced onion

1 bay leaf

1 sprig of thyme

Few parsley stems

1 teaspoon black peppercorn

REMAINDER OF DISH

8 jumbo shrimp (U15), peeled and deveined

2 whole leeks

1 small celery root

1 apple

1 cup extra virgin olive oil mayonnaise

1 dash black truffle oil

Salt and white pepper to taste

3 ounce black truffle peelings

1 cup black truffle juice

Few sprigs French mâche (rare, tender greens)

½ pound butter

12 pieces large "diver" scallops

¼ cup dry vermouth

¼ cup white wine

¼ cup fish stock

Salt and pepper to taste

2 young leeks, sliced

12 medium oysters

½ pound cinnamon honey
   cap mushroom

¼ cup truffle juice

"Diver" Scallops and Oysters Ragout with Young Leek and Cinnamon Honey Cap Mushrooms

In a sauté pan, work the butter with a spoon of water into an emulsion. Set aside.

In another sauté pan, place scallops, vermouth, white wine, salt and pepper, and fish stock. Also add the juice from the oysters. Cook slowly until scallops are nice and tender, then add the oysters. Cook 2 more minutes, then remove scallops and oysters from the pan and add the leeks and mushrooms, then truffle juice. Cook until tender, and then add emulsified butter. Check seasoning and consistency. Return scallops and oyster to the pan. Reheat slowly and serve.

YIELD
Serves 4

THE FIREHOUSE RESTAURANT

Miwok, Shonommey, and Maidu Indians first settled the Sacramento area thousands of years ago. The Europeans that eventually arrived to push these Native Americans out of Sacramento Valley were not all Spanish explorers, although it was Lieutenant Gabriel Moraga from Mission San Jose who first arrived in 1808.

Moranga found the confluence of two rivers, and named the largest one for the Spanish term for "sacrament," or "the Most Holy Sacrament of the Body and Blood of Christ." The American River was named for the new country.

Mexico's independence from Spain in 1821 opened the way for settlers from many nations to arrive in the new land. In 1833, a smallpox epidemic killed 20,000 Indians, making it all but impossible for the remaining tribe members to resist the invasion of Europeans. John Sutter came from Switzerland in 1839 and launched a trading colony in the fertile valley. He built a stockade in 1840 that he called New Helvetia ("New Switzerland"), but it would later be known as Sutter's Fort.

Sutter's Fort, which sits in the center of today's Sacramento City, was built by local Indian laborers. Sutter saw the value of their land and had thousands of fruit trees shipped in, beginning a cycle of agricultural development for the area that continues today. Expanding his new empire, Sutter built a sawmill along the American River in Coloma. In 1848, one of his employees, James Marshall, discovered gold in the river at the mill site. Sutter used his increasing wealth to found the city of Sacramento, and named it for the local river and valley. In an odd twist in history, a future Civil War general for the Union, William Tecumseh Sherman, as a very young man, helped survey and lay out the street grid for Sutter's new town.

It took a while for the news to spread, but by 1849 the California Gold Rush was on. Sacramento was the jumping-off place for tens of thousands of miners, entrepreneurs, and developers who came from all parts of the globe. They were everywhere, including where they were not supposed to be. Squatters occupied much of Sutter's land and many saw no problem with stealing his cattle for food. The onslaught that would dub California the Golden State would eventually also put Sutter in financial ruin.

Statehood in 1850 lead to the creation of various levels of new government. Since there were so many people around Sacramento due to the lure of gold, the new legislature met there. Eventually, the city would be recognized as the state capital in 1854.

There was so much lumber available in the area that the city was built largely of wood. A great fire in 1852 destroyed most of Sacramento, so in 1853 when people rebuilt important buildings, they were made of brick. The new city firehouse was erected during this time.

Built to house the fire chief and the volunteers for Engine Company #3, the firehouse received special recognition from the new state government, conveniently located in town. In 1872, the legislature made this engine company the first paid fire department in California. The firehouse served its original purpose for many decades but was abandoned in 1921 for a much larger facility.

After passing through a succession of private owners, the firehouse was bought by Newton Cope in 1959. The neighborhood along the old waterfront was a slum; citizens rallied to save it from destruction and extensive renovations began. The first restoration to reopen was this restaurant. Cope opened The Firehouse as a bar and dining establishment in 1960, with the interior designed to remind patrons of the Gold Rush Era. The entire waterfront was eventually rebuilt, creating the National Historic District of Old Sacramento.

Celebrities, tourists, politicians, and diplomats have made it a point to stop and dine at The Firehouse. Governor Ronald Reagan held both of his inaugural dinners here.

You can experience the "gateway to the goldfields" by visiting this award-winning restaurant in Old Town Sacramento.

The Firehouse
1112 Second Street
Sacramento, California 95814
(916) 442-4772

Dungeness Crab and Potato Bisque

STOCK

Clean crabs, reserving meat for garnish. Squeeze liquid out of crabmeat and reserve. Combine crab shells and liquid with all stock ingredients, and simmer on medium-high heat until reduced by one-third.

SOUP

Sauté the onion, leeks, and shallots in butter until translucent. Do not brown. Add flour and toast on low heat for 3 minutes. Add stock and incorporate, stirring briskly. Bring to a hard simmer, stirring constantly. Add tomatoes and potatoes. Cook on medium-low heat for 1½ hours or until potatoes are tender.

Using a hand blender, puree soup and strain through a fine mesh chinois.

PLATING

Finish soup by adding heavy cream and sherry vinegar. Ladle into bowls and garnish with crabmeat and fried prosciutto.

YIELD
4 quarts

CRAB STOCK

2 gallons water

30 ounces clam juice

1 tablespoon McCormick Old Bay Seasoning

4 large Dungeness crab shells and liquid

Leek tops

Thyme

Parsley

SOUP

½ pound butter

2 cups onion

2 cups leeks

½ cup shallots

½ pound flour

32 ounces diced canned tomatoes

2 pounds diced potatoes

1 cup heavy cream

1 tablespoon sherry vinegar

GARNISH

Prosciutto, browned, in pieces

½ cup Dungeness crabmeat

10–15 cooked (31-40) shrimp

½ cup lobster meat (optional)

½ cup cantaloupe melon balls

½ cup watermelon balls

2 ounces prosciutto (cooked crisp)

LOUIS DRESSING

1 cup mayonnaise

½ cup heavy cream

¼ cup sweet chile sauce, strained

1 tablespoon lemon juice

Nouveaux Louis

Toss all ingredients in a bowl with 4 ounces of Louis dressing (recipe follows). Arrange on plate using a ring mold. Top with spring mix salad lightly dressed with olive oil and sea salt. Dress plate with additional Louis dressing.

LOUIS DRESSING

In mixer, combine mayonnaise and cream. Whip for 2 minutes. Using a fine mesh strainer add sweet chile and lemon juice and mix.

THE FRENCH LAUNDRY

George Calvert Yount was born May 4, 1794, in Burke County, North Carolina. His parents moved the family to Cape Girardeau, Missouri, where he grew up to become a trapper. Eventually, his travels took him to Napa Valley in 1831. As the first white settler, he received the first land grant awarded by the Spanish government to an American citizen in Northern California.

Naming his land Caymus Rancho after a tribe of Native Americans in the area, he used this property in 1855 to lay out the boundaries of what would become Yountville. Curiously, he originally called it Sebastopol, despite the fact that there was already a town nearby with that name.

The new industry that he foresaw for the valley was grape-growing. He is credited with planting the very first vines in Napa Valley. Following his death in 1867, the second Sebastopol was renamed Yountville in honor of George Yount and all of his contributions.

Shortly after Yount's death, immigrant Gottleib Groezinger purchased 23 acres of what became known as the Gottleib Addition from the Yount estate. As a German-born vintner, he was impressed by the climate, soil conditions, and success of the grape vines and the opportunity he saw. Gottlieb built a winery, barrel room, and distillery in 1874, which operated until 1955. Now operating as the Vintage 1870 Center, it offers shopping, dining, entertainment, and special events to more than 500,000 visitors each year.

Yountville was finally incorporated into a city in 1965; its boundaries had changed very little since it was first laid out by George Yount. Railroad service and the success of wineries contributed to its growth, along with the exceptional valley weather.

On the Yountville culinary front, a Scottish man, Pierre Guillaume, built a saloon in the early 1900s. However, it was quickly put out of business in 1906 when a law was passed making it illegal to sell liquor within a mile of a veteran's home. He sold the building and John Lande used it for a French steam laundry in the 1920s, giving it a name that has stuck for almost a century. In 1978, the mayor of Yountville renovated the property and soon a restaurant was opened.

Today, reservations are difficult to get. They serve three menus a day and each meal costs $240 (as of 2007), which includes exceptional service. Unadvertised, but available by arrangement, is a

 *52*

special tasting menu with approximately twenty courses, offered at about $400. Don't be surprised if you see a celebrity at the next table.

The French Laundry
6640 Washington Street
Yountville, California 94599
(707) 944-2380

Puree of Sunchoke Soup with Pickled Red Radishes and Country Bread Croûtons

SOUP

Sweat onions in oil until completely soft. Add sugar, salt, vegetable stock, and sunchokes. Cook over medium heat until sunchokes are completely soft. The stock at this point should be reduced by half. Add water and bring to a boil.

Puree soup in blender. Pass through a fine mesh sieve.

RADISHES

Bring water and vinegar to a boil in a small pot. Dissolve sugar in the liquid and pour over the radishes. Allow to cool to room temperature, strain. Slice to desired shape.

CROÛTONS

Slice bread into small cubes. Sauté in olive oil until golden brown. Season with kosher salt and drain well on absorbent paper.

PLATING

Pour soup into warm demitasses. Sprinkle with croûtons and radishes.

YIELD
Serves 4

SOUP

3–4 ounces extra-virgin olive oil

¼ cup yellow onions

1 teaspoon granulated sugar

½ ounce kosher salt

1 quart vegetable stock

1½ cups sunchokes

3–4 ounces water

RADISHES

2 cups water

8 ounces champagne vinegar

8 ounces sugar

2 bunches red radishes, cleaned and trimmed

CROÛTONS

½ cup country bread

½ cup extra virgin olive oil

BUTTERSCOTCH

1½ ounces heavy cream

1½ ounces sugar

MOUSSE/GANACHE

10 ounces heavy cream

16 ounces Valrhona milk
chocolate or 70% dark
chocolate, finely chopped

3½ ounces heavy cream,
semi-whipped

Caramel flavoring, as needed

Chocolate Feuillentine

BUTTERSCOTCH

Boil the cream and remove from the heat.

Use a large heavy bottomed pan as the sugar will boil over when you add the cream in a smaller pan. Place enough of the sugar to cover the bottom of the pan. As the sugar begins to melt stir continuously until it is completely dissolved. Add a little more sugar and keep repeating the process until all the sugar is dissolved and it is caramel in color. Do not leave the pan unattended at any time. Carefully add the warm cream a little at a time. Bring back to the boil And then turn off the heat. Leave to cool.

MOUSSE/GANACHE

Boil the cream. Remove from the heat and add the chopped chocolate. Mix until smooth. Scale one-third of the mix into a separate bowl and fold in the semi-whipped cream. Pipe into individual molds making sure they are only half-full. Place in the fridge until set. Keep the remaining two-thirds of the ganache mix warm on the stovetop and add the caramel flavoring to it.

Use a small scoop or melon baller and scoop out the center of the set mousse and fill with the butterscotch.

Top the molds with the remaining ganache mix that you have flavored with caramel. If this has cooled too far, gently warmed it in the microwave. Freeze the completed mousses.

GLAZE

Boil the first four ingredients together and pour into bowl onto the chopped chocolate. Place the frozen ganache domes on a cooling rack with a tray underneath it and pour over the hot glaze immediately to give a smooth finish. Remove the domes from the rack and place on a sheet pan in the fridge until ready to use.

Note: A variation: Garnish with candied peanuts and chocolate décor.

YIELD
8–10 domes

CHOCOLATE GLAZE

1½ ounces heavy cream

5½ ounces flan jelly

1 ounce water

4 teaspoons sugar

3 ounces Valrhona 70% dark chocolate, chopped into small pieces

Herb-Roasted Elysian Fields Farm Lamb Rib Eye

Sautéed Panisse, Ratatouille Chutney,
Thyme Jus, and French Laundry
Garden Squash Blossoms

LAMB

1 rack of lamb rib eye, cleaned

3 ounces canola oil

Kosher salt and freshly ground
     black pepper

2 ounces unsalted butter

3 cloves of garlic,
     split and crushed

4 sprigs of thyme

LAMB

Prior to cooking, allow lamb to rest at room temperature for 1 hour. Preheat oven to 375 degrees.

Heat ⅛ inch of canola oil in a large skillet over medium-high heat. Season the lamb rack with salt and pepper and sauté for about 3 minutes to brown on the bottom. Turn the rack over and continue to cook for another 3 minutes.

Place the rack on the side and rotate it to brown the sides, another 1 to 2 minutes. The rack should be well browned but still slightly rare.

Remove most of the fat from the pan and add the butter, basting the lamb with butter as it melts. Top the lamb with the garlic and thyme. Place the pan in the oven for about 4 minutes, or until the meat is medium-rare; an instant-read thermometer should register 115–120 degrees. Remove the pan from the oven and let the meat rest for 3–4 minutes. Serve immediately. (See Plating notes below.)

PANISSE

Blend cold chicken stock with garlic in blender. While blending, add the salt and then add both the oils in a steady stream. Slowly add the chickpea flour until emulsified.

Place the blended ingredients in a cold pot, and begin to heat while whisking vigorously. Once the mixture comes to a boil, continue to vigorously whip on the heat for 2 minutes. Pour the mixture into a nonstick silicone mold and smooth with a spatula. Tap to ensure there are no air bubbles. Cool at room temperature for 20 minutes and finish cooling in the refrigerator. In a 375-degree oven, coat the green, red, and yellow peppers with olive oil, salt, and pepper and roast in the oven until soft. Let cool. Dice the roasted peppers, eggplant, tomato, zucchini, and shallots so they are all approximately the same size. Peel the orange and lemon, remove pith, and reserve ½ teaspoon of each peel. Make a sachet of the citrus peel, cinnamon, and clove.

In an appropriate-sized pot, sweat the shallots in a small amount of oil until tender. Add the tomato concasse, curry powder, and sachet and cook over medium heat until all liquid is removed. Add 2 teaspoons each of the diced roasted peppers, Cabernet Vinegar, and sugar and cook until all liquid is evaporated. In separate pans, sweat the diced zucchini and diced eggplant until tender.

Combine the eggplant and zucchini with the roasted peppers. Let the mixture cool.

THYME JUS

On the stovetop, roast the lamb bones in a large rondeaux until caramelized. Deglaze with half the water and reduce to a glaze. Re-glaze with the remaining

57

PANISSE

1¾ cups chicken stock

½ teaspoon garlic

½ teaspoon kosher salt

½ teaspoon lemon oil

½ teaspoon olive oil

3.2 ounces chickpea flour

RATATOUILLE CHUTNEY

1 green pepper

1 red pepper

1 yellow pepper

3½ ounces eggplant

1¾ ounces Roma tomato

3½ ounces zucchini

1 ounce shallots

1 lemon

1 orange

1 clove per serving

½ cinnamon stick per serving

1 pinch Madras curry powder

1 ounce cabernet sauvignon
vinegar

¾ ounce sugar

Olive oil, as needed

(continued on next page)

THYME JUS

3½ ounces lamb bones

3½ ounces water

3½ ounces chicken stock

1½ ounces leeks, rough chopped

1½ ounces yellow onions,
     rough chopped

1½ ounces carrots, rough chopped

2 each tomatoes

1 quart lamb stock

1 sprig of thyme per serving

FOR THE
SQUASH BLOSSOM

6 squash blossoms

½ teaspoon olive oil

½ ounce champagne vinegar

Salt and pepper to taste

half of the water and again reduce to a glaze. Lastly, deglaze with the chicken stock and reduce to a glaze. Add leek, onion, carrots and caramelize. Add the tomatoes and cook until the water from them deglazes the pan. Add the lamb stock, bring to simmer and reduce by one-half.

Strain the sauce through a chinois or fine mesh sieve several times until clean. Place into an appropriately sized clean pot, and reduce to sauce consistency. Strain again through a fine mesh sieve. Finish with picked thyme leaves.

SQUASH BLOSSOMS

Place squash blossoms in a small stainless mixing bowl. Add oil, vinegar, salt and pepper to taste and toss the blossoms to cover.

PLATING

Cut the panisse into desired shape and roll in flour. Shake off excess and sauté over medium-high heat until golden brown. Slice the lamb into 12 slices and serve with a tablespoon of the ratatouille chutney. Drizzle the thyme sauce onto lamb, as desired. Top with squash blossom.

YIELD

Serves 6

HOTEL LA ROSE

The earliest known inhabitants of Santa Rosa were the Pomo, Miwok, and Wappo Indians. They were displaced by the Spanish, who occupied much of present-day California in the early 1800s and made a number of land grants to encourage settlers. The first land grant in this area was given to the mother-in-law of General Vallejo, who commanded the Mexican forces north of the Presidio in San Francisco. Señora Maria Ignacia Lopez de Carrillo named her home Rancho Cabeza de Santa Rosa, or Ranch of the Santa Rosa.

Local legend says that Father Juan Amorosa was performing a baptism on the day of the Feast of Santa Rosa de Lima in the river, and so named the local river after this saint. Once the name stuck, it was also applied to the valley, and then later the town that grew. To support her ranch, Señora Carrillo built an adobe structure near the junction of the Indian trading routes. The ruins still stand today near the present-day Farmer's Lane and Highway 12, adjacent to Street Eugene's Church. The gold rush brought many people to the surrounding area, but quite a few of them realized they would probably never get rich in mining, and elected to farm the fertile valley instead.

Several enterprising businesspeople rented the Carrillo Adobe in the 1850s, opening a general goods store. To attract settlers and customers, they plotted out a town and sold lots for $25 each. Santa Rosa was born and, in 1868, the State of California officially recognized it.

The arrival of the Northern Pacific Railroad in 1870 and the Santa Rosa & Carquinez Railroad in 1887 assured the new town's success. After a fire destroyed the original stationhouse in 1903, it was replaced with the Northwestern Pacific Railroad depot. Still standing, the depot has been used as a site for scenes in movies such as Alfred Hitchcock's *Shadow of a Doubt* and *Cheaper by the Dozen*.

The same stonemasons who constructed the new train depot built the Hotel La Rose across the street. They are credited with building a number of other buildings in the area, most famously, Jack London's Wolf House. Basalt blocks for these buildings were quarried from hills to the east of the city.

When built a century ago in 1907, the Hotel La Rose cost $35,000 and had 40 rooms and a bar. The hotel was so popular that, during Prohibition, the hotel's bar continued to serve red wine, produced in copious quantities in Sonoma County. A local constable was almost tarred and feathered for trying to shut down the hotel's bar.

 *60*

The Hotel La Rose is listed with the Historic Hotels of America under the auspices of the National Trust for Historic Preservation. Guests will find many of the hotel rooms named after both illustrious and colorful Railroad Square founders. The hotel's handout offers brief biographies of these historic Santa Rosa luminaries.

Hotel La Rose
308 Wilson Street
Santa Rosa, California 95401
(800) 527-6738
(707) 579-3200

Cream of Carrot Soup

Chop 3 of the carrots and all of the celery, leek, and potato into chunks. In another bowl, shred remaining carrots and put aside. Cook leeks in butter until just turning translucent. Add remaining chunked vegetables and rice. Stir over medium heat for 3 to 4 minutes.

Add stock to vegetables and simmer for 30 to 45 minutes. Puree cooked mixture. Add cream, milk, and shredded carrots. Bring just to a boiling point and reduce heat. Season to taste with your choice of seasonings. Allow to simmer for 5 to 10 minutes. Garnish with parsley.

6 medium carrots

2 celery stalks

¼ small leek

1 medium potato

2 ounces butter

½ cup rice

2½ quarts chicken stock

1 pint heavy cream

1 pint milk

Salt, pepper, soy sauce, and
Worcestershire sauce to taste

2 tablespoons parsley, chopped

8 7-ounce beef filets

½ onion, chopped

1 tablespoon butter

1 pound mushrooms, chopped

½ cup red wine

1 tablespoon mustard

Salt, pepper, tarragon, thyme, soy
sauce, basil to taste

2 eggs

8 ounces liver pate

1 pound puff pastry dough

Duxelle, as needed
(finely chopped mushrooms
cooked in butter with
shallots and wine)

Beef Wellington

Roast or grill filets to rare. Allow to cool.

Glaze onions in butter. Add mushrooms, red wine, mustard, and spices. Simmer until wine is completely reduced. Add 1 egg and liver pate and mix well. Let cool.

Roll out puffed pastry to ⅛-inch thickness. Coat filet with duxelle and wrap it in the puffed pastry. In a small bowl, mix the second egg with a tablespoon of water. Brush the Beef Wellington with the egg wash. Bake in 425-degree oven for 15–20 minutes or until golden brown. For well-done beef, bake for an additional 10 minutes at 375 degrees.

Bread pudding

Similar in taste and fluffiness to French toast, this nut-and-fruit bread bake is perfect to serve to a group for brunch.

Cut bread into 1 inch cubes and place in a baking pan or casserole dish. In another bowl, mix all other ingredients well. Pour the custard over bread. Bake at 425 degrees for approximately 45 minutes. Serve warm.

YIELD

Serves 10

1 loaf French bread

6 eggs

6 cups milk

1 cup walnuts

1 cup almonds

½ tablespoon vanilla

½ cup sugar

3 tablespoons honey

1 cup raisins

THE HUNTINGTON HOTEL

Many people consider Nob Hill to be San Francisco's crown jewel. It has always been home to the very rich and famous; city pioneers and great railroad barons, such as Charles Crocker, Leland Stanford, Mark Hopkins, and C. P. Huntington, all built great mansions above the masses. The founders of Hibernia Bank, the Tobin family, also built a mansion there in the 1870s on the site of what is now the Huntington Hotel.

Construction of the Huntington Apartments in 1922 cost $2.5 million, a very large sum at the time. It was the first steel and brick high-rise west of the Mississippi. The *Illustrated Daily Herald* referred to this residential apartment hotel building as the last word in luxury. Offering San Francisco's first twin wall-beds or Murphy beds, Pullman kitchens with electric stoves, and inset steam radiators, The Huntington offered the finest apartment facilities with the most up-to-date hotel service. Room service for the residents was considered a unique innovation.

Eugene Fritz, a real estate developer who managed the property, purchased the Huntington Apartments in 1924, and continued the long-standing tradition of high standards and gracious service. After World War II, Fritz transformed the apartment building into the elegant Huntington Hotel. One of the most distinguishing characteristics of this change was that Fritz retained the very large size of the apartments, making the Huntington's guest rooms substantially larger than those of competitors.

Fritz's daughter Dolly took over the management of the hotel in 1950, expanding the hotel's exclusive reputation through an extensive renovation project. She lavishly refurbished the hotel's rooms and suites. Appointed with antiques, imported silks, and original artwork, she made sure that no two rooms were alike. Her commitment to service and a strong belief in a guest's right to privacy attracted patrons such as Princess Grace, the Vanderbilt family, Claudette Colbert, the Rothschilds, and many others.

Dolly also transformed the ground-floor executive offices into the Big 4 Restaurant. Named for the four great railroad barons of the Central Pacific—Huntington, Stanford, Crocker, and Hopkins—the restaurant's club-like atmosphere showcases Dolly's impressive collection of nineteenth-century railroad and early California memorabilia. Currently, a third generation of Dolly's family is actively involved in managing the property at every level.

The Huntington maintains a long-standing tradition of high standards and gracious service. Its reputation for quiet, understated luxury has made the hotel a favorite among savvy travelers who prefer individuality and elegance.

"It's simply a very romantic place. Just one look at any of those streets, and you couldn't be anywhere else—it's so beautiful, and there's that location, and the sense of the free spirit. . . . Who couldn't become ravenous in such a place?"

—Julia Child, chef

The Huntington Hotel
1075 California Street
San Francisco, California 94108
(415) 474-5400

TAMARIND-LIME DRESSING

¼ cup rice wine vinegar or Sausalito Springs watercress vinegar

½ cup lime juice

½ cup plus 2 tablespoons pureed mango

1 teaspoon tamarind concentrate or paste

2 teaspoons minced jalapeño peppers, no seeds

1 teaspoon salt

1 teaspoon curry powder

½ cup peanut oil

SALAD

1 cup cooked chicken, finely diced or shredded

1 cup sliced fresh mango

1 tablespoon mint leaves, chopped

2 tablespoons cilantro, chopped

1 tablespoon water chestnuts, chopped

¼ cup each red and green onions, diced

½ cup red bell pepper, julienned

PLATING

1 cup Sausalito Springs baby watercress

1 head of endiga or red Belgian endive

¼ cup toasted cashew nuts, chopped

Indonesian Toasted Cashew and Chicken-Mango Salad with Baby Watercress and Tamarind-Lime Vinaigrette

Puree the Tamarind-Lime Dressing ingredients in a blender until smooth. Thin out with a little water if dressing is too thick. Combine salad ingredients in a bowl and toss with enough dressing to moisten. Serve over a bed of baby watercress and endiga, with additional dressing drizzled around the plate and crushed cashews on top.

Note: Garnish with crispy rice noodles if desired.

Toasted Pecan Red Cabbage Slaw

Great accompaniment to grilled meats or fish

Place cabbage, onions, and pecans in a bowl and set aside.

In separate bowl, combine all ingredients and spices from honey through vinegars. Add olive oil, whisking continuously, until somewhat emulsified. Add most of the dressing to cabbage, pecans, and onions. Toss well. Let sit for 30 minutes before serving.

"San Franciscans are very proud of their city, and they should be. It's the most beautiful place in the world."

—Robert Redford, actor and director

1 small head red cabbage, finely shredded (about 4–6 cups)

2 cups red onion, thinly sliced

3 cups toasted pecan halves

1½ tablespoons honey

1 teaspoon caraway seeds

2 teaspoons dry mustard

½ teaspoon salt

¼ teaspoon ground ginger

Juice and zest of 2 oranges

½ cup raspberry vinegar

½ cup red wine vinegar

1 cup light olive oil

VENISON CHILI

⅛ cup cooking oil

1½ pounds ground venison meat
 (large grind)

1¼ pounds ground pork
 (large grind)

2 cloves garlic and 1 whole
 jalapeño, pureed in blender
 with ⅛ cup oil

1½ cups yellow onions, sliced

1 tablespoon chili powder

¾ tablespoon ground cumin

1 teaspoon dried thyme

½ teaspoon each dried oregano,
 celery seed, paprika,
 black pepper

⅛ teaspoon each anise seed, chili
 flakes, cayenne pepper

Small pinch of ground cloves

¾ teaspoon salt

1 bay leaf

1½ 10-ounce bottles chili sauce
 (such as Heinz)

1 28-ounce can of diced tomatoes
 in juice

⅓ cup tomato paste

2 cups chicken broth

PLATING

3 cups cooked black beans (home
 prepared or canned)

3 cups white sharp cheddar
 cheese, shredded

1 recipe Honey-Spiced Onion
 Crisps (recipe follows)

Venison Chili with Black Beans and Honey-Spiced Onion Crisps

In a 12-quart saucepan, heat oil and brown the meat. Add jalapeño-garlic mixture, onions, and spices through bay leaf. Cook for 5 minutes.

Add tomato products and stock. Stir until well combined. Bring to a boil and then simmer for about 2 hours. Add more chicken stock if mixture becomes too thick.

PLATING

Ladle chili into bowls. Top each bowl with a few tablespoons of cooked black beans (optional). Sprinkle with cheese and place under broiler or in microwave briefly to melt cheese. Top with onion crisps and serve.

YIELD
Yields 2 quarts

Honey-Spiced Onion Crisps

Heat oil for deep-frying to 325–350 degrees.

Meanwhile, in a large bowl, toss the onions with spices and honey. Flour the onions very generously, tossing them all the while, to keep them separated. Let them sit for 5–10 minutes, tossing them several times throughout.

Shake off the excess flour well.

Have a pan lined with paper towels and a skimmer ready. Fry the onions in small batches until golden.

Using a skimmer, transfer onions to paper towels to drain. Sprinkle lightly with kosher salt if desired. Serve as a garnish on top of chili.

"It is impossible to reminisce about San Francisco without thinking of food. As an international overeater, I would not hesitate to take any European gourmet and invite him to lean his paunch against the tales set by the restaurants there."

—Paul Gallico, author

2 quarts canola oil for deep frying, placed in a high-sided, 8-quart heavy saucepan

2 red onions, thinly sliced

½ teaspoon chili powder

½ teaspoon ground cumin

½ teaspoon salt

¼ teaspoon cayenne pepper

1 tablespoon honey

2 cups flour

INTERCONTINENTAL MARK HOPKINS SAN FRANCISCO

San Francisco has benefited greatly from the influx of diverse peoples. First to arrive were the Spanish explorers and then there was a flood of Europeans, a few Russians, and a great many Chinese who came to build the railroads. The Gold Rush attracted tens of thousands of new settlers from all over the world. They stayed for the climate and to enjoy the prosperity that this shipping and naval facility on America's new West Coast would offer.

The mining craze made many millionaires, both from gold and from businesses that supported the prospectors. But the railroads had perhaps the most significant impact on the city.

The Mark Hopkins is located on the site of the former 40-room mansion of Mark Hopkins, one of San Francisco's "Big Four," who founded what became the Southern Pacific Railroad. Hopkins, Charles Crocker, Collis Huntington, and Leland Stanford earned much of the credit for the economic development of San Francisco following the surge of humanity pursuing dreams of golden riches. The house was actually built by Hopkins at the insistence of his socialite wife Mary, but he died before it was finished in 1878.

After being destroyed by the great earthquake and fire of 1906, the mansion was later replaced by a more modest structure built by the San Francisco Art Association, who received the property from Mary Hopkins' second husband. The location was so admired, mining engineer and hotel investor George D. Smith, who had long admired the site, bought it in 1925 and built a luxury hotel.

When it opened in 1926, the hotel became an immediate part of San Francisco's rich and colorful history. Many events took place at the Mark Hopkins, such as some of the meetings for the historic founding of the United Nations in 1945. Since then, guests have included royalty, diplomats, political personalities, celebrities, and five American presidents and heads of state from around the world.

The Top of the Mark is a favorite watering hole for guests, tourists, and locals alike. This nineteenth-floor sky lounge atop the hotel offers a dramatic, panoramic view of the ever-changing San Francisco Bay Area landscape.

Because the Mark Hopkins is located on the top of prestigious Nob Hill at the intersection of California and Mason Streets, it is a regular stop on the California Street cable car line, just minutes away from the financial and theater districts, as well as Union Square and Chinatown.

"What I like best about San Francisco is San Francisco."

—Frank Lloyd Wright, architect

InterContinental Mark Hopkins San Francisco
Number One Nob Hill
999 California Street
San Francisco, California 94108
(415) 392-3434

2½ ounces Chopin vodka

Drop of vermouth

Tomato olive for garnish

Top of the Mark

Stir vodka and vermouth and strain into a chilled martini glass. Garnish and serve.

"I prefer a wet San Francisco to a dry Manhattan."

—Larry Geraldi, composer

YIELD

Serves 1

Only in San Francisco

Shake for 10 seconds on ice, then strain into a martini glass. Serve garnished with an orange twist.

 YIELD

Serves 1

"It is as if the entire city came from common parents— Scott Fitzgerald and Isadora Duncan."

—anonymous Hollywood writer

½ ounce Bailey's

1½ ounce Smirnoff Raspberry vodka

Orange twist for garnish

4 large egg whites (½ cup) or
    ½ cup refrigerated
    pasteurized egg whites

1 teaspoon white distilled or
    white wine vinegar

¾ cup plus about 2 tablespoons
    sugar

1 tablespoon cornstarch

1 teaspoon vanilla extract

1 cup whipping cream

Sugar to taste,
    about 2 tablespoons

3 cups sliced strawberries

1 cup mixed sliced fruit or berries

Mint sprigs

Spring Pavlova

Preheat oven to 300 degrees (275 degrees convection).

In a large bowl, with a mixer (preferably fitted with wire-whisk attachment) on high speed, beat egg whites and vinegar until foamy. Mix 1 tablespoon of the sugar with 1 tablespoon cornstarch and set aside. Gradually add remaining sugar, about 1 tablespoon at a time, beating well after each addition and scraping sides of bowl occasionally, until stiff, shiny peaks form. After beating all of the sugar into the whites, add sugar-cornstarch mixture and vanilla and beat just until blended.

Using baking sheets lined with parchment paper or silicone sheets is recommended. To make individual pavlovas, mound meringue in eight equal portions (a scant ½ cup for each) on baking sheets, spacing at least 3 inches apart. Shape each into a 4-inch round using a small thin spatula or butter knife.

Bake in preheated oven until a thin, crisp crust forms on the surface but interior is still soft when gently pressed, 20 to 25 minutes for individual pavlovas. Remove from oven and let cool completely. Carefully remove from baking sheet and transfer to a platter or plates (it's normal for crust to crack a little).

In a bowl, with a mixer on high speed, beat whipping cream just until soft peaks form. Turn mixer to low and beat in sugar to taste.

Top pavlovas with berries and sliced fruit and top with whipped cream. A sprig of fresh mint adds the perfect finish.

JACK'S GRILL

The Wintu tribe of Native Americans occupied the Redding area, until the early 1800s. Trails used by the Indians became the route for the Siskiyou Trail, which was the primary overland route for trappers moving between the Hudson Bay Company district headquarters in Southern Washington and the San Francisco offices.

One of California's early pioneers, Pierson B. Reading, received a Mexican land grant in 1844 for the land along the Sacramento River where Redding is today. The Siskiyou Trail passed through the area and the gold rush of 1849 brought many travelers. Miners founded a town along the trail that was so poor, they referred to it as Poverty Flats. When the economy of the town improved, the name was changed to Redding to honor one of the railroad men who helped develop the area. Later, citizens considered naming the town Reading after the first white settler but, when the railroad refused to acknowledge the change, the name was officially returned to Redding.

Redding incorporated with only 600 people in 1887, but grew to 25,000 before the Great Depression. Very hard times nearly caused the city to become a ghost town. Less than 300 people remained in the 1930s, due to little or no agriculture. The completion of the Shasta Dam in 1945 resulted in a surge of population and the local economy.

After prospectors failed to find major quantities of gold in the surrounding hills, Redding's main industry became lumber—and every town of lumberjacks has several saloons for entertainment. The two-story structure that houses Jack's Grill was actually built in 1935 by Bill Morrison and first served as a secondhand store. In 1938, the downstairs was leased to a World War I flying ace, Jack Young.

Redding's elders felt that there were already too many saloons in town, but Jack opened one more bar and grill. He was successful, largely because of the influx of workers for the dam, the few mines that survived, and the new railroads snaking through the area. California Street became a magnet for hotels, bars, and a number of bordellos. Even the upstairs of Jack's Grill served horizontal refreshments for a time in the early 1940s. Of all the bars opened during that era, Jack's is the only one that survived.

Jack was around just long enough to give the bar a permanent name. Jack sold the establishment to Fats Woolf in the 1940s and, when Fats died, Joe and June Stanley bought it. June was the daughter of the original builder, Bill Morrison, and she is responsible for emphasizing the restaurant aspect, adding respectability to what had been primarily a bar.

The most recent owner, Don Conley, has avoided any unnecessary modernization of Jack's. The building still has the same façade and décor of its early days, including two original Old West–style paintings. One of the paintings shows a traditional sheriff sitting in a chair. One evening, a drunk customer, just out of jail, was so enraged by the badge-wearing lawman in the painting that he shot the painting five times. All the bullets hit within 4 inches of the badge. Bullet holes in the wall behind the painting were not discovered until 40 years later.

One of the original traditions of Jack's, still observed today, is the 1-pound steak. Loggers, miners, and construction workers always wanted a substantial meal after a very long and exhausting work day, and Jack served each worker a pound of beef, and today you can get the same meal, or if you wish, a downsized version including New York strips, top sirloin, or filet mignon.

Walking into Jack's is like walking into the 1930s. Seventeen stools at the bar and old-style booths and tables accentuate the retro atmosphere. Locally owned from its very inception, Jack's is truly a part of California history.

Jack's Grill
1743 California Street
Redding, California 96001
(530) 241-9705

"Old Fashion" Old-Fashioned

Chill a large rocks glass. Add sugar, bitters cherry juice, and a splash of soda. Using a muddler, stir mixture until dissolved. Add ice and rye whiskey. Stir with a bar spoon.

Garnish with a lemon twist and cherry.

Sip and be transported to a time when life was slower and easier.

 YIELD

Serves 1

1 teaspoon sugar

Dash of bitters

Dash cherry juice

Splash of soda

1½ ounces rye whiskey

Lemon twist

1 cherry

1½ ounces premium vodka

½ ounce triple sec

½ ounce lime juice

Lime slice

Killer Kamikaze

Chill a small snifter glass. Pour vodka into a martini shaker filled with ice. Add triple sec and lime juice. Shake vigorously and pour into glass. Garnish with a slice of lime.

Proceed with caution. It's called a kamikaze for a reason.

⤚ YIELD ⤙

Serves 1

Jack's Oil and Vinegar Salad

Mix the equal parts of oil and vinegar. Toss with cold iceberg lettuce and green beans. Season and serve.

 YIELD

Serves 4–6

"We may live without friends, we may live without books, but civilized man cannot live without cooks. He may live without love—what is passion but pining? But where is the man who can live without dining?"

—Bulwer Lytton, writer

¼ cup apple cider vinegar

¼ cup good-quality salad oil

1 head cold iceberg lettuce, chopped

2 ounces French-cut green beans

Seasoned salt, such as McCormick Season-All

JIMTOWN STORE

In 1840, Cyrus Alexander was on a scouting expedition for a wealthy San Diego trader, Captain H. D. Fitch. Alexander worked for Fitch harvesting sea lions and otters at the time when Fitch decided to expand his empire. Alexander's new task was to look for unclaimed land north of San Francisco that might be suitable for raising cattle. He was expecting part of his compensation for the search to be some of that land.

His first stop was a large valley, which had already been claimed by George Yount and later was named Napa. Over the hill, he found a place that he described as "the brightest and best spot in the world." This valley, irrigated by the Russian River, became part of the Fitch empire, and Cyrus Alexander was contracted to run the operation. In exchange, he would receive both livestock and 8,800 acres in what would eventually be named the Alexander Valley.

The 1849 Gold Rush lured three brother farmers from Missouri to California. Samuel, Thomas, and Harmon Heald set out to make their fortune in the rivers and creeks north of San Francisco. Finding little success, and suffering from various medical problems, they eventually went into business supporting the prospectors and the commerce that surrounded the mad dash for gold.

Samuel bought an interest in a mill along the Russian River and Thomas became his operations manager. Then Harmon, attempting to recover from his medical problems, built a small sanitarium in the form of a squatter's cabin along the main road in the area. Passing traffic encouraged him to include a small addition that served as a general store. This enterprise became the nucleus for the town of Healdsburg.

As other settlers moved into the area, the town was eventually paid out, lots were sold, and other failed miners went into business, providing services for the few who succeeded, and for the others attracted to the quest for riches. The land itself was formally owned by Captain Fitch's widow, who was forced to sell it to pay the taxes due on the very large land holdings she inherited. While most towns in the area were named for the principal landowners, this town was named for Harmon Heald because most people thought of him as a "clean, upright, beneficent character."

Jimtown Store has been a landmark since 1895, when it served as the general store, post office, and meeting place for residents of the valley. The landmark had been abandoned for some time when the late John Werner, and his wife, artist Carrie Brown, discovered it in 1989 while visiting from New York City. Falling in love with the town, the building, and the local inhabitants, they set about reviving the former general store into a very special eating establishment. The current property includes a large general store, a renovated migrant worker's cottage, and two large barns

used as storage for antiques. Once again, this authentic country store is Sonoma County's favorite country market, just as it was in 1895.

Jimtown Store
6706 State Highway 128
Healdsburg, California 95448
(707) 433-1212

8¼-inch-thick oval slices from a baguette-style loaf of bread

Olive oil

¼ pound well-trimmed creamy blue cheese, such as Gorgonzola, at room temperature

3 tablespoons Jimtown Fig & Olive Spread

Freshly ground black pepper to taste

4 thin slices Genoa style salami, cut into matchstick pieces

Bruschetta with Fig & Olive, Blue Cheese, and Salami

For this speedy and unusually delicious nibble, toasted ovals of good bread are spread with tangy blue cheese and Jimtown Fig & Olive Spread, then topped with matchsticks of salami. This bruschetta makes a rustic starter for a country-style Mediterranean menu.

Lightly brush the bread slices all over with olive oil. Lay them on a baking sheet and toast them in a 400-degree oven, turning them once, until they are crisp and lightly browned, about 8 minutes total.

Spread the toasted bread with the blue cheese, dividing it evenly and using it all. Season generously with pepper. Spread Jimtown Fig & Olive Spread on top of cheese.

Top the crostini (toasted bread) with the salami. Serve within 30 minutes of completion.

⟞ YIELD ⟝
Serves 2–4

Potato Tomato Soup with Sage

Peel the potatoes and cut them into quarters or large chunks. Drop them into a nonheated saucepan filled with water. Add the onions, garlic cloves, sage leaves, salt, and bouquet garni of bay leaves and peppercorns. Bring to a boil over medium heat and simmer until the potatoes are tender when pierced by a fork.

While the potatoes are cooking, heat the olive oil in a sauté pan over medium heat, then add the peeled tomatoes with their juice. Simmer for 20 minutes.

The potatoes and tomatoes should be done at about the same time. Drain the potatoes in a colander set over a bowl. Reserve the liquid. Discard the bay leaf and peppercorn bundle. Allow the potatoes and tomatoes to cool for about 15 minutes.

Working in small batches in a food processor, puree the potato mixture with the tomatoes and their juice, adding a little reserved potato liquid to each batch. Transfer the pureed batches of soup into a large pot. If you haven't used all of the potato broth during the pureeing, you may use it to thin the soup to a desired consistency. Gently warm over medium heat. Taste for salt and pepper.

3 pounds Yukon Gold potatoes (or russets)

2 quarts water

2 medium yellow onions (about 14 ounces), peeled, cut into 1-inch pieces

20 cloves of garlic, peeled

24 large fresh sage leaves (approximately ½ ounce)

2 tablespoons kosher salt

4 bay leaves

8 black peppercorns (tied in a cheesecloth bundle with the bay leaves)

¼ cup olive oil

2 28-ounce cans peeled Italian tomatoes (no salt)

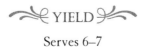

YIELD
Serves 6–7

½ cup chopped onion

½ cup chopped celery

½ teaspoon chopped garlic

2 tablespoons olive oil

1½ pounds ground turkey

½ cup breadcrumbs

1 beaten egg

1 teaspoon dried marjoram

1 teaspoon salt

½ teaspoon pepper

2 tablespoons chopped parsley

2 tablespoons dry white wine

1 teaspoon Worcestershire sauce

Tabasco to taste

1 7-ounce container Jimtown
    Roasted Vegetable Spread

Roasted Vegetable Turkey Meatloaf

A flavorful, low-in-fat update of the original!

Sauté onion, celery, and garlic in oil over medium-low heat until soft, approximately 5 minutes.

In a mixing bowl, combine all of the other ingredients with half of the Jimtown Roasted Vegetable Spread, setting aside the remaining ½ cup. Spoon into lightly oiled loaf pan (you may use vegetable spray). Bake at 400 degrees for 50–60 minutes.

Pour off juice. Top with remaining Jimtown Roasted Vegetable Spread and bake for another 15 minutes.

YIELD

Serves 4–5

MADRONA MANOR

The history of the towns in the wine country is intertwined. Indians first roamed the valley before the explorers and settlers arrived from Spain, Russia, Mexico, Europe, and other areas of the newly emerging United States. Soto, one of the leading chiefs of the Pomo Indian tribe, gave his name to later inhabitants of the region of what would later be called the Fitch Mountains.

Captain Henry D. Fitch of San Diego had been granted 48,000 acres of land in the area by the Mexican government in 1844. Fitch had hired Cyrus Alexander to survey the area and Alexander stayed to manage his property there. For his efforts, Alexander was granted 8,800 acres in this valley that would eventually bear his name.

The Fitch property was named Rancho Sotoyomi in honor of the Indian chief and the people who first settled the area. Fitch had married Josefina Carillo and they moved to the new ranch to enjoy the beautiful valley. When Fitch passed away in 1849, Josefina was forced to auction off part of the ranch several years later to pay mounting taxes.

The Heald brothers from Missouri had come to the area to seek a fortune in the gold fields, but quickly realized they were not going to get rich prospecting. Having occupied a squatters' cabin on the Rancho Sotoyomi after Fitch's death, they purchased the property they liked when Josefina offered it for sale, and set up a general store to serve the various miners and travelers in the area.

Healdsburg was named for these Missouri farmers who are credited with laying out the town. Now a community of 9,500 in the Sonoma County wine country, Healdsburg is a picturesque city with an historic town square dating back to the original town plan. The confluence of the Alexander, Dry Creek, and Russian River Valleys attracted many people, who then also attracted the Northwestern Pacific Railway in 1871. Rail service was a great step forward for the area.

John Alexander Paxton was one of the California Gold Rush success stories. He made a fortune in mining, banking, lumber, and property. In 1879, Paxton created the Madrona Knoll Rancho on 240 acres west of Healdsburg and then built a 17-room Victorian mansion.

Known as the Madrona Manor, this beautiful structure served as his country retreat on weekends. Every Monday morning he traveled to San Francisco by train or horseback to oversee his business empire, returning to the countryside on Friday evenings. Paxton established an early lifestyle of commuting to and from the big city practiced even today by many wealthy Californians.

John Paxton died in 1887 while on a steamship headed for Liverpool. His remains were returned to his country property, later to be moved to San Francisco when his wife passed away. The manor remained in the Paxton family until the early twentieth century. It continued to serve as a

 *86*

private residence until 1981, when it was renovated and converted into an elegant and romantic country inn and restaurant.

Madrona Manor
1001 Westside Road
Healdsburg, California 95448
(707) 433-4231

Pan-Seared Halibut with English Peas, Fava Beans, Olive Oil Mashed Potatoes, and Artichokes

Prepare this recipe according to the following four-step sequence below, one each for artichokes, potatoes, vegetables, and fish. (You may wish to make parts separately to serve with other foods.) You will need to start with the artichoke salad because the artichokes need to marinate for at least one hour. They will remain fine for at least 4 hours.

STEP 1: ARTICHOKE SALAD
In this salad, the artichokes are raw but "cooked" and "de-toughened" in lemon juice.

Remove tough outer leaves and stem from the artichokes so only the heart remains, making sure any green is trimmed away. Cut artichoke heart in half and remove the choke with a spoon. Rub artichokes with a cut lemon to prevent discoloration. Slice artichoke hearts paper-thin on a mandolin. Mix with sliced shallots and juice from one lemon. Let artichokes sit for one hour.

Later, when you are ready to serve the fish, mix spinach, artichokes, and the olive oil and place on top of the fish.

ARTICHOKE SALAD

2 large artichokes

2 large lemons

2 shallots sliced

½ cup baby spinach washed and stems removed

1 tablespoon extra virgin olive oil

OLIVE OIL MASHED POTATOES

2 large Yukon gold potatoes peeled and cut into ¼-inch pieces

½ cup milk

2 ounces butter

¼ cup extra virgin olive oil

Salt and pepper to taste

SPRING VEGETABLE RAGOUT

2 pounds fresh fava beans

1 pound English peas

1 bunch basil leaves

½ cup canola oil

1½ cup vegetable stock

2 tablespoons butter

Salt and pepper to taste

STEP 2: OLIVE OIL MASHED POTATOES

Replacing some of the butter with olive oil to reduce the fat, this recipe for mashed potatoes provides a healthier dish.

Cook potatoes in salted water until tender. Drain potatoes well or the mashed potatoes will become mushy and less flavorful. Put the potatoes through a food mill or a ricer. Warm the milk, add in the olive oil and butter, and stir into potatoes, making sure not to over-mix or the potatoes will become gummy. Season to taste. Set aside in a warm place until ready to serve.

STEP 3: SPRING VEGETABLE RAGOUT

This ragout features spring vegetables in an herbed vegetable broth.

Shell fresh fava beans from their pods. Quickly blanch beans in salted water, refreshing in ice bath. Remove the outer skin leaving only the inside bean.

Shell the peas. Quickly blanch in salted water and refresh in ice bath.

Blanch basil leaves in boiling, salted water for 15 seconds, then immediately refresh in ice water. Squeeze excess water out of basil and chop roughly. Blend basil and canola oil in blender on high for 2 minutes. Strain off oil (reserve for use in a salad or to flavor vegetables at a later time) and refrigerate puréed basil.

(At this point, the vegetables and basil are prepared. See Halibut section below for Vegetable Ragout finishing directions.)

STEP 4: PAN-SEARED HALIBUT

Cooking of the halibut and final plating preparations for dish.

After the artichokes, mashed potatoes, and the vegetable ragout are finished, you are ready to cook the fish. Season both sides of the fish with salt and pepper. In a nonstick pan, heat 2 tablespoons canola oil until it starts to smoke. Add the halibut and cook on high for 30 seconds; then turn the heat down to medium heat. This will ensure that the fish develops a nice crust without burning. After about 3 minutes, turn the fish over and cook on the other side for 3 more minutes.

As you are cooking the fish, heat the vegetable stock to finish the ragout and add the peas and fava beans. When the mixture comes to a boil, turn down and add butter. Just before serving, add 2 tablespoons of the basil puree to flavor the broth.

PRESENTATION

Divide vegetable ragout among four bowls. Place approximately ½ cup of mashed potatoes in the center of the bowl. Place the fish on top of the mashed potatoes. Top the fish with the artichoke salad. Serve and enjoy!

YIELD

Serves 4

89

PAN-SEARED HALIBUT

4 6-ounce halibut filets, skin and bones removed

MENDOCINO HOTEL AND GARDEN SUITES

Both the town and county of Mendocino derive their names from Cape Mendocino, which lies more than 100 miles to the north, in the next county. The cape was given its name by Juan Rodriquez Cabrillo, a sixteenth-century Spanish explorer. He discovered the peninsula in 1542 while on a voyage up the Pacific Coast and named it in honor of Don Antonio de Mendoza, the first viceroy of New Spain (Mexico), because the viceroy funded the expedition.

The Pomo Indians who were native to the area were of little concern to the Spaniards, who were out to discover the world and colonize whatever lands they found. Spanish settlers soon arrived in the area, but it was 300 years before the Gold Rush brought non-Spanish settlements into the county.

The flood of settlers hoping to get rich in 1849 forced California to organize itself. Twenty-seven counties were created in 1850 by the state legislature, including Mendocino. The county was first administered by the government of Sonoma County·until 1859, because it was so small. When the government was finally established in 1859 in nearby Ukiah, it was quickly decided that the coastal site of Mendocino would be more appropriate, and the county seat moved the following year. Logging of redwoods promised to make the town prosperous.

The life of a logger was dangerous. Add to this the Wild West nature of California with its wide-open lands, teeming with people desperate to find gold, and you get a mixture of society that was somewhat unpredictable. They all worked hard and played hard. Saloons, pool halls, and comfort houses were common in this logging town, which soon boasted a population of 20,000.

To counter this cultural depravity, settlers from the Northeast who had brought their wives and children with them began to build homes and a sense of stability. The architecture of the town today still resembles that of many New England villages.

The Mendocino Hotel was originally opened as The Temperance House in 1878. It was considered at the time to be "the one bastion of good Christian morals in a town of loggers." But as the redwood logging industry faded, then stopped completely decades later, people began to move away. The population eventually declined to about 1,000.

The original structure of the hotel remains and encompasses 26 overnight accommodations, the lobby, the lobby bar, the dining room, the kitchen, and a balcony that overlooks the Pacific Ocean and

the Mendocino Headlands. Situated on the scenic California coast, the Mendocino Hotel is the only remaining hotel from the early days when Mendocino was a booming port for the logging trade.

An extensive 1975 renovation restored the hotel to its original atmosphere adding fine art, stained glass, Oriental carpets, and period antiques. At the same time, the garden next to the hotel was designed with a large glass dome, seating for up to 100, and a dance floor to accommodate weddings, local theater, and concerts. Twenty five additional suites and a business and media center were constructed on 2 acres of lush vegetation incorporating the restored Heeser House, which was home to the original founder of the town.

Ask the front desk staff for details of the amazing collection of historical pieces in the hotel. You may also ask to be seated in the dinning room at one of the tables said to be frequented by the ghost of a Victorian lady. The staff will tell you their stories of her various appearances.

The Mendocino Hotel is about a 3½-hour drive north of the San Francisco or Oakland Airports. More than 24 wineries in the area and the breathtaking coastal scenery may make the drive longer—but once you arrive, you won't want to leave.

Mendocino Hotel and Garden Suites
45080 Main Street
Mendocino, California 95460
(800) 548-0513
(707) 937-0511

1¼ ounces Bailey's Irish Cream

½ ounce amaretto

Organic Big River Coffee

Whipped cream, optional

Mendocino Coffee

Mix Bailey's and amaretto into coffee and top with homemade whipped cream. Serve in your favorite coffee mug.

YIELD

Serves 1

"I think it must be so, for I have been drinking it for sixty-five years and I am not dead yet."

—Voltaire, writer, on learning that coffee was considered a slow poison

Roast Duck with Caramelized Apples

DUCK

Clean duckling well. Season inside and out with salt and pepper. Place orange zest and lemon zest inside cavity. On stovetop, heat oil in a roasting pan. Brown the duck. Place in preheated oven at 425 degrees. Roast for about 1 hour or until done.

STOCK SAUCE

On stovetop, place the sugar and vinegar in a pot and bring to a boil. Cook until light caramel in color. Deglaze with the orange and lemon juice. Reduce until syrupy. Add the stock and reduce by one-third.

Once duck is cooked, remove and discard the excess fat in the duck pan. Place on the stovetop and deglaze the pan with stock sauce mixture. Add red currant jelly. In a small bowl, dilute the potato starch with the orange liqueur. Bring the sauce to a boil and thicken sauce with diluted potato starch. Season and strain sauce. Add zest.

APPLES

Peel, core, and slice apples into thin wedges. Heat the clarified butter in a sauté pan. Add the apples and toss until coated. Sprinkle with sugar and cook until lightly caramelized.

PRESENTATION

Serve roasted duck with caramelized apples and citrus pan sauce neatly arranged on a plate.

DUCK

1 duckling, about 4 pounds

Sea salt to taste

Pepper to taste

½ ounce orange zest

½ ounce lemon zest

Olive oil, as needed

STOCK SAUCE

1¼ ounces sugar

2½ ounces red wine vinegar

1¼ ounces lemon juice

4½ ounces orange juice

1 pint veal stock

1 ounce red currant jelly

2 teaspoons potato starch

½ ounce triple sec

1 tablespoon blanched orange zest

1 tablespoon blanched lemon zest

APPLES

1¼ pounds apples

1½ ounces clarified butter

1 ounce sugar

2 ounces butter

2½ pounds sweet onions,
    sliced thin

3¼ quarts beef stock (canned
    stock may be substituted)

3 bay leaves

Salt to taste

Pepper to taste

2–3 ounces sherry (optional)

French Onion Soup

Heat butter in a stockpot over medium heat. Add onions and cook slowly until they are caramelized.

Add the stock and bay leaves to the stockpot and bring to a boil. Let onions simmer until the flavors are well blended, about 20 minutes. Turn heat off and season with salt, pepper, and sherry if desired.

OPTIONAL FINISH

Toast sliced French bread under broiler. Place one to two slices of toast over crocks or bowls of hot soup. Cover toast with coarsely grated Gruyère or Swiss cheese. Place under broiler until lightly brown. Serve immediately.

NAPA RIVER INN

The Napa River Inn is rich in history and architectural integrity. The cornerstone of the Historic Napa Mill, the Hatt Building was built in 1884 and serves as the primary structure of the Napa River Inn. The building was named after Captain Albert Hatt, the original owner and visionary who created a thriving business along the river. Originally from Germany, Hatt got his title as captain from sailing since the age of 14. When he arrived in Napa, he gave up the sea to build this historic property.

At the time, the river was the primary means of transportation and many businesses were located along its shores. The Napa Mill was situated in the middle of all this activity and enjoyed a booming business. Not only did the building serve as a warehouse, but it also offered recreation in the form of a roller-skating rink upstairs with a White Rock maple floor. A silo section was added in 1887 and later another building was constructed to house machinery for processing grains.

One of Captain Hatt's children, Albert Jr., did not enjoy the same success in business that the captain did. In poor health and burdened with five children and business problems, Albert Jr. hanged himself at the age of 46 from a beam in the warehouse in 1912. That area is now Sweetie Pies Bakery, a popular hangout every morning for coffee lovers. Vestiges of the old mill days still exist in the form of an old grain-bagging machine on display there.

Following Albert's suicide, Robert Keig purchased the mill from Captain Hatt in 1912.

The Keig family continued to operate the Napa Mill Feed Store until 1974.

In recent times, both Albert Hatt and Robert Keig have spawned numerous ghost stories. One of these accounts involves a woman who looks to be Albert's wife walking the halls at night. Another is that of Robert Keig. Guests at the hotel have reported talking to a man who insisted that the building was not a modern hotel, but rather a mill building—and then he disappeared. They later identified the man as Robert from an old photo hanging in the hotel.

The current Napa River Inn features oversized quarters with fireplaces, canopy beds, tufted lounge chairs, velvet ottomans, slipper tubs, and walk-in showers. In keeping with the historic restoration, rooms have maple hardwood floors and massive cove and baseboard moldings; they offer a perspective of the historic Napa Valley while providing the convenience of modern amenities. Art in the Hatt Building rooms is reflective of a burgeoning river town of the 1800s. Hatt Hall's interior appointments include the original pressed tin wall panels and deep cove moldings, originally installed in the space when it was a music room in the late 1800s.

Preservation efforts began in 1990 when Harry Price undertook his vision to restore and transform the dilapidated and abandoned warehouse property into an entertainment complex. The Historic Napa Mill project is the largest historic redevelopment undertaking in the history of Napa. The Napa River Inn is located in downtown Napa near all major transit points.

The Napa River Inn
500 Main Street
Napa, California 94559
(707) 251-8500
(877) 251-8500

Braised Lamb Shank with Winter Root Vegetables

Dust lamb shank with flour and season with salt and pepper. In a large braising dish, pan sear until golden brown. Remove lamb from pan, then add carrots, onions, garlic, thyme, and bay leaves and sauté until tender. Reglaze with red wine. Reduce by half. Add veal au jus. Bring to boil. Season with salt and pepper. Return the lamb shanks to the pan, cover and braise for approximately 2½ hours, until very tender. Strain and reserve au jus; keep warm until serving.

In the meantime, peel turnips and carrots. Cook separately, with water, sugar, butter, salt, and pepper on high heat until water has evaporated and vegetables are tender. Check seasoning and set aside.

Set diced bacon in cold water for one minute. Drain, sauté in a pan until crispy, and set aside. Peel celery root and dice to ½-inch diameter, then sauté in grapeseed oil until lightly tender.

Before serving, combine all vegetables with bacon. Check seasoning. Add butter and water, so vegetables do not become too dry.

4 1-pound lamb shanks

1 ounce flour

Salt and pepper

3 large carrots, medium diced

2 large red onions, medium diced

2 heads garlic, broken into cloves, unpeeled

1 bunch fresh thyme

2 bay leaves

1 gallon of Cabernet wine (approx. five standard 750-ml bottles)

½ gallon (2 quarts) veal au jus

¼ pound baby turnips

¼ pound baby carrots

1 cup water

2 tablespoons sugar

2 tablespoons butter

1 teaspoon salt

1 teaspoon pepper

2 ounces slab bacon, diced

½ pound celery root

2 ounces grapeseed oil

1–2 pats of butter

1 tablespoon water

Chervil sprigs

PRESENTATION

Set winter root vegetables into a dish, then place braised lamb shank on top of them. Pour the pan braising jus over the lamb shank and vegetables. Place a sprig of chervil on the lamb shank. Serve hot.

YIELD

Serves 4

Double Chocolate Bread Pudding

LOAF

Whisk together the cocoa and water until smooth. Cool. Add the vanilla and eggs and mix lightly. In mixing bowl combine the dry ingredients and mix on low speed for 30 seconds with the paddle. Add the butter and half the chocolate mixture. Mix on low speed until moistened. Scrape. Increase to medium high speed and mix for 1 minute. Scrape. Add the remaining chocolate mix in two batches, beating for 30 seconds after each add. Pour into loaf pan with parchment paper on the bottom and bake for about 1 hour or when skewer inserted in center comes out clean. Let cool and remove from pan.

TOASTING BREAD

Cut bread into 1-inch pieces and toss with melted butter and sugar. Put onto sheet tray and bake in 350-degree oven for 20–30 minutes or until dry. This can be done days ahead and stored in plastic.

PUDDING

Scald cream and milk with vanilla bean in heavy sauce pan. Melt chocolate over simmering water. Whisk yolks with sugar, temper with the hot liquid. Add the remaining liquid to the yolks. Slowly whisk the yolk mixture into the chocolate, be careful not to burn the chocolate. Strain.

LOAF

3 tablespoons +
  1½ teaspoons cocoa

3 tablespoons boiling water

1½ teaspoons vanilla

3 eggs

1¼ cup sifted cake flour

¾ cup + 2 tablespoons sugar

¾ teaspoon baking powder

¼ teaspoon salt

6½ ounce soft butter

PUDDING

3 cups heavy cream

1 cup milk

½ vanilla bean split and scraped

8 ounces bittersweet chocolate

8 yolks

8 ounces sugar

TO ASSEMBLE BREAD PUDDING

Place the toasted bread into the ramekins. About 5-6 pieces would be good. Fill with custard, cover with plastic wrap and let sit for about 30 minutes or until the bread has softened. You may need to top off the custard before baking if the bread has absorbed some of the custard. Cover with foil and bake in a water bath for about 40 minutes or until custard is set. Remove the foil and continue to bake for another 10 minutes until the top is a dark rich color. Remove from the water bath and let cool. May be served at room temperature or warm.

PALACE HOTEL

William Chapman Ralston left his home in eastern Ohio to join the hoards of people clamoring to make a fortune in the gold fields. His ultimate success, however, came from the discovery of silver from Nevada's Comstock Lode, ten years after gold was discovered at Sutter's Mill.

Ralston's sizable fortune permitted him to open the Bank of California in 1864. The bank and other business interests led to bigger dreams. Ralston wanted to turn the city from its roots as a gold rush boom town into a thriving metropolis. To do this, he chose to erect a hotel of timeless elegance and unprecedented luxury.

Ralston hired an architect to research the finest hotels in Europe. His goal was to make them all pale in comparison to his dream. After taking on Senator William Sharon as a business partner, Ralston began to pour his personal wealth into constructing the $5 million Palace Hotel.

His Bank of California had grown in value with the success of the various mining operations but not all of them were profitable. Over time, the bank was forced to take back several worthless properties and write off a number of bad loans. Also, the national depression of 1873 had weakened many banks and forced the closing of some of the larger eastern establishments.

The downhill trend accelerated for Ralston when he got involved in other business deals that turned bad. Just weeks before the hotel was to be completed, Ralston was given the unfortunate news that his bank had to close, cutting off his funding source, and forcing him into personal bankruptcy.

The next day his body was found floating in San Francisco Bay. Although Ralston often took a swim in the Bay, and some friends speculated that he may have had a heart attack, most observers believe that he had committed suicide.

The loss was great for the city. It was estimated that 50,000 people turned out for his funeral. But the construction of the Palace Hotel continued under his partner, Senator Sharon, who acquired many of Ralston's assets. The hotel opened on October 2, 1875, with great fanfare.

As the largest hotel in the world, the Palace attracted guests from all over. They were fascinated by the hotel's four "rising rooms," referred to today as elevators. There would be no more tedious climbing of stairs to get to the spectacular views from the top floor. And when a guest needed something, they only had to activate the call button in each room. Service was taken to a new level.

The Great Earthquake of 1906 did some damage to the property, but the resulting fires finished it. The entire hotel was gutted by the flames. It took three years for a replacement to rise from the ashes.

The original hotel entrance was the Garden Court, where graceful carriages arrived with San Francisco's most prestigious citizens. After the fire and renovation, the Garden Court was enclosed and now serves as one of the most elegant public meeting places in the world.

In 1919, President Woodrow Wilson hosted two Garden Court luncheons in support of the Versailles Treaty, which ended World War I. In 1945, the official banquet honoring the opening session of the United Nations was held in the Garden Court. Any trip to San Francisco deserves a stop in the historic Palace Hotel, and most importantly, you must see the Garden Room.

"There are only three great storybook cities in America—
New York, San Francisco, and New Orleans."

—Tennessee Williams, author

Palace Hotel
2 New Montgomery Street
San Francisco, California 94105
(415) 512-1111

Jumbo Lump Crab Cake

In food processor, combine cold scallop and halibut scraps. When pureed, add in whole egg and slowly add cream until balled mix runs smooth.

Place crabmeat in an ice-cold bowl. Add scallop mousse to the crab one tablespoon at a time. Sprinkle with cilantro and chives. While being careful not to break up crabmeat, fold mix together until it is combined.

Portion cakes into a small size, about 1½ ounces each. Reserve in cooler until ready to serve.

In hot sauté pan, add clarified butter. Place seasoned cake in butter and turn when golden on one side.

Immediately following, squeeze fresh lemon juice on crab cake, add cube of whole butter and baste cake with spoon over heat until butter turns brown. Place cake on plate with paper towel to drain.

MOUSSE

½ pound U-10 scallops, ice cold

½ pound halibut scraps, ice cold

1 egg, whole

1 cup heavy cream

CRAB CAKE

2 pounds jumbo lump crabmeat, shelled

2 tablespoons chives, minced

2 tablespoons cilantro, chopped

FINISHING

2 tablespoons clarified butter

Lemon juice

1 pound whole butter, cubed

Salt and pepper to taste

3 tablespoons tarragon vinegar

2 egg yolks

3 cloves garlic, minced

2 anchovy filets, minced

1 tablespoon fresh tarragon, minced

½ cup fresh parsley, minced

1½ teaspoon lemon juice

2 finely minced green onions

2 tablespoons white onion, finely chopped

1 tablespoon chives, chopped

2¾ cups olive oil

Salt and pepper to taste

Green Goddess Dressing

Created by Executive Chef Philip Roemer in honor of actor George Arliss between 1915 and 1920. Arliss stayed at the Palace while starring in William Archer's play, "The Green Goddess."

Combine vinegar, egg yolks, garlic, anchovy filets, tarragon, parsley, lemon juice, onions, and chives. Make sure to beat until very fine. For premium results, use a blender.

Once ingredients are well mixed, slowly add olive oil until sauce begins to thicken. Add salt and pepper to taste.

YIELD
Yields 3–4 cups

California Strawberries Romanoff

Pastry Chef Lucien Heyrault invented this dessert at the Palace in the 1960s, which has now become a world-famous dessert.

Squeeze the orange and retain the juice. Combine juice with the curaçao, kirsch, and sugar. Mix well.

Marinate the cleaned fresh strawberries in the mixture for one hour. Make sure to refrigerate.

Place all liquor and 3 berries per person into a blender. Run the blender at high speed until pureed. Keep the remaining whole strawberries refrigerated.

Whip the heavy cream until thick and fold into the strawberry puree.

Before serving, immediately place 6 strawberries into individual dessert dishes. Top strawberries with the cream and decorate with the remaining strawberries. Serve very cold.

1 orange

6 tablespoons curaçao

6 tablespoons kirsch

3 tablespoons fine granulated sugar

3 pints fresh ripe strawberries (about 60 total)

1 cup heavy cream

THE RITZ-CARLTON, SAN FRANCISCO

The great earthquake fires that destroyed much of San Francisco in 1906 comprised perhaps the most significant event of its kind in the history of the world. What those 60 seconds of tremendous shocks did not destroy, the subsequent fires burned. No one could tally an accurate account of the dead but casualty estimates run as high as 2,000 to 3,000 souls. Although felt all the way to Los Angeles, southern Oregon, and central Nevada, this disaster was not able to completely wipe out the city.

Citizens quickly began to recover from the devastation by rebuilding. It is perhaps due to the massive insurance claims that brought this western city's and Nob Hill's attractions to the attention of the Metropolitan Life Insurance Company.

Nob Hill was named for the numerous nabobs who congregated here. A *nabob* is an Indian word for someone who has made a great fortune or is a very rich and powerful person. The Gold Rush produced a number of those, and they all flocked together on the same hillside. Average people concluded that the area was Nob Hill, and the name stuck.

After the quake, Met Life built an enormous office building on Nob Hill in 1909. This served as their foothold on the financial district of the city and their western headquarters until it was sold in 1973.

Cogswell Technical College bought the Met Life Western Headquarters to expand their educational operations. The college was named for Dr. Henry Daniel Cogswell, one of the city's first millionaires from the Gold Rush. Descended from Alfred the Great and Charlemagne, his family moved to America in 1635 from England. When he arrived to San Francisco in 1849, Dr. Cogswell chose to practice dentistry, rather than mining. Amassing a fortune through work and investments in mining stocks, he set up a private high school to offer technical training. Growing into a technical college, the school had originally occupied facilities in the Mission District, gradually growing into larger buildings. In 1985, the college moved to Cupertino and, in 1993, the campus was located in Sunnyvale, where today it focuses on digital and software engineering for television and movie productions.

After several years of sitting idle, and following a complete four-year renovation, this historic Nob Hill landmark reopened as The Ritz-Carlton, San Francisco in April 1991. This neoclassical landmark is a renovation of one of the city's architectural treasures.

"San Francisco has only one drawback—'tis hard to leave."

—Rudyard Kipling, author

The Ritz-Carlton, San Francisco
600 Stockton Street at California
San Francisco, California 94108
(415) 364-3437

1 cup orange juice

Olive oil

1 pound Nantucket Bay scallops

Salt and white pepper

6 tangerines

Nantucket Bay Scallops with Winter Citrus

On stovetop, reduce orange juice to ¼ cup. Once reduced, whisk in olive oil to taste.

Season scallops with salt and white pepper. Sear in hot pan until lightly brown or as desired.

Segment the tangerines. Place segments on plate with scallops on top. Drizzle plate with orange oil.

YIELD

Serves 4

Seared Toro with Matsutake Mushrooms, Edamame, and Mirin Reduction

Blanch the edamame, set aside. Slice the shallots paper thin and put them in a stainless or non-reactive pot. Add the mirin and reduce until it becomes a syrupy consistency. Add brown chicken stock and let it simmer 5–10 minutes. Strain and set aside.

Season the toro lightly with salt. Sear lightly in a pan.

Using a mandolin or a very sharp knife, shave the matsutake very thinly and place on a flat layer on a plate. Warm the edamame beans, then place them on top of the mushrooms. Slice toro and fan out on the plate.

Re-heat the mirin reduction and mount with butter; drizzle on plate. Sprinkle with vanilla sea salt and Muntock white pepper. Serve.

2–3 tablespoons edamame beans

2 shallots

¼ cup mirin

½ cup brown chicken stock

4 2-ounce pieces toro

1 matsutake mushroom

1 tablespoon butter

1 tablespoon cracked Muntock white pepper

1 tablespoon vanilla sea salt

THE SAINTE CLAIRE

Real estate mogul T. S. Montgomery created a master plan for the town of San Jose. The Sainte Claire was to be Montgomery's crown jewel and serve as a focal point for the town's social and cultural life. It was to be followed by a new civic auditorium that would also serve as a convention center. Montgomery's untimely death and the Depression postponed the auditorium until 1934.

In 1923, Montgomery bought the Eagle Brewery to serve as the site of his new hotel. The Eagle had been closed by prohibition in 1918. Montgomery attracted investors who had holdings in the immediate area, convincing them their property values would rise. Stock subscribers included Charles P. Weeks and W. P. Day, the architects of the Mark Hopkins in San Francisco and the Beverly Wilshire in Los Angeles.

Construction finished in September 1926 at a cost of approximately $750,000. The equipment and the furnishing brought the price tag to an even $1,000,000, making it known as "San Jose's Million-Dollar Hotel." Built in a Spanish-Revival Renaissance style with a blend of Moorish, Spanish, and French-Italian influence, the hotel offers an exterior fashioned to imitate an Italian palazzo created with buff brick and terra-cotta.

A ventilating and heating system in the basement washed every cubic foot of air used in the 200 guest rooms, as well as through the public areas of the entire six-story hotel. The Sainte Claire also had its own deep well and subjected it to a water softener, as well as the latest charcoal water filter, which made the water absolutely pure. At the time, The Sainte Claire had the largest kitchen in Northern California, and it was the biggest and best hotel between San Francisco and Los Angeles. The tile fountain in the enclosed courtyard was custom-built by Albert Solon, the internationally known ceramist, whose work also adorned Hearst Castle and the Mark Hopkins Hotel in San Francisco.

The new hotel opened in 1926 with great fanfare, with a black-tie party for 500. By the next day, many felt that San Jose had risen above its "prune town" image and might someday rival San Francisco for sophistication and elegance. Society women came for lunch or afternoon tea. Some years later, the patio and courtyard were covered over and a dance floor was installed, creating the ballroom.

The hotel lobby had a newsstand selling magazines, cigars, and novelty gifts. The marble-floored walkway lead to the coffee shop, flower shop, barbershop, travel agency, and gift shop. The coffee shop, patronized mostly by the affluent, had two levels of chairs and tables, a higher level

along the walk and a step down leading to the street entrance. The lunch counter was very popular with area merchants. A local radio station broadcasted from the basement.

When Prohibition was repealed, Montgomery would not allow a cocktail lounge on the first floor of the hotel but agreed to open one on the second floor. Known as The Padded Cell, it was especially popular with military officers during World War II. The bar eventually moved to replace the lounge, which had earlier replaced the coffee shop.

Over the years, downtown San Jose declined as residents abandoned it for the suburbs. The early 1980s saw redevelopment of the downtown area and The Sainte Claire was partly restored by a local developer. Passing through several owners, additional renovations included bringing back the courtyard that had once been the historical heart of the hotel. The vibrantly colored, hand-painted Spanish ceramic tiles were uncovered and restored. The courtyard was painstakingly reconstructed so that natural light could once again stream through the oval windows in the lounge, lobby, and arcade areas.

During the 1960s, original Moorish-style ceiling decorations were painted over. In some areas of the ceilings, up to six layers of paint had to be removed to recreate the atmosphere of the original hotel.

Many prominent movie stars and dignitaries stayed at the hotel: Judy Garland, Clark Gable, Eleanor Roosevelt, Will Rogers, Bing Crosby, Dorothy Lamour, Susan Hayward, Betty Grable, Frank Sinatra, John Wayne, Bob Hope, and the Rolling Stones, to name just a few.

The Hotel Saint Claire was also the home of a personal pet. Bobo the Monkey lived on the fifth floor and had his own room and bath. Bobo was known to wander the halls, unscrewing light bulbs and flushing them down the toilet.

The hotel was one of the first buildings in San Jose to be built on a moving foundation system or "rollers." During the 1989 Loma Prieta earthquake, the hotel suffered only slight damage to the terra-cotta façade. The hotel has never had a major fire.

Anchored by the award-winning Il Fornaio Cucina Italiana, the hotel service includes the 150-seat Il Fornaio dining room.

 *112*

Founder T. S. Montgomery wanted no expense spared in "fitting out a house which would be a byword for the most luxurious and at the same time the most homelike of hotels." That standard still fits San Jose's grandam—The Sainte Claire Hotel.

The Sainte Claire
302 South Market Street
San Jose, California 95113
(408) 295-2000
(866) 870-0726

Pasta Ribbons with Fava Beans Pecorino and Aged Ricotta

Mince 1 garlic clove and smash the other 2. Set aside.

Bring 5 quarts of water and the 5 teaspoons of salt to a boil in a large stockpot over high heat. Add the fava beans and return to a boil. Remove immediately with a skimmer and leave the water in the pot. Remove the skins from the beans and discard. Place the beans in a small bowl and set aside.

Heat 2 tablespoons of the olive oil in a large sauté pan over medium-high heat. Add the shallot and smashed garlic. Cook until soft, about 1 minute. Add half of the basil and half of the fava beans and sauté 1–2 minutes. Add the wine and cook until evaporated completely, about 3 minutes. Cook until reduced by half, about 5 minutes. Transfer the mixture to the bowl of a food processor and puree.

Heat the remaining ⅓ cup of olive oil in a large sauté pan over medium-high heat. Add the minced garlic and the remaining basil. Cook 1 minute. Add the remaining cooked beans. Add a pinch of salt and pepper. Cook for 2 minutes. Add the pureed beans and mix well.

Return the fava water in the stockpot to a boil. Add the pasta and cook until al dente. Transfer to a colander to

3 garlic cloves

5 teaspoons sea salt, plus extra for seasoning

4 pounds fresh fava beans, shelled

⅓ cup plus 2 tablespoons olive oil, divided

1 small shallot, minced

6 fresh medium basil leaves, torn into small pieces

½ cup dry white wine

2 cups water

Freshly ground pepper and salt, to taste

1 pound dry tagliatelle

⅓ cup extra-virgin olive oil

1 ripe large tomato, peeled, seeded, and diced

½ cup pecorino Toscano or pecarino Romano, freshly grated

2 tablespoons ricotta salata, shaved

drain. Add pasta to the pan with the fava bean sauce. Add the extra virgin olive oil, tomato, and pecorino. Toss to mix well. Top with the ricotta salata.

YIELD

Serves 6

Pasta Strands with Garlic, Olive Oil, and Dried Red Pepper

Bring 5 quarts of water and 5 teaspoons of the salt to a boil in a large stockpot over high heat. Add the pasta and cook until al dente.

While the pasta is cooking, combine the olive oil with the garlic and pepperoncini in a large sauté pan. Cook over medium-high heat until the garlic begins to brown, about 3 minutes. Add the parsley and the remaining ½ teaspoon of salt.

Transfer the pasta in a colander to drain, reserving ¼ cup of the cooking water. Add the pasta to the pan with the olive oil–garlic mixture. Add the Parmigiano, extra-virgin olive oil, and a pinch of pepper. Toss to mix well. If it seems dry, add a little of the reserved cooking water.

YIELD

Serves 6

5½ teaspoons sea salt, divided

1 pound dry spaghetti

⅓ cup olive oil

5 garlic cloves, minced

2 dried pepperoncini, broken into small pieces

2 tablespoons Italian parsley, chopped

½ cup Parmigiano-Reggiano, chopped

3 tablespoons extra-virgin olive oil

Freshly ground pepper

2 pounds plum tomatoes, cored, halved, and seeded

½ cup plus 2 tablespoons olive oil, divided

5 teaspoons sea salt, plus extra for seasoning tomatoes

½ cup garlic cloves

¾ cup blanched almonds, sliced

2 cups fresh basil leaves, loosely packed

Freshly ground pepper and salt, to taste

¾ cup pecorino Romano, freshly grated

1 pound dry linguine

Pasta Ribbons Dressed with a Roasted Tomato and Basil Pesto

Preheat oven to 500 degrees.

Arrange the tomatoes in an ovenproof sauté pan. Brush with 2 tablespoons of the olive oil and sprinkle generously with salt. Bake for 15 minutes, and then place under the broiler for 6 minutes.

Heat the remaining ½ cup of olive oil in a large sauté pan over medium heat. Add the garlic and reduce the heat to low. Cook until tender, about 15 minutes. Add ½ cup of the almonds. Cook until browned, 3 to 5 minutes. Remove from the heat. Add the basil and pinch of salt and pepper. Let sit 5 minutes. Transfer to the bowl of a food processor; add the tomatoes and ½ cup of the pecorino cheese and puree. Return tomato-basil sauce to the sauté pan and keep warm over low heat.

Bring 5 quarts of water and the 5 teaspoons of salt to a boil in a large stockpot over high heat. Add the pasta and cook until al dente. Transfer to a colander to drain, reserving 1 cup of the cooking water. Add the pasta to the sauté pan with the warm tomato pesto and toss to mix well. If the pasta sticks together because the sauce is too thick, add the reserved water, ¼ cup at a time. Transfer to a serving dish and sprinkle with the remaining almonds and pecorino cheese.

YIELD

Serves 6

SILVERADO RESORT

John Franklin Miller was born and raised in South Bend, Indiana in 1831. After receiving a law degree in New York, he returned briefly to practice in Indiana before moving to Napa, California, shortly after the start of the Gold Rush. A successful lawyer wherever he went, Miller served as the county treasurer in Napa before returning to Indiana.

At home in both states, Miller was elected to the State Senate in California in 1860. The election of Abraham Lincoln to the presidency later that year was the final straw for Southern states intending to break away. After eleven states had seceded from the Union, the Governor of Indiana appointed Miller as a colonel in command of the 29th Indiana Infantry. Serving under Buell's Army of the Ohio, Miller's regiment saw action in the Battle of Shiloh and the Siege of Corinth.

After several engagements, Miller was both wounded and promoted. When the war ended, he was a major general, but declined an appointment in the Regular Army. Accepting the position of collector of customs for the Port of San Francisco, Miller returned to California.

In 1869, Miller turned to business interests. He took an interest in the booming fur industry by becoming president of the Alaska Commercial Company, just two years after the United States purchased Alaska from the Russians. With little cash available, the Alaskan stores specialized in trading such things as fish, gold, and fur pelts for goods. Thriving during the Klondike Gold Rush, these stores eventually became part of the Nordstrom chain.

Miller also began to acquire land in Napa Valley. Between 1869 and 1881, he assembled several pieces of acreage, comprising the land that is the current site of the Silverado Country Club. Miller named the property La Verge, after one of the battles he fought. Today, the mansion that he and his wife built in the 1870s houses the registration facilities, the Royal Oak Restaurant, a lounge and meeting space, and a terrace overlooking the golf courses and mountains to the east.

Miller went on to serve in the U.S. Senate representing California from 1881 until his death in 1886. When Miller's daughter, Mary Eudora Miller, inherited the property, she hosted a number of distinguished guests, including President Theodore Roosevelt and General John J. Pershing. In 1932, the property was sold to private interests and was later acquired by the Silverado Land Company in 1953, who renamed the property.

The Silverado Resort is located in Napa Valley 50 miles northeast of San Francisco and 60 miles southwest of Sacramento. Situated on 1,200 acres within easy driving distance of many of Napa

Valley's most popular wineries and other attractions, Silverado, operated by Xanterra Parks & Resorts, offers lodging, spa facilities, excellent dining, and outdoor recreation, such as championship golf, tennis, and swimming.

Silverado Resort
1600 Atlas Peak Road
Napa, California 94558
(707) 257-0200

Stir-Fry of Minced Chicken and Vegetables in Crisp Lettuce Cups with Roasted Pine Nuts

Season the chicken with salt and pepper. In very hot wok, stir-fry until half done, and take out. Sauté the celery, onion, and mushrooms in the wok and then season. Mix water and cornstarch until smooth. Add the chicken back to the wok. Add black bean sauce and cornstarch/water mixture. Put on sheet pans to cool.

After cooling, add sirachi (in very small increments). With large wire basket, deep fry moo shu skins until crisp. Roast pine nuts in oven until golden brown.

Heat up chicken mixture with a little chicken stock if needed. Place fried basket-shaped moo shu wrapper on a plate, with a little cream cheese on the underside to hold in place. Place chicken mixture into moo shu cup and garnish with pine nuts and scallions. Arrange butter lettuce leaves on side.

YIELD

Serves 6

5 pounds chicken thigh meat, diced

Salt and pepper, to taste

2 cups celery, diced

2 cups onion, diced

2 cups shiitake mushrooms, quartered

1 ½ cups water thickened with ½ cup cornstarch

3 cups black bean sauce

Sirachi (spicy Thai chili sauce), to taste

6 moo shu skins (thin Chinese pancakes)

Pine nuts

Cream cheese, as needed

Chiffonade of scallions

Crisp butter lettuce leaves

DRESSING FOR GREENS

1 cup rice wine vinegar

2 shallots, minced

2 tablespoons each chopped
   parsley, chives, and chervil

3 tablespoons Dijon mustard

1½ cups grapeseed oil

Salt and pepper to taste

TUNA

12 ounces sushi-grade tuna,
   diced ½ inch

MARINADE FOR TUNA

¼ cup Ko-choo-jung
   (Korean hot bean paste)

⅛ cup Dijon mustard

1 teaspoon roasted sesame seed,
   pulverized

1 teaspoon red wine vinegar

2 tablespoons minced scallions

FINAL PLATING

½ cup organic micro greens

8 wonton skins, cut into quarters,
   fried and seasoned

Fried taro strips

Poke of Tuna with Crispy Wonton Chips and Grapeseed Oil Salad

Whisk first four dressing ingredients together. Slowly drizzle in oil until an emulsion is formed. Season.

In another bowl, combine marinade ingredients and check for seasoning. Mix diced tuna with marinade.

Toss micro greens with dressing. Assemble five quarters of wonton on a 10-inch plate. Place micro green salad and tuna poke on wonton. Garnish with marinade and fried taro strips.

YIELD
Serves 4

The Ultimate Surf and Turf
Cervena Venison Medallion and Butter Poached Shrimp with a Creamy Goat Cheese Remoulade

In a 6-inch skillet, bring wine and butter to a boil, stirring rapidly to form an emulsion. Turn down to a simmer. Add shrimp, salt, and pepper to season. Cook for about 2 minutes, stirring and tossing the shrimp. Cool down in butter broth.

Season the venison strip loin with salt and pepper. In a 6-inch skillet, melt butter and grapeseed oil together.

On medium-high heat, sauté venison strip loin to medium rare (about 2 minutes per side). Cool and let rest.

Mix together goat cheese, lemon juice, and herbs until smooth. Add crème fraiche and fold in—but do not whip! Season with salt and pepper and reserve.

PLATING

Slice venison into 8 medallions. Place shrimp on top of venison and spoon about 1½ ounces of remoulade on top. Garnish with little micro greens and edible flowers for a nice presentation.

YIELD

Serves 6–8 as an appetizer

SURF AND TURF

2 ounces white wine

1 stick (¼ pound) unsalted butter

8 pieces peeled, deveined, tail-off shrimp (21–25)

Salt and pepper to taste

1 piece Cervena venison strip loin

1 ounce unsalted butter

1 ounce grapeseed oil

REMOULADE

6 ounces goat cheese (set at room temperature for 2 hours)

1 lemon, juiced

1 tablespoon each chervil, chives, and parsley, finely chopped

6 ounces crème fraiche

Salt and pepper to taste

THE STANFORD COURT, A RENAISSANCE HOTEL

"You can't have a bad meal in this town."

—Emeril Lagasse, chef

The Ohlone Indians settled in the Bay Area several thousand years ago but, like numerous other Indian tribes in California, they were no match for invading Europeans. Don Gaspar de Portolà arrived in San Francisco Bay in November of 1769. The year 1776 saw the establishment of a Spanish fort, followed by Mission San Francisco de Asís.

The mission claimed great tracts of land in the area that were eventually taken from it when Mexico secured its independence from Spain. All missions were secularized in 1834, and the land turned over to private interests. In 1835, Englishman William Richardson built a homestead outside the mission and laid out a street plan for the nearby pueblo named Yerba Buena or "good herb" for the wild mint found there.

The population of Yerba Buena grew further as a Mormon colony moved in, establishing one of the early Mormon enclaves in the West. After California was claimed by the United States, Yerba Buena was renamed San Francisco, after the mission. It remained a relatively small settlement, for several years, functioning as a shipping port and naval base.

The Gold Rush of 1849 saw drastic changes for the town. When word was passed of the find at Sutter's Mill, nearly every able-bodied man and a few women left town for the gold fields, seeking their fortune. Town leaders at first feared for the survival of the community, but they soon thought otherwise.

After word traveled back east and on to Europe of the gold discovery, tens of thousands of people flooded the area on their way to the mill. Land values skyrocketed due to demand and many businesses were born. Hundreds of ships sat rotting in the harbor because their crews had abandoned them to seek gold. Tent cities were erected to accommodate the influx.

San Francisco became so important economically that a fort was built at the Golden Gate. The military also erected a fort on Alcatraz Island to defend the Bay. California became a state in 1850.

After a time, things quieted down as many miners gave up, but the discovery of silver in California and Nevada in 1859 gave the city another economic boost. Wells Fargo opened a bank, Levi Strauss began a dry goods business, and Ghirardelli started a chocolate factory. Waves of Chinese immigrants arrived to work on the railroads and created the city's Chinatown. Once the railroad was completed, and the West Coast was linked to the East Coast overland, the city's future was assured.

Wealthy residents began to congregate on Nob Hill, so called because the rich "hobnobbed" there. They built large and expensive mansions that were admired by everyone, even if many working-class folks resented then. The city's Big Four—Mark Hopkins, Charles Crocker, Collis Huntington, and Leland Stanford—led the way of developing the area.

As the state's first governor, Leland Stanford was driven to live the good life. His mansion, built at a staggering cost of $2 million, was the first to be erected. It was considered at the time to be the finest home in the nation, if not the most expensive. Many other mansions followed on Nob Hill, but most were severely damaged or completely destroyed by the great earthquake and fire of 1906. Part of Stanford's mansion wall and the fence that surrounded it remain today along the eastern side of the Renaissance Stanford Court Hotel.

Following the destruction in 1906, Lucien Sly bought the property and erected the Stanford Court apartment building. Later, that building was gutted, leaving only the shell, and the Stanford Court Hotel opened in 1972. When the management under Stouffer hotels combined with Renaissance Hotels, the name was changed.

The Renaissance Stanford Court Hotel is truly a grand part of the history of the city of San Francisco and a landmark in its own right.

The Stanford Court, A Renaissance Hotel
905 California Street, Nob Hill
San Francisco, California 94108
(415) 989-3500

3 eggs, separated

⅓ cup cake flour

¾ cup ricotta

¼ cup butter, melted

2 tablespoons sugar

¼ teaspoon salt

2 tablespoons grated lemon zest

RASPBERRY SYRUP

¾ cup light corn syrup

¾ cup fresh raspberries

3 teaspoons lemon juice

Lemon Soufflé Pancakes

Separate the eggs and beat the egg whites until they hold stiff peaks. In another bowl, stir together the egg yolks, flour, ricotta cheese, butter, sugar, salt, and lemon zest until well mixed. With a large spoon or a spatula, fold the egg whites into the yolk mixture.

Gently stir; there should still be small pieces of egg white showing. Heat a skillet or griddle over medium heat. Grease the pan lightly and spoon out about 3 large tablespoons of batter for each pancake. Cook slowly for about 4½ minutes, then turn the pancake over and cook for another 30 seconds.

Keep the pancakes warm in 250-degree oven until ready to serve. Serve with raspberry or maple syrup and fresh raspberries. (The recipe for Raspberry Syrup follows.)

RASPBERRY SYRUP

Combine syrup and raspberries and bring to a boil. Simmer for 5 minutes and remove from heat. Allow to cool, then add lemon juice. Strain through a fine mesh strainer, pushing hard to remove seeds.

YIELD

Yields twelve 3-inch pancakes

"All happiness depends on a leisurely breakfast."

—John Gunther, journalist and author

Artichokes Ala Romana

Trimming an artichoke can take time but is not difficult. Hold an artichoke on its side; with a sharp knife, trim the leaves away as close to the bottom as possible, turning the artichoke as you work. Cut the leaves off the top just above the artichoke bottom. Using a teaspoon, scoop out the choke and discard. Trim the remaining greenish leaves and pieces away, leaving the bottom. Pare any tough outside fibers from the stem.

Preheat oven to 350 degrees.

To mix the marinade, grind the parsley, garlic, and anchovy fillets together. Stir in the lemon juice, wine, olive oil, water, and salt to taste. Mix and blend well.

Put the artichokes in a cooktop-safe casserole or pan. Try to place the artichoke bottoms in one layer, close together. Pour the marinade over the artichokes, then place on top of the stove over high heat, to bring to a boil. Cover and transfer to the oven. Cook covered, turning and basting the artichokes every 15 minutes, for 45 minutes to 1 hour, or until the stems are tender.

Make these at least a day in advance of serving so the flavors mellow. Serve at room temperature or slightly warmed.

8 good-sized artichokes
(about 8 ounces each)

1 cup parsley

6 large cloves garlic, peeled

5 tablespoons anchovy fillets
(oil included)

½ cup lemon juice

½ cup white wine (Chablis)

3 cups olive oil

3 cups water

Salt to taste

THE WESTIN ST. FRANCIS

"In all my travels I have never seen the hospitality of San Francisco equaled anywhere in the world."

—Conrad Hilton, hotelier

The turn of the century saw a surge in hotel construction in the thriving city of San Francisco. Leading the construction boom were the heirs of the Charles Crocker family fortune who announced plans to build The Westin St. Francis. Crocker had been one of the original Forty-niners, but quickly decided that mining was no way to make a fortune, and so he opened a store in Sacramento.

By 1854, Crocker was one of the wealthiest men in the area and had a strong business relationship with Mark Hopkins, Collis Huntington, and Leland Stanford. Together, they became known as the Big Four for their prominence in California's rapid economic development.

Following Crocker's death in 1888, the guardians of his estate set a vision to make San Francisco the "Paris of the West." Their stunning Union Square hotel would be the flagship.

Following a careful study of Europe's grand hotels—from Berlin, Vienna, and Monaco to Claridge's in London and The Ritz in Paris—construction on the original St. Francis began. Two years and $2.5 million later, the doors of The St. Francis opened in March of 1904. Early that evening, carriages and automobiles stretched for three blocks waiting to approach her entrance.

The hotel was so popular that the owners quickly announced plans to add a third wing, two floors of apartments, and a ballroom. The St. Francis had become the center of the city's social, literary, and artistic life.

The earthquake of 1906 destroyed most of the city and The St. Francis was not spared. Fires spawned by the quake destroyed the interior of the hotel's original 250 rooms, along with all early records of the hotel. Determined to recover quickly, the owners erected a temporary hotel of 110 rooms in a court around the Dewey Monument in Union Square, and The St. Francis continued as a focal point of the city. The square was soon dubbed The Little St. Francis because hotel residents occupied the shelter.

The hotel interior was rebuilt, refurbished, and reopened late in 1907, with 450 guest rooms. The long-planned third wing opened in 1908 and more additions followed on Post Street, making this the largest hotel on the Pacific Coast. The Pacific Tower opened in 1971, adding a vast new complex of guest rooms, suites, and venues and banquet facilities.

An enduring symbol of the hotel, as well as the meeting point for generations of guests and locals alike, is the famed Magneta Grandfather Clock. Installed in the hotel's Powell Street lobby in 1907 following the earthquake, it serves as a master clock, controlling all the other clocks in the hotel. The common refrain of "Meet me at the clock!" has echoed throughout the halls for a century. The first master clock brought to the West, the Magneta Grandfather Clock is an enduring symbol of the hotel's longevity and history.

The Westin St. Francis
335 Powell Street
San Francisco, California 94102
(415) 397-7000

3 pieces celery hearts,
    about 5 inches long each,
    cleaned and trimmed

1 quart chicken stock

18 pieces shrimp (16-20), peeled
    and deveined, tail on

6 leafs Bibb lettuce

12 pieces tomato wedges

3 ripe avocados, peeled, halved,
    sliced, and fanned

12 pieces hardboiled egg wedges

12 strips anchovies

6 sprigs chervil

Shrimp Celery Victor

With a red fez set rakishly atop his head and a persona larger than life, chef Victor Hirtzler reigned over the Hotel St. Francis in San Francisco from 1904 to 1926. Hirtzler was a native of Strasbourg, France, a former taster for Czar Nicholas II, and once chef to King Carlos I of Portugal. Among the astonishingly varied, European-inspired creations Hirtzler named after himself, Celery Victor (ca. 1910) may be the most enduring. The simple and delicious poached vegetable dish hails from the days before raw greens defined a salad. We've added shrimp for substance and capers for spark.

Poach celery hearts in strong chicken stock until soft. Allow to cool in the broth.

When chilled, remove celery from the stock and gently squeeze out excess liquid. Cut in half lengthwise and arrange on plates.

Dip the shrimp in Tarragon Vinaigrette (recipe follows) and broil over an open-flame BBQ until cooked.

Arrange the poached celery with Bibb lettuce, the broiled shrimp, tomato wedges, a sliced and fanned half avocado, and the hardboiled egg wedges. Crisscross the anchovy strips over the celery heart and spoon the tarragon dressing over the celery and lettuce. Garnish with a fresh chervil sprig.

YIELD

Serves 6

Tarragon Vinaigrette

Combine all ingredients and blend well.

4 ounces olive oil

2 ounces tarragon vinegar

1 ounces shallots, chopped fine

Salt to taste

Fresh ground pepper, to taste

½ ounces parsley, chopped fine

¼ ounces chervil, chopped fine

10 ounces all-purpose flour

2 teaspoons baking powder

½ teaspoon salt

4 ounces sugar

4 ounces butter, cold

2 ounces dried currants

1 egg

2 egg yolks

7 ounces milk

Very Traditional English Scones

Place flour, baking powder, salt, sugar, and cold butter in mixing bowl. Mix on low to cornmeal stage, as with pie dough. Add currants and mix just to distribute evenly. With mixer on low, slowly add combined liquid ingredients (egg, yolks, and milk) just until it comes together. Do not over-mix. (At this point, the dough can be frozen and used as needed.)

Roll on generously floured surface to 1 inch thick. Cut into circles with biscuit cutter and place on greased cookie sheet. Brush lightly with beaten egg and let rest for a half hour.

Bake at 400 degrees for about 10 minutes or until golden brown. Let stand for 15 minutes before serving.

YIELD
Serves 12

Central California

The jewel of the Central Coast is Monterey Bay. In 1797, Mission San Juan Bautista was founded near Monterey Bay by the Spaniards and is now the highlight of a state historic park and plaza. Cannery Row in Monterey was made famous by author John Steinbeck and is home to quaint restaurants and shops. The Mediterranean villa, Hearst Castle, former home of the great newspaper publisher, is located in San Simeon. The first motel in America is in San Luis Obispo, a one-day's drive from Los Angeles in the early 1900s.

The Central Valley, or California's breadbasket, stretches for 450 miles down the center of the state from Orland to Bakersfield. Vast expanses of vegetable fields give way to some of the largest vineyards in the state. Huge farms of almonds, raisins, and prunes are fed by the San Joaquin, Merced, Kings, and Kern rivers.

THE AHWAHNEE HOTEL

Before the Gold Rush brought Europeans to the Yosemite Valley, the Southern Sierra Miwok Indians lived here. They called the valley "Ahwahnee," which means "land of the gaping mouth," and they called themselves the Ahwaneechee or "the people of Ahwahnee." Fish and game were plentiful and the Indians had little reason to leave the valley. They enjoyed a peaceful existence for several thousand years until the foreigners came.

Outsiders arrived in waves as the discovery of gold in the Sierra foothills brought hoards of miners to the area. While the Indians initially assisted the miners and worked with them to extract gold, they later became hostile, as their tribesmen were indiscriminately murdered and their land became overrun with settlers. The Mariposa Indian War of 1851 resulted in many deaths on both sides; the settlers eventually prevailed.

The beauty of the valley attracted tourists as early as 1855. Only nine years later, at the height of the Civil War, President Lincoln was persuaded to grant title to Yosemite Valley to the state of California. This act was the foundation for all future national and state parks, as Yosemite became the nation's first public preserve. Control of the park reverted to the federal government in 1906 when it became Yosemite National Park.

In 1916, the first director of the newly created National Park Service, Stephen Mather, wanted to upgrade the park's accommodations to encourage tourists. He ordered the building of a luxury hotel that would attract wealthy and influential people to the park year-round. Plans were drawn for an extensive structure costing $525,000. When construction was completed seven months later in July of 1927, the final cost was $1,250,000. The Ahwahnee Hotel was born.

This impressive wilderness retreat has a six-story central tower, with three huge wings extending from it. In response to the risk of fire in a forest, the new hotel was built of concrete, steel, and granite. To ensure that it fit in with the surroundings, the exterior was stained to resemble redwood. The main building is 150,000 square feet and includes 99 rooms. Eight cottages on the grounds house twenty-four additional rooms. The dining room features granite pillars and a dramatic 34-foot-high ceiling with large sugar pine trestles.

Like many other resorts in America, The Ahwahnee Hotel served as an R&R center during World War II. The U.S. Navy turned it into a hospital and the Great Lounge became a dormitory,

with 350 bunk beds. By the time the war had ended, the hotel had played host to 6,752 patients while the National Park offered rest and relaxation to 90,000 service members.

Completely renovated, The Ahwahnee Hotel is located in Yosemite Valley, approximately 1 mile east of Yosemite Village. Surrounded by the world famous scenery of Yosemite National Park, the hotel offers views of Half Dome, Glacier Point, Royal Arches, and Yosemite Falls. While there, join one of the free historic hotel tours to learn more about its fascinating past.

The Ahwahnee Hotel
Yosemite National Park
(866) 875-8456
(559) 253-5676

Cheddar Cheese Soup

Heat a 6-quart stockpot over a medium heat and add the diced bacon. Cook until bacon is two-thirds done.

Add the butter, onions, and garlic and continue cooking for an additional 3 minutes or until the onions are translucent.

Mix in the flour to make a roux, and cook for an additional 3 minutes.

Using a whisk, slowly add the vegetable broth and heavy cream until it has all been incorporated. Bring contents of stockpot to a boil. Add the Worcestershire sauce, horseradish, mustard, and bay leaves. Reduce heat and simmer for 20 minutes.

Add the ale and Cheddar cheese. Whisk soup until smooth and all the cheese has melted and has been thoroughly incorporated. Remove the bay leaves, adjust the seasoning, and keep hot until you are ready to serve.

YIELD

Serves 8

6 slices bacon, diced

1 tablespoon butter

½ cup onion, finely diced

1 tablespoon garlic, minced

½ cup all-purpose flour

1½ quarts Vegetable Broth (recipe follows)

2 cups heavy cream, such as Producers brand

2 tablespoons Worcestershire sauce

2 teaspoons prepared horseradish

2 tablespoons Dijon mustard

2 bay leaves

1 12-ounce bottle pale ale, such as Sierra Nevada Pale Ale Beer™

½ pound shredded Cheddar cheese, such as Fiscalini Farms™

Salt to taste

Pepper to taste

SACHET OF HERBS

10–12 parsley stems

3-4 sprigs thyme

2–3 bay leaves

12 black peppercorns

3 whole cloves

1 tablespoon toasted fennel seeds

BROTH

2 cups onions, coarsely chopped

2 cups leeks, root end removed,
    washed thoroughly,
    coarsely chopped

2 cups celery, coarsely chopped

2 cups carrots, peeled,
    coarsely chopped

2 cups parsnips, peeled,
    coarsely chopped

2 cups tomatoes,
    coarsely chopped

4–5 garlic cloves crushed

¼ cup trans fat–free vegetable oil

4½ quarts cold water

Kosher salt

Vegetable Broth

A sachet is a combination of various herbs and spices. Combine sachet ingredients and tie up in a cheesecloth bag. Set aside.

Toss all vegetables and garlic in oil. Lay on sheet tray and roast at 400 degrees. Turn frequently to make sure all exposed surfaces brown well.

Place roasted vegetables in a stockpot, add water and sachet, and simmer for 30 to 40 minutes.

Remove sachet and discard. Strain the stock through a fine chinois and adjust seasoning.

❦ YIELD ❧

Yields 1 gallon

The Ahwahnee Boysenberry Pie

FILLING

In a saucepan on a low heat, add frozen boysenberries and slowly cook for 5 minutes. In a bowl, combine sugar, gelatin, and salt. Add sugar mixture to saucepan. Cook for another 5 minutes. Stir often to avoid burning. Set aside and let cool.

PIE DOUGH

In a food processor, add flour, salt, sugar, and softened butter. Mix ingredients until they are evenly distributed. Then add water all at once. Turn off food processor as soon as the dough binds and comes away from the sides of the bowl. Roll into a ball and refrigerate for one hour.

Roll out dough on countertop and form dough into 10-inch pie pan. Preheat oven to 350 degrees and bake pie shell for 5 minutes. Meanwhile, roll a top for the pie and cover with a towel. Mix egg and water together to create an egg wash.

Place berry filling in shell and place dough on top of pie, egg-washing the pie rim to seal. Cut 4 slits in the top of the pie and egg wash the top. Place in the 350-degree oven and bake until golden brown (around 15 to 20 minutes). Cool and serve.

FILLING

1½ pounds frozen boysenberries

¾ cup sugar

1¼ ounces clear instant gelatin

Pinch of salt

PIE DOUGH

9 ounces all-purpose flour

Pinch of salt

1½ tablespoons sugar

4½ ounces soft butter

1½ ounces very cold water

1 egg

1 tablespoon water

CHAMINADE

The many thousands of Native Americans that Spanish explorer Don Gaspar de Portolà encountered in 1769 were part of a larger group referred to as "Costenos," or "coastal people." Their name eventually changed to "Costanoan," until their descendants elected to call themselves Ohlones.

Portolá discovered what the local Indians had known for thousands of years: The land was lush and fertile and had a magnificent river, which he named in honor of St. Lawrence. Virtually everything that the Spanish explorers named followed their practice of giving honor to someone or something representing the Catholic Church, and the rolling hills above the river were called Santa Cruz, or "holy cross."

As the Spanish population grew with many settlers arriving in Alta California, they began to push the Native Americans off their land. They colonized the coastal area with a series of 21 missions, each often sprouting a pueblo or a nearby presidio. Mission Santa Cruz, built in 1791, was the twelfth to be erected.

The established missions quickly provided aid to the newest colony, and the area attracted a large influx of more settlers. At the time, the Spanish government was worried that the English or Russians might try to seize part of their new land. The Marqués de Branciforte, viceroy of Mexico, elected to formalize the pueblo at Santa Cruz to help fortify the coast. Not surprisingly, it was named Villa de Branciforte, but it did not serve a noble purpose.

Not everyone who arrived at Villa de Branciforte was guided by religious principles and the mission fathers were not happy to have this community nearby. Most of the original occupants were convicted of petty crimes elsewhere in New Spain and banished to Alta California. Branciforte became a haven for gambling and smuggling, and attracted the pirate Bouchard in 1818, who attacked the entire Monterey Bay. The mission declined in influence until 1840 when a tidal wave and earthquakes destroyed it. The existing Mission Santa Cruz is a recreation of the original.

Chaminade is named for William Joseph Chaminade, a French Roman Catholic priest who survived persecution during the French Revolution. France was running out of money and decided their best source of new funds would be the Catholic Church. In 1791, they insisted that all clergy swear an oath to the king, effectively removing the Vatican as their source of direction. Chaminade refused, first going underground and then moving to Spain to continue his ministry.

About the time that France sold the Louisiana Purchase to America for $23 million in 1803, Chaminade had reentered France at Napoleon's invitation, and took an interest in schools. The resulting religious foundation was named the Society of Mary, with Chaminade as the head.

As the society (also called the Marianists) expanded, they arrived in the new land of California in 1884. Realizing the need for a school, they seized the opportunity to purchase the current 300-acre site of Chaminade for $50,000 in 1923. After using the existing structure for several years, the brothers elected to build a high school.

In 1930, the ground floor was completed and the Chaminade Boys High School opened. Examination of the building will show very sturdy construction, designed to hold the weight of a second floor, which was not completed. This structure is the current main building, where the resort's meeting rooms and restaurants are located.

During World War II, the high school became a center for training priests in the Marianist order. In the early 1970s, Chaminade became a religious retreat and, in 1979, it was converted into a hotel and conference facility.

Located on a mountain ridge overlooking Monterey Bay only 90 minutes south of San Francisco, Chaminade offers 300 acres of luxury in the foothills of the Santa Cruz Mountains. Set in the mild climate and scenic beauty of this resort community, Chaminade offers casual light meals in Linwood's, breakfast, lunch, and dinner buffets in the Sunset Dining Room, and fine dining in The Library.

Chaminade
One Chaminade Lane
Santa Cruz, California 95065
(800) 283-6569

Chicken Stuffed with Prosciutto, Pears, and Brie

4 chicken breasts (Ask the
   butcher for half breasts
   with the wing tip attached.
   He will cut the wing off
   to the nub. This makes a
   nicer presentation. Leave
   the skin on.)

½ small red onion, julienned

2 shallots, minced

1–2 tablespoons olive oil,
   as needed

1 brown/Bosc pear, sliced,
   skin on

½ bunch thyme, minced

2 ounces red wine to deglaze
   (or balsamic vinegar)

4 thin slices parma prosciutto
   (or ham, but the taste will
   be different)

1 ounce Brie, skin on,
   cut into 4 rectangles

Sea salt and white pepper

Make a small pocket in the side of the chicken, approximately 1 inch wide by 1 inch deep. Set chicken aside.

Sauté onions and shallots in olive oil until translucent and slightly brown in color (caramelized). Add pears and sauté quickly. Add fresh thyme and deglaze with wine or balsamic vinegar. Reduce until almost dry. Take off heat and cool.

In the pocket of the chicken, press in prosciutto slice. Add Brie and the pear mixture. Close slit in chicken with toothpick. Lightly salt and pepper outside of chicken.

Heat a heavy skillet and sear chicken on skin side. Remove from skillet. Finish cooking in oven, covered for 25 minutes at 375 degrees.

Use some of the extra pear mixture to top chicken when it comes out of the oven.

⟞ YIELD ⟝

Serves 4

Roast Lemon Vinaigrette

Chef's Note: This is my most popular vinaigrette! There are a few steps you need to go through, but the results are awesome!

ROASTING LEMONS

Toss lemons with the salt and sugar. Cover with aluminum foil and roast in pan for approximately 1 hour in a 325-degree oven. The lemons should be soft and able to squeeze easily. Be careful not to burn them: Check lemons after 30 minutes. Uncover and cool; save all of the pan juices.

VINAIGRETTE

Add vinegars, champagne, honey, and mustard to blender. If it is too much for the blender, puree in batches. Return to blender and slowly drizzle in some oil and then some water. If too thin, add more oil; if too thick, thin with water.

Season with salt and pepper. Add minced tarragon at the end.

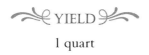

YIELD

1 quart

4 whole lemons

¼ cup salt

¼ cup granulated sugar

7 ounces white wine vinegar

7 ounces apple cider vinegar

2 cups champagne

3 tablespoons honey

1 tablespoon Dijon mustard

1–2 cups corn oil

1½ cups water

Sea salt and white pepper

1 tablespoon fresh
    minced tarragon

Macadamia Nut Encrusted Brie with Spicy Chili Glaze

BRIE

½ cup all-purpose flour

2 whole eggs

1 ounce water

1 ounce macadamia nuts, toasted and ground to powder

1 ounce breadcrumbs

1 small, 2-ounce wheel Brie (or cut Brie into sections)

Crisco shortening

CHILI GLAZE

½ cup prepared sweetened chili paste (recommend to use Sambal chili paste, sweetened with honey in a 1:1 ratio)

1 cup orange marmalade

1 ounce orange juice

BRIE PREPARATION

You will need 3 shallow bowls. In bowl 1, place flour. In bowl 2, place egg mixed with water and slightly beaten. In bowl 3, mix macadamia nuts and breadcrumbs.

Dip Brie into flour and coat well. Dip into egg mixture, again coating well. Next, dip in macadamia-bread-crumb mixture. Set aside and refrigerate to chill.

FINAL PREPARATION

To make sweet chile glaze, blend all ingredients in a blender until smooth.

Heat the Crisco in a deep skillet. When very hot (test with water droplet), place Brie in oil using a slotted spoon. Quickly fry on all sides until soft and nuts are golden. Take out of oil and drain on paper towels.

You can also bake in the oven. To do so, spray the Brie, as well as the pan, with cooking spray, then cook in a 400-degree oven for 10 minutes or until Brie is soft.

Serve sweet chili glaze on the side or drizzled on the Brie.

FURNACE CREEK INN
& RANCH RESORT

The incomparable Death Valley is the setting for the Furnace Creek Inn & Ranch Resort. First inhabited by Panamint Indians from the Shoshone Nation, Death Valley National Park holds the title as the hottest, driest, and lowest spot in the Western Hemisphere. It offers more than 3 million acres of breathtaking vistas across mountains, rolling hills, snow-covered peaks, beautiful sand dunes, rugged canyons, and a valley that is mostly below sea level.

Geologic patterns full of colorful minerals and rock formations offer a detailed history of the area, as well as the formation of the valley of salt. Geologists believe that shifting tectonic plates caused the mountains to rise at about the same time the valley floor dropped to a low of 282 feet below sea level. Seawater trapped in the area deposited salt that is up to 1,000 feet thick in some places.

While Telescope Peak, the park's highest point, is more than 11,000 feet above sea level, the bedrock under the valley floor is up to 9,000 feet below sea level, covered by centuries of erosion from surrounding hills. Death Valley is one of the best places on earth to view stream formations known as alluvial fans. Created by even small amounts of infrequent rain rushing down the steep canyons scouring rocks, boulders, soil, and debris, alluvial fans are the result of repeated deposits of this sedimentary fill near the valley floor at the canyon's mouth.

The Timbisha Tribe of the Shoshone Nation occupied the area for centuries and left petroglyphs in several of the remote canyons in Death Valley. Settlers first discovered the area in 1849. Pioneers heading for the gold fields attempted to find a shortcut and entered the 130-mile-long valley rimmed by high mountains. Search parties eventually found a way out, but one weary woman offered a parting comment, that she was glad to be leaving "death valley" behind. The name has stuck ever since.

Hopes of finding great gold and silver deposits were never realized, but minor discoveries kept prospectors looking until they discovered "white gold," better known as borax. W. T. Coleman built the Harmony Borax Works in 1882, and introduced the 20 mule teams that were popularized in the 1950s by the TV program *Death Valley Days* and its host, Ronald Reagan. The mule-drawn wagons hauled borax more than 165 miles to the railroad stop in the Mojave Desert for several years until the operation was moved to Daggett, California.

After the turn of the century, the Pacific Coast Borax Company returned to Death Valley to resume borax mining. In 1927, the company followed the lead of the successful Palm Springs Desert

Inn and entered the tourism business by opening The Furnace Creek Inn. The mission-style structure was set into the low ridge overlooking Furnace Creek Wash. Adobe bricks were handmade by Paiute and Shoshone laborers, while a Spanish stonemason created the Moorish-influenced stonework. Meandering gardens, Deglet Noor palm trees, and more rooms were added and other improvements were made for its completion in 1935 with 66 rooms.

Warm springs continuously flow to the facility, keeping the swimming pool at a constant 84 degrees and providing all of the moisture necessary for the inn, its surrounding gardens, a forest of date palms, and the nearby ranch, which was added in 1933. A lush 18-hole golf course at the ranch, the lowest-elevation course in the world, is situated next to an airport that services small planes, some of which just stop for the food. Wild but lazy coyotes on the course have been known to walk off in broad daylight with those little white balls that resemble bird eggs.

Hiking, horseback riding, and tennis are also popular with guests—but be prepared. Whether you are walking or driving, pack lots of water, then pack some more. Summer temperatures (measured 5 feet above the ground) can average about 120 degrees with humidity below 10 percent. Surface temperatures are considerably hotter. Hats and sunscreen are also recommended for most activities.

Other area attractions include the 2,000-year-old Ubehebe Crater, a relic from an explosive steam eruption when rising magma met an underground lake. Dante's Peak on the eastern border of the valley offers a mile-high vantage point toward the southern portion of the park; it also overlooks Badwater, so named because of the reaction thirsty animals had to the salt-filled springs.

Scotty's Castle (built by Walter Scott, also known as Death Valley Scotty) is a testament to what a determined con man can accomplish. Scotty did most everything in life with other people's money, often obtaining the funds through deceit. A wealthy Chicago insurance man named Albert Johnson invested in Scotty's "gold mine," but quickly became disillusioned with the results. When he finally traveled to Death Valley to inspect the "mine," he discovered two things: Scotty had lied to him about the investment and his health greatly improved with the climate change. Thus began a lifelong friendship and partnership. Johnson eventually financed more than $2 million in construction overseen by Scotty, leading most people to believe that the property was his. Tours are available daily but are quite limited in size, so plan ahead.

The Furnace Creek Inn provides a list of more than four dozen movies filmed at least in part in the area. These include *Star Wars*, *Spartacus*, and *King Solomon's Mines*. Television shows filmed here include *Tarzan*, *Death Valley Days*, and an episode of *The Twilight Zone*.

President Hoover named Death Valley a national monument in February 1933. In 1994, Death Valley became a national park, making it the largest park in the continental United States.

High summer temperatures discourage many visitors. Most tourism is in the winter, spring, and fall, and the inn is available to guests from mid-October through mid-May. In the hot months, from mid-May through mid-October, all operations are consolidated at the Furnace Creek Ranch. The mission-style inn is a AAA four-diamond property. The nearby Furnace Creek Ranch offers 224 family-oriented accommodations.

The Furnace Creek Inn & Ranch Resort offers the perfect vantage point to explore the beauty of a region that is virtually untouched and extraordinarily distinct.

Furnace Creek Inn & Ranch Resort
Highway 190
Death Valley, California 92328
(760) 786-2345

1 jar nopalito cactus (found
    in ethnic food section of
    grocery store)

1 cup flour

1 tablespoon Cajun seasoning
    (chile, garlic, white pepper,
    cumin, and paprika)

Salt and pepper

Crispy Cactus Appetizer

Drain cactus well. Combine dry ingredients in large bowl. Toss cactus thoroughly. Shake off excess flour. Deep fry in very hot oil until crispy, about 2 minutes.

Serve with your favorite dipping sauce.

Chef's Note: At Furnace Creek Inn, we use three sauces: yellow tomato salsa; guacamole and sour cream mixture; and prickly pear and jalapeño jelly mixture.

Rattlesnake Empanadas

Grind rattlesnake and chicken fat together until it looks like ground pork. Sauté peppers, cactus, and ground meat together for about 15 minutes.

Add seasonings and lime juice to the skillet. Cook for 15 to 20 minutes more.

Drain and let cool.

Add shredded cheese to mixture. Spread out pastry sheet and cut in 4-inch circles (use a biscuit cutter, fancy tart cutter, or can). Brush pastry with egg wash. Place a tablespoon full of mixture in middle of circle, fold pastry over and crimp closed with fingers or fork.

Cook in 350 degree oven for about 12 minutes.

Plate on top of salsa. Top with guacamole, sour cream, or ranch dressing.

1 pound boneless rattlesnake meat (found at gourmet stores or online)

3 ounces chicken fat to bind (can use chicken meat)

½ cup each red, yellow, and green bell peppers, chopped fine

½ cup diced nopalito cactus (found in ethnic food section of grocery store)

1 tablespoon ground cumin

1 teaspoon salt

1 teaspoon pepper

1 teaspoon granulated garlic

1 teaspoon chile powder

¼ cup lime juice

⅔ cup shredded Colby cheese

2 boxes puff pastry sheets, defrosted

Egg wash (one egg, fork whipped with 2 tablespoons water)

1¼ pounds semisweet chocolate

1 cup heavy cream

2 ounces crème de menthe

3 ounces unsalted butter, melted

1 pound unsweetened chocolate, for dipping

8 ounces cocoa powder

For garnish: chopped almonds, Oreo cookie crumbs, and white chocolate; sauces of your choice

Chocolate Truffles

Melt semisweet chocolate in a large double boiler. Meanwhile, in a separate pot, bring cream to a soft boil (not rolling). Once cream is hot, add crème de menthe. In a large bowl, combine melted butter, melted chocolate, and hot cream mixture. Fold or whisk until completely and evenly mixed.

Pour into a 2 or 4-inch pan and cool in refrigerator for 24 hours or until set.

After ganache is set, scoop into a ball and roll in cocoa powder (use your hands—it's a messy job but well worth the effort).

Place unsweetened chocolate in double boiler and melt until runny. Dip rolled truffles in melted chocolate and set on papered sheet pan.

For presentation, place truffles onto plates with different sauces (white chocolate, dark chocolate, raspberry, or any other), and sprinkle with garnishes.

Cheesecake Pie

Choice of lemon or orange.

Cut pastry into 4 equal pieces. Using a large cupcake pan, spray the pan and press dough into the pan, leaving parts hanging over the edges.

Soften cream cheese. Blend well with beaters or mixer, then add all other ingredients until very smooth. It should look like cake batter. Pour batter into the uncooked pastry shells.

This is a very important step: Add water to a larger pan and place the cupcake pan into the larger pan. Cooking in a water bath ensures even temperatures throughout. Set the cupcake pan in about 2–3 inches of water.

Bake at 350 degrees for 1 hour, then place straight into freezer for up to 4 hours or overnight, for up to a week unwrapped. (This process stops the cooking and produces air bubbles for a light and fluffy texture.)

When ready to serve, you can thaw out for 1 hour or pop in microwave for about 30–45 seconds. Top with your favorite sauces.

1 package puff pastry sheets

24 ounces cream cheese

6 eggs

Zest from an orange or lemon

1 teaspoon lemon or orange extract

1 cup canned mandarin oranges or prepared lemon pudding

1 cup sugar

Pinch of salt

LA PLAYA HOTEL

The Spanish influence in California began with the very first explorers who landed here in 1602. Friar Sebastian Vizcaino named this area for his patron saint, Our Lady of Mount Carmel. When they started building missions along the California coast, the mission at Carmel became the second in a series of 21 embassies to be erected. Father Junípero Serra, who supervised the entire mission-building project, was so impressed with the beauty of the Carmel area that he made it his headquarters and his home. Built in 1770, it was named the Mission San Carlos Borromeo de Carmelo.

The inspiration for all of the early construction in Alta California derived from Spain. Adobe buildings, haciendas, and virtually every structure built for any purpose was modeled after the grand churches and missions in Europe.

When Christopher Jorgensen married into the famous Ghirardelli chocolate clan from San Francisco in 1905, he felt the need to build a home in Carmel for his new bride. Today, the section of that structure still standing is part of La Playa Hotel. The original building had a star-shaped stained glass window facing the street and steps leading up to a nonexistent bell tower, a style inspired by the design of the missions.

The Jorgensens enjoyed this home for several years. When they chose to leave Carmel, the property went to Alice Signor. La Playa remained in her family for many years, and they converted it into a small hotel for area visitors. Guests often arrived by train into the Monterey station, to be met by the hotel's pickup truck to carry steamer trunks full of clothes.

Carmel-By-The-Sea, originally started as an artist community in 1904, soon attracted people of all kinds. As the city grew, the hotel was expanded to accommodate an increasing number of guests. Connected to the original mansion, the second building, erected in the 1920s, housed most of the guest rooms.

La Playa eventually passed through several owners until the Cope family bought it in the 1980s. They installed a two-level brick patio and replaced the old wrought-iron gazebo with a larger one. The surrounding gardens and landscaping were upgraded and expanded. Guest rooms were repainted and refurbished to complement the stunning views of the ocean, garden, and patio. Numerous pieces from the family collection of European antiques, artwork, and California memorabilia were imported to enhance the property's decor.

La Playa Hotel and Cottages-by-the-Sea is a great place to stay while visiting the numerous area attractions, such as the Carmel Mission, 17-Mile Drive, Monterey Bay Aquarium, and the many Monterey and Carmel Valley wineries.

La Playa Hotel
Camino Real at Eighth Avenue
Carmel-By-The-Sea, California 93921
(831) 624-6476

½ pound Dungeness crabmeat

½ pound shrimp meat

⅓ cup egg whites

½ cup onion, finely diced

½ cup carrot, finely diced

½ cup celery, finely diced

½ cup chives, finely diced

3 tablespoons ginger or thyme

Panko or breadcrumbs

Crab Cakes

Clean the crabmeat. Puree the shrimp and egg whites until a paste forms.

Mix crab, shrimp, and all ingredients except panko. Divide mixture into 12 equal patties. Bread with the panko or bread crumbs before cooking.

Pan sauté or cook in a preheated oven at 350 degrees for approximately 10 minutes. Serve with your favorite accompaniment as an entrée or alone as an appetizer.

YIELD
12 cakes

Mixed Greens with Goat Cheese, Roast Beets, and Balsamic Vinegar

CROUTONS

For the croutons, slice the baguette lengthwise, ⅛ to ¼-inch thick horizontally. This will leave you with 20 to 30-inch-long slices of baguette that are ⅛–¼ inch thick. Brush the baguette slices with clarified butter or olive oil (herbs may be added).

Wrap bread around the side of an aluminum soda or beer can loosely, so a small finger can be inserted between bread and can. (The baguette will expand as it bakes, and this space allows room for the size increase.) Overlap the end 2 inches over the beginning (loosely) and trim any extra.

Place on sheet tray, with the seam side down. Bake at 350 degrees until light brown. Remove. Carefully slide crouton off can. This leaves you with a circular crouton with a hole in the center for salad.

May be stored 3 days in airtight container.

BEETS

Rub each beet with 1 ounce of olive oil and roast in oven at 300 degrees until toothpick tender. Remove and chill.

Peel and slice beets ⅛ to ¼-inch thick. May be prepared up to 2 days ahead.

1 sweet baguette
    (20–30 inches long)

2–3 ounces butter, melted
    (or olive oil)

Herbs (optional)

6 12-ounce aluminum cans

3 beets (size of a medium orange)

3 ounces olive oil

1½ quart mixed greens

4 ounces goat cheese

1–2 ounces balsamic vinegar

⅓ cup tomato, diced

⅓ cup confetti flower
    (or flowering herbs)

PLATING

To assemble the dish, lay the beet slices overlapping in a circle, allowing a space in the center for the crouton to set.

Set the crouton vertically. Toss or spray mixed greens with herbed olive oil and place inside the crouton tower. Crumble cheese on top. Drizzle beets with balsamic vinegar. Garnish with diced tomatoes and confetti flowers.

⚜ YIELD ⚜

Serves 6

MISSION RANCH

Spain first laid claim to the California coast in 1542 when Juan Rodríguez Cabrillo sailed by Carmel, but did not land. Some sixty years later, Friar Sebastian Vizcaino landed at Carmel in 1602 and named it for his patron saint, Our Lady of Mount Carmel. The local Ohlones Indians were not too happy to see the Europeans arrive, particularly after they discovered that they brought all kinds of new diseases with them, which would eventually decimate the tribe.

When the Spanish started building a series of 21 missions along the California coast, the mission at Carmel was the second to be built. Built in 1770, Father Junípero Serra named it the Mission San Carlos Borromeo de Carmelo.

Missions were routinely built in conjunction with garrisons or forts nearby. The Carmel Mission shared the peninsula with the presidio in Monterey. The U.S. Army would later build Fort Ord on this peninsula to help secure California for the new nation.

The beauty of the area, combined with the presence of Father Serra and the military stationed here, caused the government of New Spain to place its capital of Alta California in Monterey. When New Spain gained independence in 1821 and became Mexico, the capital remained in Monterey. It was not until California became a state in 1850 that the capital was moved to Sacramento.

Every mission was expected to be self-sufficient. This was accomplished by hiring the local Indians to plant and tend the fields and to care for the livestock raised on the vast tracts of land claimed by the missions. But when New Spain became Mexico, the new government secularized the missions, giving most of their land to private individuals in the form of land grants.

Agriculture remained the primary focus of landowners in the valley, but some focused on farming. Juan Romero, a Native American who apparently worked around the Carmel Mission, is the first recorded owner of the section of land where the Mission Ranch is today. A dairy was erected here in the 1850s and it supplied most of the cheese and butter for the area. The creamery is now the Mission Ranch restaurant.

By the 1920s, competition closed the dairy and the ranch became a private club, until Bert and Maggie Dienelt turned it into a restaurant and resort. The ranch also served as an officers' club during the war but remained open to the public.

Carmel-By-The-Sea was established in 1904, primarily as an artist's colony. The beauty of the seascapes along the coast, combined with the seclusion of this out-of-the-way historic village, made it perfect for creative activities. The Depression and the Dust Bowl of the 1930s forced thousands of Midwesterners to greener pastures, and the agricultural centers of California absorbed most of

them. John Steinbeck wrote classic literature about these people. *Grapes of Wrath* and *East of Eden* were two of his major works. His *Cannery Row* focused on the very difficult work performed around the wharfs of Monterey Bay.

In 1950, at the outbreak of the Korean War, Clinton Eastwood Jr. was an army draftee stationed at Fort Ord on the Monterey peninsula. Working as a swimming instructor for the army, he occasionally visited the restaurant at Mission Ranch and was very impressed with both the food and the service. He had not forgotten the area when he became a world famous movie star and, in 1986, after being elected mayor of Carmel-By-The-Sea, he bought the Mission Ranch.

Renovation of the deteriorated property was a major priority. Eastwood hired the best craftsmen around to rebuild and repair every structure to match the style of the original buildings. The restored bunkhouse nestled among the cypress is the oldest structure. With the historic creamery as the restaurant, cottages doted around the property, and the century-old Martin farmhouse functioning as a bed and breakfast, the Mission Ranch offers visitors a glimpse of old California.

Food served at "The Ranch" (as the locals call it) is not the fancy gourmet fare offered at exclusive restaurants in the area. They serve "real food" such as steaks, prime ribs, and potatoes. The large crowd of locals drinking at the bar and eating in the dining room could be the best indication that the Mission Ranch has consistently provided exceptional atmosphere, entertainment, and food for decades.

Mission Ranch
26270 Dolores Street
Carmel-By-the-Sea, California 93923
(800) 538-8221
(831) 625-9040

Sea Horses with Citrus Cilantro Sauce

Skewer each prawn, stretching it from its natural shape into that of a seahorse. Steam the prawns in the white wine and Old Bay seasoning until they are three-fourths of the way done (approximately 3 minutes).

Slice each prawn down the middle of its back to create a pocket. Stuff each prawn with 1 tablespoon of goat cheese.

Set up these four-part coating stages: Pour flour into a bowl. Combine eggs and milk into another. Coat each stuffed prawn first in flour, then egg mixture, sesame seeds, and last coconut flakes. Sear for approximately 1 minute on each side. Serve drizzled with Citrus Cilantro Sauce (recipe follows).

CITRUS CILANTRO SAUCE

Reduce white wine down to 2 cups. Reduce vegetable stock down to 2 cups. Mix the two and continue to simmer. Add butter, citrus juices, salt, and pepper and simmer 5 minutes more.

Add cornstarch to the sauce, which should come to a slightly thicker consistency. Simmer for 5 minutes, then add the zests, stir, and add the cilantro.

Drizzle over the prawns. Serve, perhaps with risotto and sautéed spinach.

24 Mexican prawns,
     peeled and deveined

8 cups white wine

4 tablespoons McCormick's
     Old Bay Seasoning

1 pound goat cheese

1 pound flour

4 eggs

1 cup milk

½ pound sesame seeds

1 pound coconut flakes

CITRUS CILANTRO SAUCE

8 cups white wine

8 cups vegetable stock

1½ pounds butter

3 limes, juiced

3 lemons, juiced

1 orange, juiced

2 pinches of salt

Pinch of pepper

2 tablespoons cornstarch

Zest of limes, lemons, and orange

3 tablespoons cilantro, chopped

YIELD

Serves 4

158

3 cups white wine

3 cups vegetable stock

4 bay leaves

Pinch of salt

Pinch of pepper

1 pound unsalted butter

2 tablespoons capers

3 lemons, juiced

1 bunch chopped parsley

2 pounds jumbo scallops

Scallops

For the sauce, combine the white wine and vegetable stock into a large saucepan. Add bay leaves to the simmering liquid. Reduce to 1 cup and strain. Add salt and pepper. Gradually add the butter at medium heat, stirring constantly. Add capers and lemon juice. Simmer on low heat for 3 minutes. Add parsley.

To plate, sear the scallops 2 minutes on each side for a golden brown color. Pour sauce over scallops and serve.

YIELD
Serves 4

"One cannot think well, love well, sleep well, if one has not dined well."

—Virginia Woolf

The Sprawling Claremont Resort & Spa was built in 1915 in Berkeley. Courtesy of The Claremont Resort & Spa.

The majestic Fairmont is located at the only spot in San Francisco where each of the city's cable car lines meet. Courtesy of Fairmont Hotels & Resorts.

Renovations have revived the Fairmont Sonoma Mission Inn & Spa back to its 1920s gran-deur. Courtesy of Fairmont Hotels and Resorts.

Napa River Inn is the cornerstone of the Historic Napa Mill, built in 1884. Photo by Fred Lyon.

The Ahwahnee Hotel is located in Yosemite Valley and is surrounded by the world famous scenery of Yosemite National Park. Photo by John Bellenis Photography.

The incomparable Death Valley is the setting for the Furnace Creek Inn & Ranch Resort. Courtesy of Xanterra Parks & Resorts.

Potential patrons of The Steinbeck House in Salinas can look forward to a unique luncheon experience in this literary landmark. Photo by Steve Bauer.

Renowned for its magnificent architecture, San Diego's Hotel del Coronado is equally well known for its legendary guests. Courtesy of Hotel del Coronado.

The Biltmore Hotel in Los Angeles features the opulent architectural style of the Spanish-Italian Renaissance to reflect the Castilian heritage of California. Courtesy of the Millennium Biltmore Hotel.

The stunning Mission Inn in Riverside is an assemblage of arcades and gardens, turrets and domes, flying buttresses and spiraling staircases, catacombs and carillon towers. Courtesy of the Mission Inn Hotel & Spa.

The romantic coastal charm of the property has made The Pierpont Inn a favorite location for weddings, reunions, retreats, and splendid overnight getaways for over 95 years.

Since The Queen Mary arrived in Long Beach, it has had its insides modified once more to serve as a floating hotel, restaurant, shopping area, and museum. Courtesy of the Queen Mary.

The Santa Ysidro Ranch is located in the exclusive enclave of Montecito, just minutes from downtown Santa Barbara. Courtesy of the San Ysidro Ranch.

The US Grant opened with great fanfare in October 1910 at a final cost of $1.9 million, a staggering sum at the time. Courtesy of the US Grant Hotel.

POST RANCH INN

When the Spanish explorers arrived in the Big Sur area, they discovered the Costanoan Indians. Having lived there peacefully for several thousand years, the Costanoans were perhaps too friendly with the newcomers. Associating with them in their missions and working for them in their agricultural pursuits led to the introduction of new diseases.

Smallpox, measles, and other diseases caused tremendous loss of life among the native populations and, of course, more settlers arrived. Eventually, the Indians were greatly outnumbered; when their land was taken away by the new state of California in 1850 and 1851, the treaties they signed left them with little to show for their existence in Central California.

The Indians held small portions of the vast land holdings they had originally inhabited. Most of the rest of their land was taken first by the Spaniards who became Mexicans and then by the European settlers. Big Sur remained relatively devoid of inhabitants until the 1860s, when the first American pioneers arrived on the scene. Following the rush to the gold fields up north, settlers began to spread out over other parts of the state in search of land.

William Brainard Post, an 18-year-old from Connecticut, arrived in Monterey in 1848 by ship. An enthusiastic explorer and entrepreneur, Post spent years along the California coast hunting grizzly bears and deer. He later turned from buckskin hunter to businessman, opening the first grain warehouse in Moss Landing and the first butcher shop in Castroville.

Post married Anselma Onesimo, who was of Costanoan descent, in 1850. They had five children and the family needed a place to grow. Perhaps with the encouragement of his new bride and because of her ancestry, he made a claim on 160 acres of land in Big Sur. They opened one of the region's first homesteads. With the help of his sons, he built a cabin that would remind him of his own roots in Connecticut. The red New England-style house, which is a registered historical landmark, still stands today along scenic Highway 1, across from the entrance to Post Ranch Inn.

The Post family took up his entrepreneurial ways, raising cattle and hogs and exporting apples from their prolific orchard. Their youngest son, Joe, married a neighbor of Cherokee descent, and harbored the same homesteading instincts as his parents. After buying up numerous claims from both of their families, he eventually accumulated nearly 1,500 acres, including the area of the Post Ranch Inn.

Together Joe and his wife ran their extensive land holdings and acquired substantial portions of the wilderness around Big Sur. Their son Bill continued the family entrepreneurial tradition, attacking various opportunities and working as a cowboy and rancher. On one trip where he was

driving the stagecoach between Monterey and Big Sur, Bill met Irene Fredericks. She was a city girl whose attraction to Bill turned her summer visit to Big Sur into a lifelong stay. The couple opened Rancho Sierra Mar, a small resort and café near the Post family home, which they ran with the help of their two children, Billy and Mary.

Billy has spent most of his life in Big Sur. After working there as a child, then serving in the Marine Corps in World War II, Bill came home to run the ranch. He met and married Luci and together they continued the family tradition of ranching in Big Sur.

As the world progressed, it grew more difficult to hold onto the old style of living. A friend and neighbor approached Bill and Luci, suggesting they turn the land into an inn that would preserve the integrity and history of the Post family's property. After shaking hands on the deal in 1984, they sealed the Post partnership with a shot of Jack Daniels, which has since become the Inn's unofficial drink. When a formal agreement was finally signed several years later, the partnership bought Bill a tractor, which he used to do nearly all the excavation and grading to build the Inn.

The Inn has been a Post family project from the start. Bill decided to honor the early history of Big Sur by using the ranch cattle brands as the logo. He also named each guest room after Post family and friends. Luci was responsible for putting together the library. And Bill's sister, Mary Post Fleenor, ran the Rancho Sierra Mar café.

For many years Bill Post lead nature walks around the property, describing all manner of plant and animal life, while also relating stories about the Post family. What better way to learn about a place than with someone who has been exploring it for more than 80 years? He no longer leads the walks but, if you find him at the bar, you may get a great story or two out of him.

The Post Ranch Inn is located 30 miles south of Carmel on the west side of Highway 1, directly across from the entrance to the Ventana Inn.

Post Ranch Inn
Highway 1, PO Box 219
Big Sur, California 93920
(800) 527-2200
(831) 667-2200

Toasted Barley "Risotto"

Preheat oven to 350 degrees. Place barley in a single layer on a sheet pan and toast in oven for 15 minutes. The barley should be lightly browned and have a nutty aroma when done.

Heat the oil in a small pan over medium heat; add onion and sauté until translucent, about 2 minutes. Add the barley and stir to coat with oil. Add hot chicken stock or water to the barley, enough to just cover the grains and then reduce heat to a simmer. Continue adding the stock to keep the grains covered throughout the cooking process. When all the stock is incorporated, add the Mushroom Jus and continue to cook until the barley is still slightly chewy and has a creamy texture. Add the mushrooms and cook 1 minute more; then add salt, pepper, lemon juice, butter, and the truffle butter. Adjust seasoning if needed. Serve immediately.

YIELD

Serves 6

1 cup pearl barley

2 tablespoons canola oil

¼ cup yellow onion, diced

1½ cups chicken stock or water, hot

¾ cup Mushroom Jus (recipe follows)

1 cup pan-roasted chanterelle mushrooms

1½ teaspoons salt

¼ teaspoon black pepper

1½ teaspoons lemon juice

2 tablespoons butter

1 tablespoon truffle butter

¼ cup dry porcini

1 cup hot water

3 tablespoons canola oil

2 cups yellow onions, julienned

2 cloves garlic, chopped

6 cups assorted mushrooms, sliced

¼ cup tomato paste

1 cup sherry wine

6 cups water

10 sprigs thyme

1 tablespoon soy sauce

Mushroom Jus

Soak the dry porcini in hot water until hydrated.

Heat the oil in a heavy-bottom pot over high heat. Add the onions and reduce heat to medium. When the onions begin to brown lightly, begin stirring frequently with a wooden spoon, scraping the bottom to loosen up any browned bits and redistribute into the onions. Occasionally add a few tablespoons of water and scrape the bottom to completely deglaze.

Once the onions are golden brown, about 20 minutes, add the garlic and assorted mushrooms. Cook until the mushrooms have given up all of their liquid and begin to caramelize (this takes about 10 minutes).

Add the tomato paste and cook about 5 minutes more or until it begins to caramelize on the bottom of the pan. Immediately add the sherry wine and porcinis with their liquid, being careful not to include the sediment at the bottom. Scrape the bottom of the pan with a wooden spoon and deglaze again, allowing the sherry and porcini liquid to reduce until almost dry. Add the water and thyme and bring to a simmer for 45 minutes. Strain liquid through a fine chinois and add soy sauce.

YIELD

4 cups

Butternut Squash and Pear Soup with Chestnut Cream

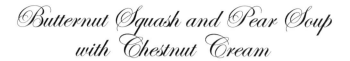

Chef's Note: Every chef has his or her favorite soup, and during the winter months, this soup is one of mine. I am not alone in this thought, as this is the most requested Sierra Mar recipe to date. A hint of pear divides the linear richness of butternut squash with a balance of sweet and slightly acidic undertones, adding another flavor dimension to this recipe.

SQUASH FOR VESSEL

Preheat oven to 350 degrees. Cut off the bottom ends of each squash just enough to create a flat surface for the squash bowl to sit flat. Cut each squash in half across and remove seeds. Brush inside flesh of squash with oil. Place cut side up on a silicone-pad-lined sheet pan. Bake for 35 minutes or until done; set aside and keep warm.

SOUP

Preheat oven to 350 degrees. Cut butternut squash in half lengthwise and remove seeds. Brush with oil and place cut side down on a baking sheet; bake until soft to the touch, about 35 minutes. Remove from the oven and let cool.

Scoop out flesh with a spoon and discard peel. Melt butter in a pot over medium heat. Add shallots and sauté until translucent, about 3 minutes. Add squash pulp, pears, and water; bring to a boil and then reduce heat. Simmer for 30 minutes.

SQUASH FOR VESSEL

3 medium acorn squash

¼ cup canola oil

SOUP

1 large butternut squash (about 2 pounds)

1 tablespoon canola oil

2 tablespoons butter

½ cup shallots, julienned

2 ripe d'anjou pears, peeled, cored, and chopped

6 cups water

Salt and pepper

Fresh nutmeg

Transfer to a container of a blender, cover, and run on high until smooth. Season with salt, pepper, and fresh nutmeg. Keep warm.

PLATING

Fill the acorn squash vessels with hot squash soup. Top with a dollop of Chestnut Cream and serve.

YIELD

Serves 6

Chestnut Cream

Place the heavy cream and chestnuts in a small saucepan and simmer over medium heat for 5 minutes. Transfer to the container of a blender; cover and puree until smooth, adding a little more cream if needed.

Place cooled cream mixture and crème fraiche in a stand mixer with the whisk attachment and whip to soft peaks. Add salt, white pepper, and nutmeg to taste.

YIELD

1 cup

¼ cup heavy cream

¼ cup steamed chestnuts, chopped

½ cup crème fraiche

Salt

Pinch of white pepper

Pinch of nutmeg

SIERRA RAILROAD DINNER TRAIN

Like so many other historical sites in California, the Sierra Railroad was born from the great influx of settlers looking to get rich in the gold fields. Formed in 1897 to connect the San Joaquin Valley to the foothills of the Sierra Nevada Mountains, the Sierra Railroad is the third oldest railroad in North America.

An early railroad pioneer, Thomas S. Bullock, determined that a railroad to the Sierra Nevada foothills was sorely needed and economically feasible. The railroad would carry passengers, freight, supplies, ore, lumber, and cattle. Bullock convinced Prince Andre Poniatowski, a descendant of the king of Poland, of the value of this project. Poniatowski went to William H. Crocker for financing.

William was the son of Charles Crocker, one the Big Four businessmen who are credited with the economic revival of San Francisco after the Great Earthquake and fires that almost destroyed the city in 1906. William was the founder and president of Crocker National Bank and agreed to fund the project. On February 1, 1897, the three formally incorporated the Sierra Railway Company of California.

The railroad started in Oakdale and regular gauge track was built eastward to the foothills in Jamestown. Bullock provided most of the equipment and rail from his defunct railroad in Arizona that became unprofitable when Santa Fe built a track parallel to it. The Sierra's first passenger train arrived at the Jamestown depot and roundhouse on November 8, 1897.

As operations expanded, the railroad's terminus was later moved to Sonora. While the Sierra trains continued to move goods between the valley and the foothills, they also built branches to surrounding areas. One went deep into Yosemite National Park.

However, as the nation became more mechanized and built many roads and highways, railroads like the Sierra were struggling to survive. Fortunately for the Sierra, it was discovered by Hollywood. With the growth of the motion picture industry, a new era began as the Sierra became commonly known as The Movie Railroad.

With its unparalleled scenery, this railroad has been singled out by movie producers from around the world as a preferred location for filming. Featured in more than 300 motion pictures, television programs, and commercials, the Sierra has been immortalized on the silver screen.

The first film was a silent movie made in 1919, *The Red Glove*. Then came the first *talkie* filmed on the railroad, *The Virginian* (1927). Other famous films include *Dodge City* (1939), *High Noon*

(1951) with Grace Kelly and Gary Cooper, *The Great Race* (1966), *Finian's Rainbow* (1969), and *Back to the Future III* (1989).

Movie stars such as John Wayne, Michael Landon, Clint Eastwood, and Michael J. Fox have all played a part in the Sierra Railroad's storied past. Even today, Sierra Railroad continues to haul freight, carry passengers, make Hollywood movies, and play an important role in California.

In the 1970s, the Sierra Railroad launched the first dinner train in North America. Mimicking the famous Super Chief—the flagship of the Atchison, Topeka, and Santa Fe Railway—the Sierra Railroad launched the Supper Chief. Never before had a railroad offered passengers the opportunity to enjoy the charm and nostalgia of railroads as a regular attraction rather than a cross-country voyage. When the railroad was sold by the Crocker Family in 1982, the dinner train was discontinued but, by then, it had launched an industry that now has dozens of dinner trains operating throughout North America.

Following an extensive renovation of the track and the introduction of new equipment, the modern-day Sierra Railroad Dinner Train was launched in 1999 by the Hart brothers to bring tourism back to the railroad. Every week of the year, the Dinner Train offers romantic dinners, fun murder mysteries, lunches, Sunday brunches, Wild West shows, wine tastings, and more. The train station in Oakdale is about one hour from the San Francisco Bay Area or Sacramento, on the way toward Yosemite National Park.

Sierra Railroad Dinner Train
330 South Sierra Avenue
Oakdale, California 95361
(209) 848-2100
(800) 866-1690

CHICKEN

4 8-ounce chicken breasts,
    boneless and skinless

Flour, as needed

Egg wash, as needed (1 egg and
    1 tablespoon water)

Panko breadcrumbs, as needed

2–3 tablespoons olive oil

HONEY MUSTARD SAUCE

½ cup honey

¼ cup Dijon mustard

¼ cup lemon juice

2 teaspoons poppy seeds

1 teaspoon pepper

Honey Mustard Chicken

Prepare the chicken through three dredging stages: dust the chicken breasts in the flour; dip in the egg wash to coat well; then coat well with breadcrumbs. In a sauté pan, lightly brown the breaded chicken breasts in oil on both sides. Remove from oil and finish cooking in a 350-degree oven for about 20 minutes.

To make the honey mustard sauce, combine honey, mustard, lemon juice, poppy seeds, and pepper. Stir together well and heat slightly. Serve drizzled on chicken.

Note: For a deeper honey mustard flavor, add 2 tablespoons honey and 2 tablespoons Dijon mustard to the egg wash.

YIELD
Serves 4

Tomato Basil Soup

In a stockpot with oil, sauté the onion, carrots, and celery for 3 minutes on medium-high heat. Add the garlic and sauté for an additional 1 minute.

Add the diced tomatoes, tomato sauce, dried basil, salt, and pepper. Bring to a boil, reduce heat, and simmer for 1½ hours.

Puree the tomato mixture in a food processor or blender until smooth and return to the stockpot.

With a wire whisk, add the heavy cream and adjust seasonings.

4 ounces oil

16 ounces yellow onion, chopped

8 ounces carrots, diced large

8 ounces celery, diced large

1 tablespoon garlic, chopped

56 ounces canned, diced tomatoes with juice

16 ounces tomato sauce

½ cup dried basil

1 tablespoon salt

½ tablespoon pepper

16 ounces heavy cream

Wildflower Spring Salad with a Champagne Vinaigrette

½ cup olive oil

¼ cup champagne vinegar

1 tablespoon shallots, finely diced

Salt and pepper

Spring-mix mesclun, as needed

½ cup fresh strawberries, sliced

½ cup red onion, sliced

Edible flowers, as needed

Whisk the olive oil, vinegar, and shallots until well incorporated. Season vinaigrette with salt and pepper as desired.

Combine the spring mix, strawberries, red onion, and edible flowers in a salad bowl and toss with the champagne vinaigrette. Serve immediately.

THE STEINBECK HOUSE

"When I was a child growing up in Salinas, we called San Francisco 'The City.' Of course it was the only city we knew but I still think of it as The City, as does everyone else who has ever associated with it."

—John Steinbeck

Author John Steinbeck was the third of four children. Born on February 27, 1902, in the room to the immediate left as you enter the front door, John would spend all of his formative years here.

This Queen Anne-style Victorian home was built in 1897 by J. J. Connor and was purchased by John Ernst and Olive Hamilton Steinbeck in 1900. The second floor had never been finished by the original owner, so Mr. Steinbeck built "climbing things" for the children to enjoy, and it became an indoor playground until finished as a bedroom and bath in 1906.

The future Nobel Prize and Pulitzer Prize winner began his education at the "Baby School," located only five blocks from home. He went on to attend the West End School and eventually graduated from Salinas High School in 1919. He had taken an active roll at Salinas High, performing in the school play, serving as president of the senior class, working as a member of the yearbook staff, and participating on the track and baseball teams. He went on to attend Stanford University but left without a degree.

John was an active, strong-minded person but was greatly influenced by his father, who encouraged him in his writing efforts. He no doubt lavished extra attention on John because he was his only son, and they were greatly outnumbered by the four women in the house. His mother, however, was much more inclined for John to "be something decent like a banker."

In his 1952 novel, *East of Eden*, John describes his boyhood home: "On an impulse he turned off Main Street and walked up Central Avenue to number 130 . . . it was an immaculate and friendly house, grand enough but not pretentious, and it sat inside its white fence surrounded by its clipped lawn and roses and cotoneasters lapped against its walls." He also describes the room he was born in: "The pleasant little bedroom was crowded with photographs, bottles of toilet water, lace pin cushions, brushes and combs and the china and silver bureau-knacks of many birthdays and Christmases."

Dining at The Steinbeck House is a must for anyone traveling through the area. Menus are changed every week to take advantage of both the seasonal produce from the fertile Salinas Valley and the wines of Monterey County. Sunday tours of the house are available during the summer months.

The restaurant itself was opened February 27, 1974, on John Steinbeck's birthday, by a non-profit organization, the Valley Guild. Formed by eight civic-minded women who shared a common interest in cooking and showing off the bounty of the valley, the guild quickly raised the $80,000 needed to purchase the house. Remodeling and renovations were true to the period, and patrons can look forward to a unique luncheon experience in this literary landmark. It is open Tuesday through Saturday for lunch and reservations are highly recommended.

The Steinbeck House
132 Central Avenue
Salinas, California 93901
(831) 424-2735

Stuffed Mushroom Appetizers

Select firm, fresh mushrooms that are larger than a nickel, up to the size of a quarter. Break off the stems, reserving them for soup or stew. Wash mushroom caps. Dry on paper towels.

Combine bread, cheese, and garlic early in the day so garlic has time to permeate the bread. Add enough melted butter to hold crumbs together well. Pack stuffing into mushrooms.

Place stuffed mushrooms on a greased cookie sheet and add another dab of butter on top of each. Preheat oven to 350 degrees. Bake mushrooms 10 to 15 minutes until soft.

"There is no such thing as a little garlic."

—Anonymous

50 mushrooms

1½ cups grated day-old sourdough bread

½ cup freshly grated Romano or Parmesan cheese

2–3 fresh garlic buds pressed through a garlic press

½ cup melted butter

8 spears fresh broccoli

8 raw, skinned, boned chicken
    breasts

29 ounces cream of chicken soup

1 cup mayonnaise

1 teaspoon lemon juice

½ teaspoon curry powder

1½ cups sharp Cheddar cheese

1½ cups soft bread cubes

¼ cup Parmesan cheese

Poulet de Broccoli

Parboil or barely cook the broccoli spears. Slash the stems for even cooking. Put in a buttered casserole or ramekin. Top with chicken breasts.

Mix the cream of chicken soup, mayonnaise, lemon juice, and curry powder. Pour over chicken breasts. Cover this sauce with Cheddar cheese. Top with bread cubes and Parmesan cheese. Bake for 30 minutes at 350 degrees.

YIELD
Serves 8

Cranberry Pecan Pie

In a large bowl, beat eggs slightly. Add sugar and salt and mix until sugar dissolves. Stir in corn syrup and melted butter and mix well. Stir in chopped cranberries and pecans. Pour into unbaked piecrust. To prevent overbrowning, cover edge of piecrust with foil.

Bake at 325 degrees for 45 minutes or until knife inserted in center comes out clean. Cool thoroughly. Garnish with whipped cream.

3 eggs

⅔ cup sugar

⅛ teaspoon salt

1 cup dark corn syrup

⅓ cup melted butter

1 cup fresh cranberries, coarsely chopped

1 cup pecan halves chopped

1 unbaked 9-inch piecrust

Whipped cream, for garnish

STOKES RESTAURANT & BAR

Stokes began as an adobe building, constructed in 1833 as a single-room structure by Hoge and Benjamin Day. In four short years, it passed through several hands, until it was purchased by an English sailor-turned-doctor, James Stokes. Stokes married a Californio (a Spanish-descended native of Alta California) named Josefa Soto de Cano. Over time, their home grew as the family grew. He enlarged the old tile-roofed house until it became a gracious two-story house with seven rooms and a wing for the kitchen and storeroom. A detached shed was also added to house the press that produced California's first newspaper, *The Californian*.

The doctor and one-time mayor of Monterey included a sala, or main room, in his home to host grand gatherings of Monterey's leading citizens. He also hosted the city's Cascaron Ball. A *cascaron* is a party favor thrown at balls and festivals and is a chicken egg that has been properly cracked, emptied, thoroughly washed, brightly painted, and filled with confetti.

From 1855 to 1890, in the years after Stokes and his wife died, the adobe housed both families and businesses, including the bakery of Frenchman Honore Escolle. From 1950 to 1980, Stokes was the home of the popular restaurant Gallatin's. Employees often whispered that the upper floors of the adobe were haunted by sociable ghosts: a man in the dress of the 1800s that might be Dr. Stokes, and a beautiful woman they believed to be Dona Josefa.

Restaurants and apparitions continued to occupy the premises until 1995, when Kirk and Dorothea Probasco and Chef Brandon Miller opened Stokes Adobe Restaurant in June 1996. Located in the heart of historic Monterey, it was remodeled in 2001. A wood-burning pizza oven was added, and the establishment was reopened as Stokes Restaurant & Bar. Apparitions are still occasionally reported but do not diminish the hospitality offered by the current restaurateurs.

Stokes Restaurant & Bar
500 Hartnell Street
Monterey, California 93940
(831) 373-1110

Fava Bean Purée

Cook shelled fava beans in boiling salted water until tender. Shock in an ice water bath. Peel the beans and put aside.

Slice bread very thin, approximately ⅛ inch thick. Brush or spray lightly with olive oil and season lightly with salt and pepper. Arrange on sheet pan and toast in 350-degree oven until golden brown.

In food processor, add fava beans, garlic, and lemon thyme and puree while adding the olive oil. Season to taste. Spread fava bean puree on croutons and serve.

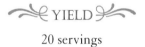 YIELD

20 servings

1 cup fresh fava beans, shelled (about 2 lbs.)

1 baguette loaf

Olive oil for toasting crostini

Salt and pepper to taste

1 clove garlic

1 tablespoon lemon thyme

⅓ cup extra virgin olive oil

Duck Confit Salad

2 tablespoons whole fennel seed

2 tablespoons whole coriander seed

4 tablespoons whole black pepper

1½ tablespoons chili flakes

1 tablespoon whole allspice

1 tablespoon whole clove

4 tablespoons kosher salt

8 duck hen legs

2 quarts duck fat

8 eggs

½ pound smoked bacon

¾ cup aged red wine vinegar

½ cup pure olive oil

8 shallots, finely diced

½ cup whole roasted garlic cloves

2 pounds clean spinach

Salt and pepper

PREPARATIONS

Lightly toast all spices and crush in a spice grinder. Add salt and sprinkle liberally on all sides of the duck legs. Layer legs in a perforated pan or colander and weigh them down over a drain pan. Refrigerate for 24 hours.

Heat oven to 300 degrees. In an ovenproof pan, heat duck fat slowly while brushing off spices from duck legs. Submerge duck legs in warm fat and cover with a tightly fitting lid. Place in the oven for 1½ hours or until thigh bone removes easily.

Drain duck fat and store separately in refrigerator. In a medium saucepan, bring 2 quarts of salted water to a boil and add eggs for 7 minutes. Drain and place in ice water to cool. Then peel and set aside.

FINALS STEPS

Cut bacon into small lardoons and cook slowly in a large sauté pan until crisp. Drain and reserve fat. In a bowl, whisk together vinegar, oil, and shallots, seasoning with salt and pepper. Add a tablespoon of the rendered bacon fat to vinaigrette.

Heat another sauté pan and add a tablespoon of duck fat, then add duck legs, skin side down. When skin is crisp, remove legs and keep warm in the oven. Place rendered bacon in the warm pan. Add garlic cloves and

spinach. Season with salt and pepper, then add vinai-grette and sauté for 1 minute.

Divide spinach between 8 warm plates and place a duck leg on each portion. Cut eggs in half and garnish each plate, seasoning with salt and pepper.

YIELD

Serves 8

Slow Cooked Lamb Shoulder
Stuffed with Winter Greens and Mint

2 bunches golden chard

1 lamb shoulder,
    boned and cleaned

4 sweet peppers,
    roasted and peeled

8 cloves garlic,
    peeled and chopped

½ cup mint, chopped

Sea salt and cracked black pepper

Butcher's twine

4 large onions peeled and
    chopped

4 medium carrots sliced

6 ribs celery chopped

1 fresh bay leaf

½ cup tomato paste

2 cups red wine

8 cups lamb or chicken stock

2 cups tomato concasse

Fresh mint

Sweet butter

Wild arugula

Preheat oven to 325 degrees.

In a large saucepan of boiling salted water, cook the chard for ten seconds and plunge into ice water. Squeeze out excess water and finely chop the chard.

On a board, lay the lamb shoulder with fat cap facing down and away from you. Evenly spread chard, peppers, garlic, and mint inside lamb. Season with salt and pepper and roll up moving away from yourself. Tie with butcher's twine and brown the lamb in a braising pan with a little oil.

Remove lamb when completely brown and then add the vegetables until caramelized. Add tomato paste and cook for two more minutes. Deglaze with wine. Add stock and bring to a boil. Return the lamb cover and put in the oven for 1½ hours or until tender.

Remove lamb and keep warm. Strain braising liquid and reduce to a sauce consistency, skimming the fat often. Add tomato, fresh mint, and a knob of butter to finish sauce.

Check seasoning and serve sauce over sliced lamb and arugula. Garnish with more mint.

YIELD

Serves 10

THE UPHAM HOTEL & COUNTRY HOUSE

When the Spanish explorers arrived in Santa Barbara, they precipitated a flood of Spanish settlers into the area. The Presidio (Royal Fort) was built in 1782 and the Santa Barbara Mission was built in 1786. The Chumash Indians had welcomed Juan Cabrillo when he arrived in 1542, and they actively worked with the new settlers around the mission, but this association would eventually cost them dearly.

The Spanish settlers eventually pushed the Chumash from much of their land and many of the Native Americans succumbed to unfamiliar diseases. The land was first given as land grants to influential members of the Spanish then Mexican governments of Alta California. After the United States won the Mexican-American War in 1848, Santa Barbara and the land around it was taken over by the U.S. government.

The Gold Rush of 1849 and statehood for California in 1850 produced a new breed of settler. People from eastern states came to California to seek their fortunes. Word traveled fast and more easterners came west for the weather, as well as the economic opportunities.

Amasa (Macie) Lyman Lincoln, a cousin of President Lincoln, left Massachusetts in 1869 and sailed to Panama with his wife, two children, and a family friend. They traveled overland to the Pacific, and then took a steamer up the coast to San Francisco. After considering several options, they finally settled in Santa Barbara, probably for health reasons. Macie wrote home to relatives about a man that had lived for a long time and left Santa Barbara to die, but wanted to be brought back there to be buried once he died. After his death, he was brought home for burial but came back to life from the good weather.

Macie's wife Abbie noted that others arriving in Santa Barbara had very few choices of where to stay. She promptly bought two lots in downtown for $300 and had a New England-style boarding house built. It was not easy in early Santa Barbara. Redwood timbers sent by steamship had to be floated to shore, as the city wharf had not been built yet. When finished, the Lincoln House offered exceptional service for travelers.

New England architecture usually included a cupola, which is Italian for "dome." The Lincoln House cupola served a very practical purpose: The Chinese chef would climb up there and watch for arriving steamships. His assistant on the dock would meet the ships and signal back to the chef as to how many guests were coming. The chef would then know how many rooms to make ready, how

many hot baths to draw, and how many meals to prepare. When the guests arrived in the house's own horse and carriage, everything would be above their highest expectations.

The Lincoln House was eventually sold and a succession of owners acquired more property nearby, expanding the size of the boarding house. Cyrus Upham purchased the house in 1898 and renamed it for himself. Upham built the two-story structure next door, still in operation today, which he called the Lincoln Building, perhaps to justify his having changed the name of the original boarding house.

When Upham died, the hotel was sold to Ira Goodridge. He and his family ran the property for several years and are responsible for adding the cottages on the property.

An earthquake in 1925 damaged or destroyed much of downtown Santa Barbara, but the Upham Hotel survived. Built of flexible redwood beams, the only significant damage was to some stone fireplaces. Over the next few days, much of the town flocked to the Upham because it was one place where hot coffee and meals were being served.

The hotel eventually passed to Carl Johnson from Pasadena, which also happened to have been the home of Cyrus Upham and Ira Goodridge. Johnson went to great lengths and considerable expense to completely restore the hotel to its original grandeur.

One of the additions was to convert the sitting room off the lobby into an eating place. Leased to Tom Gilbertson and Marcus Gatter, the restaurant was named Louie's Restaurant in honor of Marcus's favorite dog.

The Upham Hotel is the oldest continuously operated hotel in Santa Barbara and remains an integral part of its history.

The Upham Hotel & Country House
1404 De la Vina Street
Santa Barbara, California 93101
(800) 727-0876
(805) 963-7003

Shrimp and Scallop Cakes with Scallion Vinaigrette

SHRIMP AND SCALLOP CAKES

Combine all ingredients in a food processor. Form into cakes and pan sauté.

VINAIGRETTE

Whisk all scallion vinaigrette ingredients together. Drizzle over the top of the cakes.

"The only real stumbling block is fear of failure. In cooking you've got to have a what-the-hell attitude."

—Julia Child

CAKES

10 peeled shrimp

6 large sea scallops

2 tablespoons bread crumbs

1 tablespoon red pepper, finely diced

1 tablespoon green onion, chopped

Salt and pepper

1 tablespoon Parmesan cheese

SCALLION VINAIGRETTE

¼ cup lemon juice

¼ cup rice wine vinegar

¾ cup olive oil

¼ cup sliced green onion (scallions)

¼ cup sliced shallots

Salt and pepper

5 large yellow onions, coarsely chopped

2 tablespoons butter

1 large pizza crust

2 cups Gorgonzola cheese

1 teaspoon fresh thyme

1 teaspoon dried sage

Salt and pepper

Pizza with Caramelized Onion and Gorgonzola Cheese

Sauté the onions in butter until they are very soft and caramelized. Top pizza crust with onions, gorgonzola cheese, and herbs. Bake the pizza on a pizza stone or pizza pan at 400 degrees for 10–15 minutes, depending on desired crispness of crust.

Chicken Romaine Salad with Rice Noodles and Ginger Vinaigrette

Combine ginger, sesame oil, honey, canola oil, and rice wine vinegar in a food processor.

Toss with romaine lettuce, chicken, and rice noodles. Finish with roasted almonds.

YIELD
Serves 6–8

3 cups sweet pickled ginger

½ cup sesame oil

¾ cup honey

¼ cup canola oil

1 cup rice wine vinegar

1 bunch Romaine lettuce

2 cups grilled chicken, cubed

1 cup crispy rice noodles

3–4 tablespoons roasted almonds

WOLF HOUSE RESTAURANT

The original Wolf House was built to serve as the residence for a suddenly successful author. Jack London was born in 1876 as John Griffith Chaney, the apparently illegitimate son of an itinerant astrologer and journalist. Chaney deserted Jack's mother before he was born and she married John London within a year. Jack did not learn who his biological father was until two decades later.

Raised in Oakland and the surrounding towns, Jack spent some time in school but quit after the eighth grade. He would return and finish high school at the age of nineteen but his primary education came from reading. At the age of fifteen, London was sailing around San Francisco Bay, raiding oyster beds because there was so much money to be made. Trading crime for government after only one very successful year as a thief, Jack joined the California Fish Patrol and helped catch poachers.

His formal and informal education led him to join the Socialist Labor Party at the age of twenty. He was already known at the time for his curbside lectures, and the newspaper referred to him as the "Boy Socialist" of Oakland. The FBI created quite a file on him but his own writing vastly surpassed the government's efforts.

London spent a lot of time at sea, learning the ways of shipboard life and gaining many worldly experiences. One of his ventures took him to Alaska in search of a fortune during the Klondike Gold Rush. He failed to find a fortune and instead grew deathly ill from lack of fresh vegetables. Returning home, he was faced with supporting his mother since his stepfather had passed away. He took up writing.

London's first book, *The Son of the Wolf*, was published in 1900 when he was twenty-four. During the remaining fourteen years of his life, he would write more than 50 books, and have hundreds of articles published.

Success allowed him to marry (twice) and buy "Beauty Ranch," 1,200 acres on the edge of Glen Ellen. He had elected to settle there because he was so enamored with the beauty of the hills covered with ripe grapes. The construction of Wolf House began in 1911 on the ranch just outside of town. Built of stone and redwood, it took two years to complete. Just before they were about to move in, spontaneous combustion destroyed everything but the walls. London died three years later.

His property is now known as the Jack London State Historic Park. In January of 1986, Jack London was honored on what would have been his 110th birthday with a twenty-five-cent U.S. postage stamp as part of the Great American Series.

The building that the current Wolf House Restaurant is in was built in town in 1905. Every lumber and mill town had to have a saloon to entertain the loggers, and this brick building served that purpose. The Jack London Lodge and Wolf House Restaurant came along well after the Jack London Saloon, but the three offer an excellent entertainment complex for visitors and locals alike along the wooded banks of Sonoma Creek.

Wolf House Restaurant
13740 Arnold Drive
Glen Ellen, California 95442-9998
(707) 996-4401

Forest Mushroom Ragout with Crispy Parmesan and Truffle Oil

1 tablespoon unsalted butter

1 tablespoon chopped garlic

1 tablespoon chopped shallots

Salt

Pepper

1 pound mixed wild mushrooms

¼ cup white wine

1 tablespoon chopped parsley

½ cup finely shredded Parmesan

Truffle oil

Micro mixed greens to garnish

MUSHROOMS

Melt butter in a large sauté pan over medium heat. Once the butter starts to brown add the shallots and garlic, season with salt and pepper, and sauté for 2 minutes.

Add the mushrooms and turn down the heat to medium low. As the mushrooms start to wilt, add the white wine and let the mixture stew for 2 minutes or until most of the liquid is gone from the pan.

Add the parsley and set the mushrooms aside but keep warm.

PARMESAN CRISP

Place silicone baking mat on a sheet pan. Spread the finely grated Parmesan in a ⅛-inch-thick circle. Cook at 300 degrees for 2 minutes watching closely the entire time. Cheese is done when it is golden and has melted into a large chip. Let the Parmesan cool completely and break into 6 individual crisps.

PLATING

Place a large spoonful of mushrooms in the center of the plate. Lightly drizzle with truffle oil and top with a piece of the Parmesan crisp. Finish with the micro greens on top as a garnish.

Meyer Lemon and Almond Crusted Tilapia
with Melted Sorrel and Brown Butter Sauce

CRUST

Zest and juice the Meyer lemon. In a bowl, mix toasted almonds, brioche, thyme, zest, and juice. Season as needed with salt and pepper. Set aside.

TILAPIA

Separate the fillet into two pieces lengthwise. Season with salt and pepper.

ASSEMBLY

In a sauté pan over medium heat, start to sweat the chopped shallots in olive oil. Once they are translucent, add the sorrel and a teaspoon of butter and sauté until wilted. Salt and pepper to taste. Set aside.

In a mixing bowl, whip the egg with a pinch of salt until fluffy. Brush the fish fillet with the egg and place desired amount of crust on top of it. Place the crusted fillet into an oiled lukewarm sauté pan and place in broiler. Cook until golden brown.

In a small saucepot, brown the remaining butter. Be careful not to burn the whey.

1 whole Meyer lemon

¼ cup toasted almonds

2 cups brioche, large diced

1 bunch thyme

1 tilapia fillet

Salt and pepper

¼ cup shallots, chopped

Olive oil for sautéing

¼ pound sorrel

½ cup butter

1 whole egg

PLATING

Place the sorrel in the center of the plate. Set the fish atop the sorrel and finish the dish by drizzling the butter sauce over it. Garnish with fresh thyme or maybe some diced tomato.

YIELD

Serves 2

Southern California

California's heart and soul reside in San Diego. Lovely Victorian buildings and restored brownstones are part of the historic architecture. Mariachi bands serenade diners at Mexican restaurants in Old Town and visitors are delighted while Shakespeare is performed under the stars at the Old Globe.

Orange County ranges from Silverado Canyon, where stagecoaches ran more than 100 years ago, to Mission San Juan Capistrano, and to the largest concentration of Vietnamese in the United States.

To the east of Los Angeles is the Inland Empire. Palms sway in front of the Victorian homes. In the 1880s, Southern California was resplendent with thousands of acres of citrus trees due to the planting of seedlings by Luther and Eliza Tibbets in 1875. Richard and Pat Nixon married and Ronald and Nancy Reagan honeymooned at the historic Mission Inn Hotel in Riverside.

Los Angeles County includes the Antelope Valley to the California Poppy Reserve in the north, and Santa Catalina Island in the south. Herein lies the California Dream. The area resonates with history: from the historic La Brea Tar Pits—where bubbling, sticky tar trapped prehistoric creatures—to colorful Olivera Street where the city was born, to Mann's Chinese Theater in Hollywood.

The deserts to the east contrast sharply with lush Palm Springs in the west. Native Americans and Spanish explorers traveled through the area centuries ago. Today visitors enjoy the natural beauty and solitude of shifting sand dunes and majestic Joshua trees.

BEVERLY HILLS HOTEL

By the time New Spain had officially become Mexico in 1821, there were a number of Spanish settlers who had claimed land in the area now known as Beverly Hills. Homes were built and cattle ranches were created, even though the Native Indians often raided the herds.

After California became a state in 1850, there was a brief flirtation with oil drilling in 1865. Wildcatting efforts proved unsuccessful, and a series of owners tried vegetable farming and sheep ranching, until more interest in oil produced another flurry of drilling around 1900. Once again, their efforts were in vain, and the land passed to new owners determined to create a town.

In 1906, Burton Green formed the Rodeo Land and Water Company to develop the area. Laying out wide streets and large lots, the company considered its options for what to call it. Rejecting the previous name, Rancho Rodeo de las Aguas, used by the settlers, Burton suggested they call it "Beverly Hills" after his former home in Beverly Farms, in Massachusetts.

On May 1, 1912, the Beverly Hills Hotel opened with the description as "about halfway between Los Angeles and the sea." At a cost of a half-million dollars, the hotel became the social focus of the city. It not only served as the local church but also housed the only movie theatre in town. With the attention of the film industry, the hotel soon began to attract the rich and famous. Mary Pickford and Douglas Fairbanks moved to "Pickfair" in 1920 just above the hotel and it was quickly dubbed the "White House of Hollywood."

On the grounds of the Beverly Hills Hotel, the great Will Rogers was inaugurated as the mayor in 1923. Unfortunately, during the Depression the hotel was forced to close but the bungalows continued to be occupied under individual leases.

In 1941, Loretta Young, Irene Dunne, and Harry Warner were part of the group that bought the hotel. Soon the world-famous Polo Lounge was christened. Will Rogers, Darryl Zanuck, and Tommy Hitchcock enjoyed casual polo matches; the championship polo team of Charlie Wrightsman stored its elegant silver trophy bowl on the premises.

Designing Women was filmed with Gregory Peck and Lauren Bacall at the pool and cabana club. Marilyn Monroe and Yves Montand stayed in a couple of the bungalows while filming the celebrated *Let's Make Love*. In 1963, the intimate Cinema Room provided guests with a marvelous opportunity to screen films. When Charlie Chaplin returned to Hollywood to accept an Oscar award, he stayed at the Beverly Hills Hotel. The Rat Pack, W. C. Fields, and Humphrey Bogart all

enjoyed relaxing at the hotel and lounge. Marlene Dietrich eradicated the no-slacks-for-ladies rule at the lounge when she entered attired in pants. In the 1960s, the Beatles were brought to the pool through a hidden back way wearing disguises.

Neil Simon filmed his hit "California Suite" on the premises. The hotel changed hands a multitude of times—from Ben Silberstein to the Boeskys to Denver oilman Marvin Davis to the Sultan of Brunei.

The Pink Palace—with its 22 bungalows tucked away under the swaying palms, gardenias, and perfectly landscaped grounds—has been the choice for Clark Gable, Carole Lombard, Spencer Tracy, and Katherine Hepburn to enjoy themselves in this historic and one-of-a-kind setting.

In the 1990s, the Sultan of Brunei spent more than $100 million to remodel the hotel. Grateful guests are still languishing at the Polo Lounge, pool, and bungalows, enjoying the scene and unique lifestyle.

Beverly Hills Hotel
9641 Sunset Boulevard
Beverly Hills, California 90210
(310) 276-2251

Polo Lounge Country Style Meatloaf with Roast Corn Sauce

Combine the first five ingredients with an electric mixer, fitted with the paddle attachment and blend together on a slow speed. Blend for 3 to 5 minutes and then add eggs separately.

Add the breadcrumbs and continue to mix for another 5 to 8 minutes. It will be a light consistency.

Spray a medium-sized loaf pan with vegetable spray and pour in the meat mixture, up to the top. Spread the marinara sauce evenly on top of the meatloaf. This will form a flavorful crust while baking. Bake in a pre-heated oven at 350 degrees for approximately 1 hour. Serve with Roast Corn Sauce (recipe follows).

YIELD

Serves 8

3 pounds ground beef

1 pound chorizo

1½ whole green peppers, minced

1 sprig rosemary, minced

1½ whole onions, small diced

3 eggs

3½ ounces breadcrumbs

½ cup tomato marinara sauce

2 garlic cloves, minced

2 shallots, minced

1 tablespoon grapeseed oil

1 cup whole corn

1 cup tomato, coarsely chopped

2 cups veal demi-glace

¼ cup parsley, minced

2 ounces soft butter

Roast Corn Sauce for Country Style Meatloaf

In a hot saucepan, sauté the garlic and shallots in oil until golden in color. Add the corn and continue to sauté, then add the tomato.

Pour in the prepared demi-glace and bring to a boil. Adjust seasonings and add the parsley. Whisk in the soft butter and serve.

YIELD

Serves 8

Polo Lounge McCarthy Salad

Chop and combine all lettuce and place in a shallow bowl. Lay out the remaining ingredients on the top decoratively.

Serve with choice of dressing, as desired.

⅔ pound iceberg lettuce, chopped

2 ounces watercress, finely chopped

⅔ pound hearts of Romaine, chopped medium

½ pound cheddar cheese, small diced

½ pound bacon, finely chopped

3 hardboiled eggs, finely chopped

½ pound herbed grilled chicken, finely chopped

2 large vine-ripened tomatoes, peeled and seeded, medium dice cut

BEVERLY WILSHIRE

When the Spanish expedition led by Don José Gaspar de Portolá arrived in the Beverly Hills area, he discovered that the Tongva Indians were already there. They had been there for at least hundreds and perhaps thousands of years. These Native Americans were attracted to this fertile area for the same reasons the Europeans would invade their land and push them out: Water was abundant here.

Three canyons in the area, Coldwater, Benedict, and Franklin, funneled rainwater from the surrounding hills to where the various streams met near the intersection of what is now Beverly Drive and Sunset Boulevard. The area was sacred to the Indians and they called it the Gathering of the Waters. The Spanish translation, El Rodeo de las Aguas, would later lend its name to one of the most exclusive shopping destinations in the world.

The first European intruders discovered meadows of wild oats, cucumbers, and buckwheat, as well as the abundant game drawn to the dependable supply of moisture. Fields of wild roses and grapes would eventually lead to flourishing industries for California.

As the Spanish settlers gradually took firm control of the area, they erected one of their 21 missions nearby in San Gabriel. Tongva Indians were paid to work the fields and ranches of this mission and their association would cause the Spanish, and history, to refer to them as Gabriellitos. As the Indians moved nearer the mission, they abandoned their former villages and, over time, their former culture eroded.

The Europeans not only brought a major change to the natives' lives, they also brought diseases that wiped out many of the Indians who lacked any immunity to these new maladies. Smallpox killed two-thirds of the local population in 1844, and land grants sealed the fate of those who survived.

In 1838, the Mexican governor of Alta California gave a land grant to an Afro-Latina, María Rita Valdez Villa, the widow of a Spanish soldier. She called it El Rodeo de las Aguas, after its Indian namesake, and employed many cowboys to tend to her large herds of cattle and horses. Time and Mother Nature, in the form of a severe drought, forced a change in ownership several times. Wildcat oil wells were unsuccessful and the land reverted to cattle and sheep ranching. A theme park in the late nineteenth century also flopped when the national economy collapsed.

In 1906, Burton Green and his partners bought the defunct theme park land and renamed it Beverly Hills after Beverly Farms, Massachusetts. They designed and built wide curving roads that hugged the hillside and then proceeded to sell lots.

As the city grew, there was an obvious need for lodging for visitors and tourists. The Beverly Hills Hotel was built in 1912. Attracted by the glamorous lifestyle that Beverly Hills represented,

Douglas Fairbanks and Mary Pickford erected their mansion, "Pickfair," in 1919. Many other stars followed including Rudolph Valentino, John Barrymore, Will Rogers, Gloria Swanson, Charlie Chaplin, Tom Mix, Buster Keaton, and Clara Bow, to name just a few.

The excesses of the Roaring Twenties resulted in the building of a huge, banked wooden racetrack in the southern part of the city. The speedway produced entertainment for only four years before advancing development caused it to be demolished.

In 1928, the Beverly Wilshire Apartment Hotel opened on the former site of the speedway. Built in the Italian Renaissance style with Tuscan stone and Carrara marble, the hotel thrived, even as it passed to new owners who renamed it the Beverly Wilshire. The big band era ushered in a renovation that included a large ballroom. An Olympic-size swimming pool was added, and championship tennis courts were presided over by Pancho Gonzales, one of the greatest tennis champions of all time.

With Hollywood nearby, and the city full of movie stars, it wasn't long before Beverly Hills and the Beverly Wilshire would appear on screen: Jack Benny did his show from Beverly Hills in the 1950s; *Beverly Hillbillies* in the 1960s highlighted the lifestyle of some residents; and *Beverly Hills 90210* introduced a younger generation to the historic city.

In 1990, Richard Gere and Julia Roberts filmed *Pretty Woman* at the Beverly Wilshire. Warren Beatty lived in the penthouse for several years and, in the 1930s, Dashiell Hammett wrote *The Thin Man* here. Elvis Presley lived at the Beverly Wilshire for several years while making movies in Hollywood. Other long-term guests have included Elton John, Mick Jagger, Andrew Lloyd Webber, and Cary Grant. Many members of Britain's Royal Family have stayed at the Beverly Wilshire, as did Japan's Emperor Hirohito and the Dalai Lama.

In 2006, Wolfgang Puck opened a very high-end steakhouse, CUT, in the Beverly Wilshire. An all-day dining option is The Blvd, which has large windows allowing patrons to people-watch on the intersection of Wilshire Boulevard and Rodeo Drive.

Beverly Wilshire
9500 Wilshire Boulevard
Beverly Hills, California 90212
(310) 275-5200

2 pounds fresh Manila clams

2 pounds fresh black mussels

6 5-ounce swordfish steaks

Olive oil, as needed

Salt and fresh ground black
    pepper, to taste

¼ cup chopped garlic

½ cup chopped shallots

1 cup unsalted butter

2 cups white wine

½ cup chopped parsley

6 slices of ciabatta bread,
    grilled or toasted

Olive oil, as needed

Salt and fresh ground black
    pepper, to taste

Thin slices of Soria chorizo
    (or any dry-cured chorizo)

Spicy Aioli (recipe follows)

Grilled Swordfish,
Steamed Clams, and Mussels

This a great summertime backyard party dish with a good bottle of white wine.

To prepare the clams and mussels, rinse under cold running water to remove any sand, drain well, and keep refrigerated.

For the swordfish, preheat a grill or BBQ on medium-high. Rub the swordfish with olive oil and season with salt and fresh ground black pepper. Place the swordfish on the grill for about 4 minutes per side or until cooked.

In a large cast iron skillet or sauté pan on high heat, add ¼ cup olive oil. When the oil becomes very hot, add the clams and mussels and roast them in the pan for about 3 minutes. It is important that the clams and mussels be dried well to avoid any flare-up.

Then add the chopped garlic, shallots, and unsalted butter. Stir well and cook for 2 more minutes and add salt and pepper to taste.

Add the white wine and cover to steam until all of the shells have opened up. Finish with the chopped parsley and a drizzle of good olive oil.

For the bread, use ciabatta or any kind of your favorite bread. Slice and drizzle with olive oil and grill until light and crispy.

PLATING

Place the grilled swordfish in the center of each bowl; spoon the steamed clams and mussels over the top. Finish with the sliced chorizo and some fresh chopped parsley. Spoon some Spicy Aioli (recipe follows) onto the grilled bread and place on top.

 YIELD

Serves 6

"Fish, to taste right, must swim three times—
in water, in butter and in wine."

—Polish proverb

2 cups mayonnaise

2 tablespoons sambal oeleck

Salt and pepper

Spicy Aioli
Spicy Mayonnaise

Sambal oeleck is Indonesian chili paste, which is available at Asian specialty stores. Mix ingredients together with a whisk, then season to taste. The mayonnaise will keep in the refrigerator for 1 month; keep covered.

YIELD
Yields 2 cups

Ahi Tuna Sandwich

Preheat grill. Season the tuna with salt and pepper, then let stand for a minute or two. Next, slice focaccia roll in half lengthwise, brush with a little olive oil, and grill until lightly charred. Meanwhile, place ahi tuna on the grill and cook until medium rare or a desired temperature.

To build the sandwich, spread a thin layer of aioli on each side of the roll. Place the two slices of the tomato on the bottom half and top this with the grilled tuna. Mix the arugula with the remaining aioli and toss. Place on top of the tuna, followed with some mushrooms and pickled onions.

Finally, place the top roll of the sandwich and insert two toothpicks, cut in half, and arrange on a plate. Garnish with mixed greens and possibly a side of French fries.

YIELD

Serves 1

5 ounces ahi tuna steak

Salt and pepper

1 black pepper and parsley focaccia roll

Olive oil, as needed

1 tablespoon Spicy Aioli (recipe above)

2 slices heirloom tomatoes

2 ounces baby arugula, stems removed

2 ounces shiitake mushrooms, julienne cut and sautéed

1 ounce Pickled Red Onions (recipe follows)

3 medium red onions

2 cups red wine vinegar

1 teaspoon red chili flakes

2 tablespoons sugar

Pickled Red Onions

Peel and julienne the onions. Place in a medium size pot and add the rest of the ingredients. Bring up to a boil and let simmer 5 minutes.

Transfer onion and pickling liquid to an ice bath to cool. Onions will keep in the refrigerator covered for 2 months.

EL ENCANTO HOTEL AND GARDEN VILLAS

The Chumash Indians have been in the Santa Barbara area for thousands of years. Their territory extended from Paso Robles to Malibu and included several settlements on the Channel Islands.

The Island Indians were considered the mint for their tribe, as they made bead money out of shells from a marine snail called the Purple Olive. The currency they made was used by all of the tribes. The Indians in the mainland villages referred to their Island neighbors as Chumash. A loose translation of Chumash is "bead money makers."

The Chumash should also be given the credit for building the first spas in the Western Hemisphere. They built underground shelters known as sweathouses. Used primarily by the men, a sweathouse was entered by a ladder descending through the roof. They built a fire inside and heated stones to maintain a hot dry atmosphere. After spending time sweating, they would go and jump into a cold river, then return for another round. They did this for health and cleanliness reasons; they also burned aromatic plants to mask a man's scent when he went out hunting.

When the Spanish explorers arrived, they made a concerted effort to make Christians out of all the inhabitants of the area. They built missions along the coast and introduced agriculture and ranching. The Santa Barbara Mission was founded in 1785. California became a Mexican territory in 1821 and remained under its control until 1846, when Colonel John Fremont captured the area and claimed it for the United States.

Statehood in 1850 brought new settlers and development. In 1877, C. A. Storke bought 123 acres up on the hillside for $1.25 per acre. Since there was a lack of water and trees, local folks referred to his investment as Storke's Folly. But just ten years later, after the railroad had arrived, he sold the land for more than $200 an acre to a San Francisco capitalist, Walter Hawley, for a considerable profit. The area would eventually be named Hawley Heights.

Hawley's investment included all but two lots, which are the actual site of El Encanto Hotel. The hillside area was greatly desired by locals due to its fabulous vistas of the Pacific Ocean. Transportation up the hill was greatly improved when the state agreed to establish a normal college school there, with the stipulation that the city would provide the land and rail service to the campus. In 1911, an electric trolley line was completed and, in 1914, the forerunner of the University of California at Santa Barbara opened. Buses replaced the trolleys in 1930.

Housing to support the new school was built in 1912 and today is part of El Encanto (The Enchanted). Seeing the growth potential, a local banker, George Batchelder, bought the surrounding area to develop it. He is credited with planting hundreds of oak trees on the hillside, to take advantage of the new water system. He also started a trend by burying all the wires and cables for the construction underground and insisting that new buildings must not block the views of existing homes. Batchelder called his development the Riviera, since it reminded him of his trips to the Mediterranean.

After student rentals for the normal school proved to be unprofitable, plans were made to develop a cottage hotel from the student housing. Tourism was growing and, in 1918, El Encanto Hotel and Garden Villas opened.

Many improvements have been made over the years, with the hotel passing through several owners. Additional land has been acquired and many more cottages have been built. As a precursor to the modern time-share industry, many of these cottages were designed and built to serve as winter homes for the business tycoons of the day, including the founders of *Time* magazine, Pepsi-Cola, and Arrow Shirts.

During the early days of Hollywood, El Encanto was a pleasant escape from the rigors of stardom and city life for many stars, including Clark Gable, Carole Lombard, and Hedy Lamarr. When President Franklin D. Roosevelt stayed in cottage 320, it was renamed the Presidential Suite. More recent celebrities have included Diane Lane, Sharon Stone, and Barbara Streisand, among others.

Perched above the red tile roofs of Santa Barbara and overlooking the Pacific Ocean and Channel Islands, El Encanto Hotel and Garden Villas has been an integral part of Santa Barbara's social, cultural, and architectural heritage for more than 90 years.

El Encanto Hotel & Garden Villas
1900 Lasuen Road
Santa Barbara, California 93103
(805) 687-5000

Santa Barbara Shellfish Stew

Prepare all vegetables and reserve separately: chop onion, garlic, and celery; peel, seed, and chop tomatoes; and thinly slice the fennel.

Heat olive oil in a large saucepan. When hot, sauté the chorizo with the chopped onion, celery, and garlic and render until lightly caramelized. Add fennel, thyme, bay leaf, and cloves and cook on medium heat for 4 or 5 minutes.

Add the white wine, bring to a boil, and reduce the liquid by half. Stir with a wooden spoon to scrape the bottom of the pan into the liquid.

Add the tomatoes, the fish fillets, and orange zests and juice and 4 cups of fish broth. Boil uncovered for about 10 minutes.

Remove a half-cup of liquid from the stew pot. Mix saffron, salt, and pepper with the broth, then return it to the pan. Add the oysters, clams, mussels, shrimp, and the remaining fish broth.

Bring to a boil again and cook about 5 minutes longer.

At serving time, taste and correct the seasoning of the broth, adding a little more salt or pepper to taste, a touch of orange juice if needed, and a splash or two of Pernod.

Serve with croutons, Parmesan, and rouille on the side.

---

2 large onions

8 cloves garlic

2 celery stalks

4 fresh tomatoes, peeled, and diced

1 fennel head

¼ cup olive oil

4 ounces chorizo

3 sprigs fresh thyme

1 bay leaf

2 cloves

2 cups white wine

6 fish fillets, cut into 2-inch pieces (at least 3 kinds of fish—a mix between flavorful firm fish, like striped bass, haddock, halibut, snapper, or sea bass, and delicate fish, such as flounder, red snapper, or whiting; leave the skin on these delicate fish)

Peel and juice 2 oranges

8 cups fish stock or broth (can be replaced with ½ water, ½ chicken stock)

½ teaspoon powdered saffron

¼ teaspoon pepper

2 teaspoons salt

½ dozen oysters

(continued on next page)

½ dozen clams

½ dozen mussels

1 dozen shrimp peeled (with head on, if desired)

Splash of Pernod or Ricard (to taste)

GARNISH

Sliced baguette, for croutons

Parmesan

Rouille sauce

ROUILLE

3 egg yolks

½ teaspoon Dijon mustard

½ tablespoons minced garlic

1 teaspoon saffron threads

1 tablespoon warm fish broth (can be taken from the stew/ bouillabaisse broth)

¼ teaspoon cayenne pepper

1 teaspoon Pernod or Ricard

½ teasoon salt

1½ cups olive oil

Lemon juice (from 1 lemon, as needed)

CROUTONS

Slice baguette, arrange on sheet pan, and lightly drizzle with olive oil. Lightly toast in the oven until crispy. Rub each warm slice with a clove or garlic.

ROUILLE

In a blender, mix all ingredients except olive oil and lemon juice. Once well blended, incorporate olive oil slowly. Once it is all incorporated, add lemon juice; this will liquefy the sauce, so use ½ lemon at a time. Sauce should be smooth but to the consistency of a thick mayonnaise.

Note: Shell or no shell? You may want to use some of the shellfish and shrimp shells for decoration.

Chilled Avocado Soup with Citrus-Cured Santa Barbara Spot Prawn

In a blender, mix avocado pulp, juice of 2 lemons, yogurt, chicken broth, and chopped jalapeño. Add salt and pepper to taste, and more lemon if needed. Add more chicken broth, as needed, for a smooth and slightly thick consistency—keep in mind the soup will set during chilling. Chill for at least 4 hours.

About ½ hour before serving, dice prawns (¼ inch) and mix in a bowl with shallots, lime juice and zest, salt, and white pepper. Let cure for at least 15 minutes, up to 30. Right before serving, strain juices from bowl and add the chopped chives to prawns.

Ladle the chilled soup into individual soup bowl (or martini glass), and spoon the prawns in the center. Top with a couple sprigs of chives and pinch of lime and lemon zest for decoration.

SOUP

8 ripe avocados, peeled and rough chopped

2–4 lemons, juiced

1 cup yogurt

2 cups chicken broth, chilled

½ jalapeño, seeded and chopped

Salt and pepper to taste

REST OF DISH

1½ pounds spot prawns (whole), peeled

2 shallots, chopped

2 limes, juiced

1 teaspoon lime zest (and 1 teaspoon of lime and lemon zest for décor)

Salt and white pepper

2 tablespoons fresh chives, chopped (and a few sprigs for décor)

THE GRANDE COLONIAL HOTEL LA JOLLA

When it opened in 1913, The Colonial Apartments and Hotel, as it was known, was the talk of the town and a foundation for the community. Designed by Richard Requa, the original white, wood-framed building stood perfectly situated overlooking the ocean.

When George Bane became the sole owner of the Colonial in 1920, he realized the tourist potential of this picturesque seaside town and decided to give the Colonial a new look. He commissioned an architect to design a hotel that would "rival anything in the West."

The existing building was physically moved to the rear of the property and a four-story, concrete, mixed-use structure was erected in its place. With 28 apartments and 25 single hotel rooms, the new Colonial Hotel had the first sprinkler system west of the Mississippi, along with solid, unsupported, reinforced cement stairways and fire doors that can still be seen today.

Even with its new safety features, the Colonial was awesome. The design of "sunburst" windows and semi-circle domes of leaded glass above the French doors captured the sunlight, bathing the interior of the hotel. Inside, the new hotel included colonial fireplaces with marble hearths, ornate chandeliers, and richly colored sofas and chairs. Rooms rates ranged from $25 to $50 per month.

The La Jolla Drug Store, which sat next door to the Colonial, was purchased in 1926 by Kansas native Silas O. Putnam and moved inside the Colonial. The drug store became a prime location for locals to gather, talk, and watch the few passersby. The pharmacist Putnam hired considered it a big day if he filled more than three prescriptions. The pharmacist was also the father of Gregory Peck, who grew up in La Jolla. After becoming a movie star, Peck founded the La Jolla Playhouse. Charlton Heston, Dorothy McGuire, Groucho Marx, Jane Wyatt, Eve Arden, Pat O'Brien, David Niven, and many other celebrities occupied the hotel well into the late 1950s, while performing at the playhouse.

During the World War II years, the Colonial became home to many of the senior officers from nearby Camp Callan. While the men worked during the day, their wives volunteered for the local Red Cross. At night, the hotel's sunroom was partitioned to create accommodations for single servicemen.

In 1976, the Colonial was purchased by three local partners for approximately $1 million, and the name was changed to the Colonial Inn. In 1980, the space once occupied by Putnam's drug store

became Putnam's Grille. Reflecting the La Jolla of the 1920s, the restaurant was redesigned and featured dark wood paneling, wrought iron chandeliers and ceiling fans, oak dining sets, and large picture windows that created an open, fluid environment. The original soda fountain was replaced with a mirrored-back bar and alcoholic beverages were served instead of ice cream sodas. The restaurant also stayed true to its heritage by offering diners sidewalk seating, continuing the tradition of the past 65 years.

Putnam's Grille closed in 2001 and was quickly replaced by the award-winning restaurant Nine-Ten. From the ocean-view terrace, patrons can enjoy both fine dining and gorgeous California sunsets.

Just like the hotel envisioned by George Bane, The Grande Colonial La Jolla is a classic European-style lodge that strives to preserve the gracious heritage laid down by the hotel's founders more than 90 years ago. Located on popular Prospect Street in the heart of La Jolla, it is the seaside town's oldest original hotel.

The Grande Colonial Hotel La Jolla
910 Prospect Street
La Jolla, California 92037
(888) 530-5766
(858) 454-2181

2 live Maine lobsters,
    1¼ pounds each

1 cup fresh spring peas

1 cup chicken stock or
    vegetable stock

1 ruby grapefruit

2 oranges

1 tablespoon grapefruit juice

1 tablespoon orange juice

1 tablespoon minced shallots

¼ teaspoon salt

4 tablespoons light olive oil

2 tablespoons basil, julienned

2 firm-ripe avocados, diced

¼ pound pea tendrils or
    pea sprouts

1 head frisee,
    washed and trimmed

Lobster and Pea Tendrils Salad

In an 8-quart saucepot, bring salted water to a boil. Plunge lobsters headfirst into pot. Cook, covered, over high heat for 6 minutes. Using tongs, transfer lobsters to sink to drain. When lobsters are cool enough to handle, remove meat from the tail and claws, keeping meat intact. Place in fridge for later use. Lobsters may be cooked one day in advance.

Set up an ice bath. Bring a small saucepot of salted water to a boil. Add peas and blanch for 2–3 minutes. Remove from water and place in ice bath. Once peas are cooled, place in a blender with chicken stock and puree until smooth. Season with salt and pepper to taste; reserve for later.

To cut segments, cut away the bottom ends of the grapefruit and orange. Place the flat side of the fruit on a cutting board, cutting the peel around the flesh of the fruit, removing all of the pith. Then, slice next to the connective membrane on both sides of each segment, to remove each piece. Place the segments in a bowl. Reserve the liquid for vinaigrette.

In a small bowl, add grapefruit juice, orange juice, shallot, and salt and mix. Add olive oil slowly until incorporated.

TO SERVE SALAD

Cut the lobster bodies in half lengthwise. Spoon pea puree in the center of the plate creating a 4-inch circle. Place half of the lobster tail off-center of the pea puree. In a mixing bowl, add lobster meat, grapefruit and orange segments, basil, avocados, pea tendrils, and frisee and toss with dressing. Season with salt and pepper to taste. Place the salad in the center of the puree without covering the lobster. Place the knuckle and claw on top of the salad.

"Wine brings to light the hidden secrets of the soul."

—Horace

Roasted Baby Beet Salad with Pistachios and Baby Arugula

1½ pounds baby beets

½ cup sliced shallots,
    ⅛-inch thick

½ cup olive oil

2 whole oranges, segmented

1 teaspoon Dijon mustard

1 tablespoon shallots, minced

2 tablespoon Champagne vinegar

3 ounces olive oil

½ cup toasted pistachios, chopped

½ pound baby arugula

Salt and pepper to taste

Heat the oven 350 degrees. Trim the green tops and stringy bottoms from the beets. Wash beets well. In a mixing bowl, add beets and coat with oil. Season with salt and pepper. Line a cookie sheet with foil and place the beets on the tray. Place another sheet of foil over the beets and crimp the edges, creating a seal. Place the beets in the oven and cook until fork tender, about 40 minutes.

Allow the beets to cool slightly. While still warm, peel them by gently rubbing with a towel. Cut the beets into quarters.

Place shallots and olive oil in an ovenproof sauté pan and cover with foil. Place in the oven for 15 to 20 minutes or until tender. Remove shallots from oven, strain off oil and place on a plate. Let cool. Shallot-flavored oil may be reserved for other uses, if you wish.

To make orange segments, cut away the bottom ends. Place the flat side of the fruit on a cutting board, cutting the peel around the flesh of the orange, removing all of the pith. Slice next to the connective membrane on both sides of each segment. Place the segments in a bowl.

In a small mixing bowl, add mustard, shallots, and vinegar and mix well. Add oil slowly until incorporated.

TO ASSEMBLE

In a small mixing bowl, add beets, pistachios, and two ounces vinaigrette. Season with salt and pepper to taste. Using a medium-sized salad plate, place a quarter of the beet mixture in the center of the plate making a circle. Place 4 or 5 orange segments around the top of the beets. Shingle the shallot ring, as well. Do this to four plates or on one large platter. In the same bowl the beets were mixed, add arugula and 2 ounce of vinaigrette. Season with salt and pepper and mix well. Place a small pile of arugula on top of the beets. Make sure that you can see the beets and citrus. Drizzle a little of the remaining vinaigrette around the plate.

 YIELD

Serves 4

16–20 shrimp, peeled and
marinated

1 teaspoon harissa paste

2 tablespoons olive oil

16 watermelon sticks,
½ inch by 3 inch

1 ounce feta cheese

1 tablespoon chives, minced

½ cup lemon feta vinaigrette,
divided (recipe follows)

¼ cup lemon juice, fresh

¼ cup Champagne wine vinegar

1 egg yolk

1 ounce water

2 cups olive oil

1 cup feta cheese, crumbled

Harissa-Marinated Shrimp with Lemon Feta Vinaigrette

Toss shrimp with harissa and oil and let marinate for 30 minutes. In a mixing bowl, toss watermelon sticks with crumbled feta and 3 ounces of feta vinaigrette and chives. Mix carefully, so as not to break the watermelon sticks. Season marinated shrimp with salt and pepper and grill for 1–2 minutes. On an oval plate, smear a line of feta vinaigrette down the middle of the plate. On the left side of the plate, stack four sticks of watermelon nicely. On the other side of the plate, stack the shrimp as high as possible.

YIELD
Serves 4

Lemon Feta Vinaigrette

In a blender, add lemon juice, vinegar, egg yolk, and water. Turn blender on low speed and slowly add oil. When halfway finished, stop and add feta. Turn the blender back on and add the rest of the oil. Be careful to combine slowly and thoroughly. You may need to add more water while emulsifying.

HOTEL DEL CORONADO

It started with a dream. In 1888, the picturesque Coronado peninsula—surrounded by water on three sides and just a stone's throw from the developing city of San Diego—showed its promise to Elisha Babcock and Hampton Story, who dreamed of building a hotel that they envisioned would be "the talk of the western world."

The 1848 discovery of gold in northern California had attracted a substantial population to the west, but much of the nation's interior was still wild and dangerous nearly 40 years later when Babcock and Story came to Coronado to hunt. They purchased the peninsula for $110,000 and proceeded to subdivide it into lots. The lots were auctioned off in a single day for enough profit to build a magnificent hotel for the rich and famous of the era.

Originally promoted as a hunting and fishing resort, the chef was kept busy cooking the guests' catch of the day. Other amenities included separate billiard rooms for men and women, bowling, croquet, swimming, boating, bicycling, archery, golf, and fine dining, as well as special rooms set aside for smoking, reading, writing, cards, chess, and music.

Completed at a cost of $600,000 for construction, The Del was outfitted with $400,000 in furnishings. At the time, The Del was one of the largest buildings in the country to offer electric lights, telephones, and elevators. Another modern convenience was running hot and cold water combined with water pressure servicing numerous bathrooms. In deference to the guests who believed the saltwater and ocean air were health-promoting, The Del also offered hot and cold running seawater. Fine china and linens came from Europe while carpets and furnishings came from the Far West, along with many of the original employees.

Sophisticated travelers from the eastern part of the country, tired of the usual resorts, flocked to The Del. Some would stay for months at a time. A school was opened for their children, allowing them more freedom and time to relax in the temperate Southern California climate. A few of the wealthiest even arrived in the area traveling in their own rail cars.

Heir to the wealthy "Sugar King" Claus Spreckels, John D. Spreckels purchased The Del and moved his family there from San Francisco after the earthquake of 1906. Guiding it through the gilded age, he was also responsible for helping modernize San Diego, where he built a streetcar system, published two newspapers, developed real estate, ran a water company, and built his own railroad line.

After Spreckels' death in 1926, his family continued to own the hotel, but the Depression and World War II took its toll. During the war, many Navy pilots were housed at The Del, even though the hotel remained open for the very few tourists and businessmen who visited. Military weddings and honeymoons were common fare. In 1948, the family sold the property, and it passed through several owners before its recent 3-year, $55 million renovation.

Renowned for its magnificent architecture, the Hotel del Coronado is equally well known for its legendary guests. Ten U.S. presidents have stayed at the resort, starting with Benjamin Harrison in 1891. Every president since Lyndon Johnson has visited The Del.

Thomas Edison visited during 1915 and American aviator Charles Lindbergh was honored at the hotel after his successful 1927 transatlantic flight. Legendary sports figures Babe Ruth, Jack Dempsey, Willie Mays, Magic Johnson, and Muhammad Ali have graced the property with their presence.

In 1920, England's Prince of Wales visited The Del. At that time, his future wife, Wallis Spencer Simpson, was living in Coronado. Ever since then, people have wondered if the two may have met for the first time during Prince Edward's 1920 visit. Sixteen years later, Edward would give up the throne to marry the divorced Mrs. Simpson.

With its proximity to Los Angeles, the Hotel del Coronado has attracted movie stars since 1901, when the first film was made in Coronado. In 1958, *Some Like It Hot*, starring Marilyn Monroe, Jack Lemmon, and Tony Curtis, was filmed at The Del. Enormously popular, this movie was recently named number one on the American Film Institute's list of the 100 best comedies of all time.

Early Hollywood visitors included Rudolph Valentino, W. C. Fields, Douglas Fairbanks Sr., and Charlie Chaplin. Despite the Depression, the Del also hosted Mary Pickford, Al Jolson, Greta Garbo, Mae West, Rita Hayworth, and Clark Gable. Following the war, television made stars out of such regular guests as Carol Burnett, Donna Reed, Raymond Burr, Doris Day, and Dinah Shore. Modern celebrity guests include Oprah Winfrey, Bruce Willis, Sylvester Stallone, and many more.

One guest who arrived in 1892 may still be here. Kate Morgan checked into the hotel apparently brokenhearted and alone after a quarrel with her estranged husband. Only five days later, she was found dead on the beach, a gunshot wound to her head. Since then, guests, employees, and even paranormal researchers have sworn that Kate's former room is still haunted by her spirit.

The world-famous Crown Room was built as the original dining room in 1888. Whimsical crown-shaped chandeliers, designed by frequent guest *Wizard of Oz* author L. Frank Baum, drop from the glowing sugar-pine ceiling. Spacious windows circling the room offer some of California's most radiant views. The Crown Room hosted the site of the largest state dinner held outside the White House, which was given in 1970 by Richard Nixon in honor of Mexican President Gustavo Díaz Ordaz.

The Crown Room still serves as the premier dining facility of The Del, offering an award-winning Sunday Brunch, holiday celebrations, and special events.

Hotel del Coronado
1500 Orange Avenue
Coronado, California 92118
(800) HOTELDEL
(619) 435-6611

1-inch round slice seedless
watermelon, peeled

¼ fresh papaya, peeled, seeded,
and cut into parallel slices
lengthwise (leaving intact
at the base, fan-style)

¼ cantaloupe, peeled, seeded,
and cut into parallel slices
lengthwise (leaving intact
at the base, fan-style)

3 slices pineapple, peeled

4 sections pink grapefruit

3 sections orange

1 kiwi, peeled and cut into
3 slices

¼ plum, unpeeled, pitted,
and sliced, fan-style

1 fresh blueberry, for garnish

4 mint sprigs, for garnish

6 fresh raspberries, for garnish

Debbie Reynolds' Fresh Fruit Fantasy with Pecan-Yogurt Dressing

Debbie Reynolds and Donald O'Connor performed at The Del's centennial weekend celebration. They sang and danced their way to a standing ovation from the 700 guests who enjoyed their combined performance. Ms. Reynolds, clad in a skin-tight, royal blue sequined gown and known to be a health-conscious star, chose the Del's Fresh Fruit Fantasy for dinner before her spectacular performance.

Cut watermelon slice into quarters and place in the center of the plate. Arrange papaya fan on the center of watermelon, on the right side. Arrange cantaloupe fan on the center of watermelon, on the left side. Arrange pineapple slices on top of the watermelon slice, below the papaya and cantaloupe.

Arrange pink grapefruit sections on top of the watermelon slice, two on each side. Place the orange sections at the twelve o'clock position. Place the kiwi slices down the center of the plate. Place plum fan atop pineapple slices. Arrange the blueberry at the base of plum. Garnish with sprigs of mint placed at the 3, 6, 9, and 12 o'clock positions. Place 2 raspberries in the center of each kiwi slice.

Serve with Pecan-Yogurt Dressing (recipe follows) on the side.

YIELD

Serves 1

Pecan-Yogurt Dressing

In a small mixing bowl, combine all the ingredients thoroughly. Transfer to a small serving bowl, cover, and refrigerate for at least 2 hours (or overnight). Serve in a small bowl to accompany Fresh Fruit Fantasy.

YIELD

Yields about 1¼ cups

1 cup plain yogurt

1 tablespoon honey

2 teaspoons lemon juice

¼ cup finely chopped pecans

3 pounds chicken wings, disjointed

2 teaspoons salt

¼ teaspoon pepper

3 tablespoons canola oil

1 clove garlic, peeled and minced

1 teaspoon onion powder

1 teaspoon Chinese
   5-spice powder

1 teaspoon honey

½ cup soy sauce

1 teaspoon ground ginger

¼ cup ketchup

½ cup dry sherry wine

Dionne Warwick's Oriental Chicken Wings

Dionne Warwick was one of the celebrities who performed a star-studded musical review held after the centennial dinner. During her rehearsal, the hotel employees who were setting up the ballroom for the performance stopped simultaneously to listen to the songbird, spellbound by her talent. After her rehearsal, she retired to her suite and ordered the Del's Oriental Chicken Wings for a snack before her evening performance.

Preheat the oven to 375 degrees.

Place the chicken wings in a 13 × 9 × 2-inch baking pan. Sprinkle with salt and pepper. Brush on oil. In a medium-size bowl, combine garlic, onion powder, Chinese 5-spice powder, honey, soy sauce, ginger, ketchup, and wine. Blend thoroughly, then pour over wings. Bake uncovered for 50 minutes, basting frequently. Remove from the oven and serve on a heated serving platter or chafing dish.

Note: These chicken wings may be served as an hors d'oeuvre. They may be prepared and cooked in advance, then wrapped in foil and frozen. To serve, remove from freezer and open foil wrapping. Allow chicken wings to reach room temperature, then place in a preheated 300-degree oven for 15 minutes or until heated through.

Note: To disjoint chicken wings: Cut wings off at the joint (do not use the tips). Loosen the meat away from the bone. Pull back all of the skin and meat.

 YIELD

8 servings

INGLESIDE INN AND MELVYN'S RESTAURANT

Palm Springs was first populated by the Cahuilla Indians, a group of Native Americans who had inhabited the area for more than 2,000 years. This local tribe is the namesake to the enormous Lake Cahuilla, which went dry several hundred years ago when the Colorado River shifted.

Europeans discovered the Cahuillas in 1774 when the Spanish explorer Juan Bautista de Anza was searching for a suitable trade route between Mexico and the seaport of Monterey, California. Up to this time, all exploration and colonization of Alta California had been concentrated along the seacoast. Since the Cahuilla Indians were living well inland in the desert, which the Europeans deliberately avoided, the natives had almost no contact with outsiders.

It was not until the 1840s that Europeans came to stay. One of the early pioneers was Daniel Sexton, who befriended the Cahuilla tribal chief, Juan Antonio. The chief also gave aide to an Army expedition commanded by Lieutenant Edward F. Beale, shielding the expedition against Ute Indian assaults. The lieutenant rewarded the chief with a set of military uniform epaulets, which he proudly wore to demonstrate their friendship.

Sexton married into the tribe and, through the local medicine man, discovered minerals nearby. Tin mines and miners flocked to the area, making more fortunes for those selling mining claims than those actually doing the prospecting. The Gold Rush added to the hoards of settlers, and the influx of European people brought misery with them: A smallpox outbreak in 1863 devastated the tribes and killed Chief Juan Antonio.

The U.S. government decided that development of the frontier took precedence over the land claims of a couple of thousand Native Indians. Cahuilla land was divided into one-mile-square sections, giving every other one to the Indians, and encouraging the Southern Pacific Railroad to use the others for expansion of the train routes through the desert. Indian reservation boundaries were formally established in 1877, leaving the Cahuillas with only part of their original land.

Today, the Cahuilla occupy nine reservations in Southern California, including Agua Caliente and Augustine, the smallest federally recognized Native American tribe—it has only six persons, as of the 2000 census.

One of the former Cahuilla tribes was located at the hot springs known today as the nearby town of Indio.

Palm Springs derives its name from the water that supported the palm trees growing here. Spanish explorers referred to the area as "the palm of God's hand." Later, government surveyors identified the local springs as being at the base of "two bunches of palms." The completion of the railroad brought Judge John Guthrie McCallum of San Francisco and his family in 1884. McCallum hired local Indians to build a 19-mile stone-lined ditch from the Whitewater River into Palm Springs, bringing in pure, precious water for irrigation and giving him the title of founder of Palm Springs.

By 1915, Palm Springs was a small desert town with great potential. Humphrey Birge, the founder of the Pierce Arrow Motor Car Company, visited Palm Springs and decided he loved the area. He built a Spanish-style home in 1925 and lived there for ten years. Upon his death, the estate was sold to a city council member, Ruth Hardy. She turned the place into a twenty-room inn, which was so exclusive, one could not even make a reservation. You had to be invited to come and stay and any guest you might bring to dinner had to be personally approved by Ruth. Should she decide that you were not suitable company, you would simply be told there was "no room at the Inn."

The Inn was a private club and she usually closed it for six months of each year. Ruth was meticulous in her supervision of the restaurant. She did not have a liquor license, though guests were permitted to bring their own spirits. Their informal "happy hour" was held in what is now the Library Room of the Inn. The Inn hosted such notable figures as Howard Hughes, Salvador Dali, Norman Vincent Peale, and Spencer Tracy, among others.

Ruth passed away in 1965 and the Inn passed through two owners before Melvyn Haber bought it after arriving as a tourist in 1975. He completely renovated the property, creating Melvyn's Restaurant and the Casablanca Lounge.

Today, Palm Springs is growing rapidly, due in part to the climate and in part to its star-quality prestige. Al Jolson, Greta Garbo, Cary Grant, Steve McQueen, Liberace, Bob Hope, Elvis Presley, Debbie Reynolds, Lucille Ball, Desi Arnaz, Sonny Bono, Cher, Kirk Douglas, Jack Benny, Frank

 *226*

Sinatra, and Dean Martin have all owned homes in Palm Springs, giving the town the sobriquet the Playground of the Stars.

The Ingleside Inn should prove to be as attractive to you as it was to the famous diva Lily Pons and her husband Andre Kostelanetz, who came for one night and stayed thirteen years.

Ingleside Inn and Melvyn's Restaurant
200 West Ramon Road
Palm Springs, California 92264
(800) 772-6655
(760) 325-0046

Banana Squash Soup

Sauté the onions until caramelized. Pour in the sherry wine and cook until reduced.

Add the chicken broth and banana squash. Boil for 45 minutes to 1 hour.

Add the chicken base, brown sugar, and heavy cream. Cook for 20 minutes. Blend together and use cornstarch to thicken. Serve and enjoy!

YIELD
Serves 6
(Cut recipe in half for the home cook.)

10 whole yellow onions, sliced

16 ounces sherry wine

1½ gallons of chicken broth

10 pounds banana squash, peeled

4 ounces chicken base

1 pound light brown sugar

1 gallon heavy cream

Cornstarch as needed

2 ounces peanut oil

3 (U-15) shrimp

2 3-ounce medallions of pork

Flour, as needed

2 ounces shallots

2 ounces brandy

Salt and pepper, to taste

5 ounces heavy cream

3 ounces light brown sugar

Medallions of Pork and Shrimp

Pour peanut oil into a hot pan. Place the shrimp in the pan. Sauté for 1 minute on each side, then remove from the pan and set aside.

Powder both sides of the pork medallions with flour. Sauté for 1½ minutes in saucepan. Remove the medallions from the pan, set aside, and drain and discard the oil.

Place the shrimp and pork together in the same pan. Add the shallots to pan. Remove the pan from the heat; add the brandy and slowly put the pan back to heat. Leave on the stove for 30 seconds.

Add a pinch of salt and pepper, the heavy cream, and brown sugar. Reduce for 3 minutes. Serve and enjoy!

YIELD
Serves 2

Navy Bean Soup

In a large pot, add the chicken broth and navy beans and cook for 1 hour.

In a separate pan, cook the bacon. Add onions, carrots, and celery. Cook with bacon for 10 minutes. Put this mixture into the bean pot. Stir in the tomato paste and chicken base. Cool for 20 minutes until the tomato paste is liquefied and blended in. Serve and enjoy!

YIELD
Serves 10
(Cut recipe in half for the home cook.)

2½ gallons chicken broth

2 pounds navy beans

1 pound sliced bacon

2 whole onions, diced

8 carrots, diced

1 bunch celery, diced

16 ounces tomato paste

8 ounces chicken base

THE INN AT RANCHO SANTA FE

The first residents of this Southern California area were a group of Native Americans we now call the San Dieguito. Named for the major waterway in the area, San Dieguito, meaning "Little San Diego," referred to the area north of San Diego, where the San Dieguito River empties into a lagoon and then flows into the ocean, just north of today's city of Del Mar.

Juan Cabrillo's discovery of San Diego in 1542 prompted Spain to claim the area, and Gaspar de Portolá's 1769 expedition opened the new territory for European settlement. Shortly after Mexico (or "New Spain") declared its independence from Spain, the Mexican governor gave a provisional land grant of the area now called Rancho Santa Fe to Lebrado Lilva. Later, when that governor was overthrown, his successor gave the interim land title to Juan Maria Osuna.

Osuna, an early settler in San Diego, was a corporal in the local military. Born to a Spanish father and an Indian mother, Osuna took part in the Mexican Revolution of 1821 and later became a district elector in 1830. After retiring from the military, Osuna built a three-room adobe house on the plains of San Diego.

In 1833, Osuna led a committee that convinced the governor to establish a local government for San Diego Pueblo, to replace many years of military rule. When this was accomplished, Osuna was elected the first alcalde or mayor of San Diego Pueblo. That same year, Osuna was granted the interim title to Rancho San Dieguito by the governor. Interestingly, as alcalde, Osuna had already approved his own application for the land. What had originally been an Indian rancheria was now two square leagues (about 8,800 acres) that comprised Rancho San Dieguito.

The center of this rancho would be near today's Rancho Santa Fe. To the north, a 4,431-acre parcel of land was given to Don Andres Ybarra in 1842, and this was called Rancho Las Encinitas. These two ranchos and some surrounding land became known as San Dieguito.

Osuna raised cattle and horses on the ranch, but he had a weakness for gambling. He was forced to sell part of his land to pay off his debts. In 1845, the new governor awarded him full title to the land but he wouldn't enjoy it for long. Osuna remained loyal to the fledgling government of Mexico during the Mexican-American War from 1846–1848. After the war, Osuna faired poorly under U.S. rule because he didn't understand U.S. law, and he didn't speak English. He died in 1851.

His son, Leando, took control of the property, but treated the Native Americans very harshly. Legend has it that they eventually poisoned Leando, then told him how he was about to die a miserable slow death. Leando promptly committed suicide.

Between 1906 and 1917, the Santa Fe Railway acquired all of the lands that made up the original San Dieguito Land Grant. The railroad company intended to plant 4,000 acres with 3,000,000 eucalyptus tree seedlings to produce railroad ties. Many of the trees were planted, but the project was abandoned when they discovered that eucalyptus would not hold the spikes. The railroad company turned to development.

The Lake Hodges Dam solved the flooding problems and opened the region to agriculture and residential development. The area was renamed Rancho Santa Fe and the railroad formed the Santa Fe Land Improvement Company, which laid out estates and constructed roadways for new home sites. Most importantly, they established deed restrictions, which even today control most every aspect of land use and building design and construction in Rancho Santa Fe, the oldest planned community in the nation.

The first structure erected by the Land Company, a guesthouse in the Spanish Revival style, was called La Morada, or "the house of many rooms." Originally intended to provide lodging for prospective buyers, La Morada became a clubhouse. It was sold in 1940 and the named was changed to The Inn at Rancho Santa Fe. Osuna's adobe house, overlooking the San Dieguito River Valley, was restored and is now part of The Inn at Rancho Santa Fe.

Lilian Rice returned to her family home near San Diego in 1910, fresh out of the University of California at Berkley. As an architect, she was hired by the Land Company, and soon found herself in charge of the Rancho Santa Fe development project. Responsible for the overall plan and supervision of this new community, Rice designed many of the town's buildings as well as a number of residences. She remained the driving force for the community's development until her death in 1938.

If you feel comfortable, inspired, or renewed at The Inn, it's for a reason. As Lilian said, "I have found real joy at Rancho Santa Fe. Every environment here calls for simplicity and beauty: the gorgeous natural landscapes, the gently broken topography, the nearby mountains. No one with a

sense of fitness, it seems to me, could violate these natural factors by creating anything that lacked simplicity in line and form and color."

The Inn at Rancho Santa Fe
5951 Linea Del Cielo
Rancho Santa Fe, California 92067
(858) 756-1131

Braised Short Ribs with Creamy Polenta and Thyme Sauce

SHORT RIBS

Cut ribs into single bones and season with salt and pepper. Sear ribs in a hot pot with a little olive oil. Allow to brown on all sides. Once browned, remove from pot and then add mirepoix (chopped carrots, celery, and onion). Allow vegetables to brown. Deglaze pot with red wine, add garlic and tomato paste, and allow to reduce. Add the ribs back to the pot and cover the ribs with cold water (just enough water to slightly cover ribs). Add spices and herbs through rosemary, then allow to simmer for 3–4 hours or when ribs become fork tender. (Do not boil; this would make the ribs dry.)

When finished, remove herbs, adjust seasoning, and then finish with parsley and thyme.

CREAMY POLENTA

Combine chicken stock (or water) and garlic together in a saucepot, then bring to a boil. Add polenta and cook slowly, stirring continuously until combined, and then simmer 30 minutes. At this point, polenta can be put in the refrigerator for use the next day.

Reheat if necessary. Add cream to create a saucy consistency. Finish with Parmesan cheese and parsley.

SHORT RIBS

4 pounds 2-inch trimmed short ribs

Salt and pepper

Olive oil, for searing

3 carrots

3 stalks celery

1 onion

6 ounces red wine

½ bulb garlic

2 tablespoons tomato paste

2 cloves

7 black peppercorns

2 bay leaves

1 sprig thyme

1 teaspoon parsley

½ teaspoon rosemary

1 teaspoon thyme, chopped

1 tablespoon parsley chiffonade

CREAMY POLENTA

2 cups chicken stock (or water)

1 teaspoon garlic, finely chopped

½ cup polenta, medium style

2 ounces cream

2 ounces Parmesan cheese

1 tablespoon parsley, chiffonade

YIELD

Serves 6

Gnocchi with Garlic, Basil, and Tomato

GNOCCHI

2 potatoes

½ pound all-purpose flour

¾ pound Parmesan cheese, grated

1 egg

1 egg yolk

Pinch nutmeg

Salt and pepper

Olive oil

FOR EACH SERVING

Olive oil, to sauté

Pinch shallot, diced

Pinch garlic, diced

2 Roma tomatoes, peeled, seeded, rough cut

3 ounces Jus de Poulet

Pinch mixed herbs, chef's choice

Pinch basil

Pat of butter

Parmesan cheese

GNOCCHI

Bring potatoes to a boil in cold salted water with skins on.

Once potatoes are tender, carefully remove from water and peel. Dry the potatoes out in the oven for a few minutes.

Meanwhile, bring a pot of water to a boil.

Pass hot, peeled potatoes through a food mill and place on the counter or table. Sprinkle potatoes with one-third of the flour and all of the cheese. Work potato mix with a plastic scraper and continue to add flour until it is in a firm dough consistency. Work in eggs and seasonings. Once dough is complete, cut, roll, and shape gnocchi. Keep gnocchi well floured.

Cook gnocchi in boiling, salted water. When gnocchi floats to the top, remove and shock in ice water. Drain well and toss with olive oil. Store as needed.

FINAL DISH

Sauté gnocchi on the grill, dabbed with olive oil, on all sides until golden brown. In a small sauté pan, sweat garlic and shallots in olive oil. Add rough-cut Roma tomatoes and allow to simmer. Deglaze with Jus de Poulet; simmer. Add browned gnocchi to sauce.

Finish dish by adding mixed herbs, basil, and butter. Season with salt, pepper, and Parmesan cheese. Serve hot.

LA VALENCIA HOTEL

When the Spanish explorer Juan Rodriguez Cabrillo discovered Alta California in 1542, he landed in San Diego Bay. Thinking he had found a new tract of land in the Pacific Ocean, maps were marked to indicate that Alta California was an island. Other expeditions on behalf of the king of Spain extended their knowledge of the new territory, but they did not attempt to exploit the land until 1768 when the Russians were discovered to be seal hunting off the coast.

To settle the land in the name of the king of Spain, and to convert the Native Americans already living there, the government of New Spain (modern-day Mexico) was directed to establish missions and pueblos along the coast. The Franciscans were selected to lead these expeditions and they built the Mission San Diego de Alcalá in 1769.

As the birthplace of Christianity in the Far West, this would be the first church in the state. The mission would eventually anchor El Camino Real—a series of twenty-one missions built over a period of 54 years, stretching to Sonoma, north of San Francisco.

Several square miles of surrounding land were incorporated into the Mission San Diego de Alcalá, to be used for ranching and agricultural support of the Mission. This did not include La Jolla, as there was very little water available there at the time. Once California became a state in 1850, La Jolla was incorporated into the city of San Diego, although it remained a barren area for several more years.

In 1869, Daniel and Samuel Sizer each bought 80 acres in La Jolla from the city for $1.25 an acre, but failed to develop their new property. Frank Botsford arrived in 1886, also purchased land, but went on to develop it with his partner, George Heald, from the Heald family in Healdsburg. Lots were subdivided and resold at a considerable profit. Today, each acre would sell for well over a million times more than its original price of $1.25.

La Jolla, which means "the jewel" in Spanish, grew with the influx of settlers following the Gold Rush up north. The arrival of the railroad in the 1890s produced a land boom, which continues to this day, interrupted only by the Great Depression. Ellen Browning Scripps, heiress to the newspaper empire, arrived in 1896. She would be known for funding an ocean research center, later to be named after her family. It is now part of the University of California at San Diego.

In December 1926, MacArthur Gorton and Roy Wiltsie opened the La Valencia Apartment-Hotel, overlooking La Jolla Cove. Just two years later, they expanded the property by adding more rooms, a lounge, an outside balcony, and its distinctive tower.

The lavish grand opening attracted the rich and famous. Many of their autographed pictures still hang in the lobby today. By the 1930s, the hotel, with its surrounding beaches and sea vistas, attracted many of Hollywood's biggest stars. Charlie Chaplin, Groucho Marx, Greta Garbo, Lillian Gish, and Mary Pickford all discovered the beauty of the hotel and its surroundings. Their attraction to the area would eventually spawn the La Jolla Playhouse, allowing Gregory Peck, Charlton Heston, Ginger Rogers, David Niven, and many others the opportunity to work where they played.

Over the next few years, the patios and gardens were added. But the most popular additions have been the Whaling Bar & Grill, The Sky Room, and Café La Rue. They have become the centerpiece of the hotel, both for guests and for locals who visit. Colonel Billy Mitchell donated the unique barrel clock located behind the bar. The last major addition to the hotel was when it acquired the Cabrillo Hotel next door in 1956. This addition increased the room count to 100.

The staff of La Valencia goes out of their way to ensure that every guest is treated as though he or she is someone special. If they can satisfy celebrities, you too are likely to enjoy a visit to La Valencia.

La Valencia Hotel
1132 Prospect Street
La Jolla, California 92037
(858) 454-0771
(800) 451-0772

Paella Valencia

RICE

Heat 2-quart saucepot with oil over moderate heat. Add rice and sauté until all oil has been incorporated with rice. Add chicken stock and saffron and let mixture come to a tumbling simmer. Cover, turn down heat, and let it cook for 5 minutes. Remove from stovetop and let cool.

PAELLA

To make paella, the overall plan is to add all ingredients in sequence. Usually this is done slowly over low heat. Moderate high heat is optional, but you must carefully monitor the pan at all times while sautéing to avoid burning ingredients, especially garlic and chorizo.

Heat oil in 10-inch-round sauté pan over moderate heat. Add diced chicken and sauté until almost done. Add chorizo and garlic for a minute, stirring all three ingredients. Toss in mélange of bell peppers. Let it sauté for a couple of minutes more.

Next, begin to add remaining ingredients: mussels, clams, fish pieces, shrimp, and sea scallops. Allow this to cook for several minutes again with moderate flame. Add pork sausage, optional.

SAFFRON RICE

1 tablespoon olive oil

1½ cup Uncle Ben's polished rice

¾ cup chicken stock or water

1½ teaspoon saffron

PAELLA

1 tablespoon olive oil

2 ounces diced chicken breast

1 ounce chorizo, chopped

1 teaspoon chopped garlic

½ cup tricolor bell peppers, diced

3 black mussels

3 mahogany clams

1 ounce sea bass (or assorted
    fish pieces)

3 large shrimp

2 large sea scallops

1 2-ounce link of pork sausage
    (optional)

1½ cup clam juice or chicken
    stock

¼ cup raw English peas

1 tablespoon basil,
    freshly chopped

Kosher salt and white pepper
    to taste

Finally, add cooked saffron rice, chicken or clam broth, peas, basil, salt, and pepper to taste. Let simmer (or bake in preheated 375-degree oven) for 10 to 15 minutes until broth is completely absorbed into paella. Bon Appétit!

"The discovery of a new dish does more for the happiness of mankind than the discovery of a new star."

—A Brillat Savarin

Snow Creek Oyster Au Gratin

With an oyster knife, remove the top shell of the oyster and cut the oyster away from the attaching muscle. Wash off any bits of shell under cold running water. Return oyster to its half-shell and place on a sheet pan lined with parchment paper. Clean all oysters in this manner. Reserve in the refrigerator.

In a medium saucepan, cook the speck until crisp and golden brown. Remove from pan and place on a paper towel to absorb excess fat. In the same pan, add the celery and onion and sauté until soft. Remove from heat.

Preheat oven to 375 degrees. Remove oysters from refrigerator and place a small amount of cheese and celery-onion mixture in each oyster. Sprinkle a small amount of panko on top. Place in the oven and bake until cheese has melted.

Remove from oven and squeeze fresh lemon juice on each oyster. Garnish with a piece of speck and micro watercress. Season with salt and pepper. Serve.

12 Snow Creek oysters

6 thin slices of speck (Italian bacon, similar to prosciutto)

2 stalks celery, small diced

¼ small sweet onion, small diced

¼ cup Roquefort blue cheese

¼ cup panko (Japanese bread crumbs)

2 tablespoons fresh squeezed lemon juice

¼ cup micro watercress

Salt to taste

Fresh cracked pepper

1-kilogram wheel Brie cheese
(about 2¼ pounds)

1 cup plus 1 teaspoon brown
sugar, divided

1 cup blanched almonds, sliced

4 cups fresh cranberries

Zest and juice of 1 orange

Baked Brie with Cranberries and Orange Zest

Preheat oven to 375 degrees. Place the Brie wheel on a cutting surface and remove the top rind layer with a sharp kitchen knife. Be sure to only remove the rind, leaving the cheese in tact.

Place the Brie in a large round glass or ceramic baking dish, just deep enough and wide enough for the cheese wheel to fit neatly in (usually a 9-inch dish). Sprinkle 1 cup of brown sugar and almonds over the top crust of the Brie. In a saucepan, combine the cranberries, orange zest, orange juice, and 1 teaspoon of brown sugar. Turn to medium heat and melt the cranberries down until soft. Remove from heat and let cool.

Once the cranberries have cooled, with a spoon place the scoops of the cranberry mixture around the top of the Brie. Place in an oven and cook until golden brown and bubbling (approx. 15–20 minutes). You may have to poke the edges of the Brie with a butter knife in order to force it to settle into the cooking dish.

Top with candied orange peels, fresh cranberries, or other garnish of your choice. Serve immediately with crackers or toast points and a glass of Champagne.

Note: Brie should be placed into hot oven 15–20 minutes prior to guests' arrival.

MILLENNIUM BILTMORE HOTEL LOS ANGELES

With its grand architecture and impressive list of guests including presidents, royalty, and celebrities, the Millennium Biltmore Hotel opened as the "Host of the Coast" on October 1, 1923—and remains so to this day.

The Biltmore Hotel features the opulent architectural style of the Spanish-Italian Renaissance to reflect the Castilian heritage of California. Detailed ceiling frescoes depicting mythological themes were executed by "modern-day Michelangelo" Giovanni Battista Smeraldi, whose work also graces the White House and the Vatican. Accenting these fresco murals are the wall reliefs, sculpted columns, and bronze work throughout the hotel.

Legends and traditions thrive within the embellished walls of the Biltmore Hotel, as it has played host to the people and events that contribute to the history of Los Angeles. From Cary Grant to Brad Pitt, countless movie stars have passed through the doors of the Biltmore Hotel, reflecting the Hollywood culture of Los Angeles. The monumental decision to found the Academy of Motion Picture Arts and Sciences was made in the hotel's own Crystal Ballroom with many of its corresponding Oscar Awards ceremonies taking place in the Biltmore Bowl.

In addition to its connection with the Hollywood film industry, the Biltmore has also welcomed public figures such as John F. Kennedy and the Duke and Duchess of York to enjoy the historic and beautiful facilities offered by the hotel.

A downtown Los Angeles landmark since its completion, and the "star" of numerous movies and TV shows filmed at the property, the Millennium Biltmore has long been the meeting spot for high society, celebrities, and conventioneers from around the globe. The stately 683-room property celebrated a landmark 80th anniversary by bringing back jazz to its grand Gallery Bar, daily high tea in the Rendezvous Court, and establishing a "historic corridor" for guests to relive its colorful history.

The Biltmore's Crystal Ballroom was the site of several early Academy of Motion Picture Arts and Sciences banquets, and the 14,000-square-foot Biltmore Bowl recently reopened after a $3 mil-

lion renovation to prepare the grand venue for another century of memorable events. The hotel also features two restaurants, including Sai Sai, which serves authentic Japanese cuisine.

Millennium Biltmore Hotel Los Angeles
506 South Grand Avenue
Los Angeles, California 90071
(213) 624-1011

Kaki Shishito

Pan-fried oyster on the half shell with Japanese green pepper and tomato yuzu salsa

Mix all salsa ingredients well together in a bowl. Set aside.

Dust the oyster with plain flour and pan-fry in a little oil until one side is golden and crisp. Turn it and leave it for 10 seconds in a hot pan. We just want to cook one side of the oyster.

Pan-fry shishito peppers to make them softer.

PRESENTATION

Place kaiso seaweed on the shell, creating a bed on which to sit the oyster (crispy side up); top with a spoon of tomato salsa and garnish with a pan-fried shishito.

YIELD
12 oysters

TOMATO YUZU SALSA

½ cup white onion, finely chopped

1 green jalapeño chile, seeded and chopped

¼ bunch of cilantro, chopped

1 cup cherry tomatoes, chopped

½ teaspoon chopped fresh garlic

6 tablespoon yuzu (Japanese citrus) or juice of 3 lemons

OYSTERS

12 live oysters, cleaned, with reserved half-shell for serving

Flour, as needed for coating

Light oil, as needed

GARNISH

12 shishito (Japanese green peppers)

Kaiso (Japanese fresh seaweed)

CEVICHE

2 lbs center cut yellow tail,
    cut into 6 pieces
    (approx. 3 inches thick)

12 cucumber sticks

Kaiso (fresh seaweed)

1 jalapeño chile, sliced

Cilantro sprigs

1 red onion, sliced thin

1 lemon, sliced, for plating

DRESSING

6 tablespoons yuzu (Japanese
    citrus) or lime juice

6 tablespoons ponzu sauce
    (citrus-soy dipping sauce)

1 tablespoon hichimi (a peppery
    blend of seven spices)

Yellow Tail Ceviche

Sliced fish with jalapeño, red onion, and yuzu-ponzu dressing

Each ceviche roll should be prepared as follows: Lay out a slice of yellow tail. On top of the fish, place 2 cucumber sticks, a pinch of seaweed, a slice of jalapeño, 2 slices of red onion, and a sprig of cilantro. Roll the yellow tail to produce the ceviche roll.

To make the dressing, place yuzu, ponzu, and hichimi together in a small bowl. Mix well.

PRESENTATION

Layout six ceviche rolls on a cold plate. Each roll should sit on a slice of lemon.

Cover each roll with one tablespoon of dressing.

Note: Yuzu, ponzu, hichimi, and fresh seaweed (kaiso) can be purchased in Japanese stores.

YIELD

Serves 6

Tiradito de Salmon

Seared salmon with garlic ponzu dressing

To make ponzu sauce, in a saucepan, bring soy sauce to a boil. Add bonito flakes to the pan, then turn off heat and set aside to cool.

Strain and retain the soy sauce. Mix soy sauce, vinegar, and lemon juice. Add garlic last.

PRESENTATION

Prepare salmon to be seared by spreading garlic onto each side. In a pan, heat olive oil to smoke point. Place salmon in pan to sear, turning once.

Place seared salmon on a plate. Add ponzu sauce and sprinkle with sesame seeds. Garnish with organic salad and serve.

YIELD

Serves 1

PONZU SAUCE

1 cup soy sauce

½ cup bonito flakes (pink flakes of dried tuna)

¼ cup rice wine vinegar

¾ cup lemon juice

2 garlic cloves

SALMON

2½ ounces salmon, thinly cut

1 tablespoon garlic puree

1 tablespoon olive oil

2 ounces ponzu sauce

1 tablespoon sesame seeds

Organic salad (baby mixed green or micro green)

5 ripe tomatoes

2 medium cucumbers, peeled,
    seeded, and diced

½ medium red onion, small diced

2 jalapeño peppers, diced

½ cup chopped cilantro

2 ounces Champagne vinegar

1–2 limes

Salt and pepper

1 teaspoon cilantro oil, prepared
    in advance (recipe follows)

1 ounce crabmeat

1 cilantro leaf

Dungeness Crab Gazpacho

For the gazpacho, peel tomatoes and put into a strainer. Over a bowl, squeeze out seeds and juice. Discard the seeds and juice. Puree half of the tomatoes. Dice the remainder. Combine all tomatoes, cucumbers, onions, peppers, cilantro, vinegar, and juice from one lime. Juice from a second lime is optional, to taste.

Refrigerate overnight. Season with salt and pepper.

PRESENTATION

Place 6 ounces of gazpacho in a dish. Drizzle with cilantro oil. Put crabmeat on top of gazpacho in center of dish. Top with cilantro leaf.

Cilantro Oil

In boiling water, blanch bunch of cilantro for 15 seconds, then put into ice water to shock. Dry cilantro. Place cilantro into blender and add 4 ounces of olive oil. Puree for 30 seconds. Pour into stainless steel container. Add the remaining olive oil and let set over night. Strain through a coffee filter.

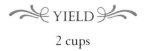 YIELD

2 cups

1 bunch cilantro with stems

2 cups olive oil

MISSION INN

The Spanish missions built along the coast in the mid and late 1700s were expected to be self-sufficient. They all claimed lands around them and used the fields to raise livestock and crops. No mission was built in the Riverside area, but the San Gabriel Mission, fifty miles away, used the land in this area for its ranching. The fertile valleys, lakes, and sub-desert climate in the area would eventually attract many settlers. Over the years, the Riverside area experienced the land-grant boom, the challenges of new statehood, and the developments of the railroad.

After the Civil War, Judge John Wesley North and a group of abolitionists came to Riverside to establish a community that did not suffer from the moral degradation of the big cities on the East Coast. They also hoped to prosper in the real estate boom that California promised.

North and his group laid out a one-mile-square plot of land on the Jurupa Rancho that would become the center of modern Riverside. Referred to now as Mile Square, this new community was known to take a very dim view of anyone who drank liquor or partook of other common vices.

It didn't take long for the settlers to discover that citrus crops grew quite nicely in this rich valley. Soon the countryside was covered with naval orange trees and the owners prospered beyond their wildest dreams. By the time Riverside County was created by the California Legislature in 1893, it was thought that the town had become the wealthiest city per capita in the country.

One of the settlers was a civil engineer. Christopher Columbus Miller did some work for the new town and was compensated with part of the town's land in 1876. He immediately set out to build a 12-room, two-story adobe boarding house that he called the Glenwood. In 1880, his son Frank purchased both the hotel and the surrounding property.

Attracted to the area by the prosperity of the citrus farmers, wealthy easterners and tourists flooded the area. They became so numerous that Frank decided he needed a bigger hotel. In 1902, he constructed a much larger four-story hotel enclosing a large central courtyard. The next thirty years saw three wings added to accommodate even more growth in tourism: The Cloister Wing was erected in 1910, the Spanish Wing in 1914, and the International Rotunda Wing in 1931. Also, in the 1920s, the Spanish Wing was expanded to include Author's Row and Miller's own private suite. Designed with reclusive writers in mind, Author's Row offers a secluded setting for your next great novel, whether you are writing it or just reading it.

The third wing filled out the original city block. It included the St. Francis Chapel, designed specifically to accommodate a massive eighteenth-century gold-leafed cedar altar from Mexico and seven equally impressive Louis C. Tiffany stained glass windows.

Miller hosted President Theodore Roosevelt soon after the 1903 Mission Wing was built. Frequent visitors included Maude Adams, Sarah Bernhardt, and Madame Modjeska, who played to Riverside audiences in the Loring Opera House. Hamlin Garland, Pulitzer Prize–winning author, wrote portions of his latest works in the Inn's Alhambra Suite. Visiting members of the royal houses of Sweden, Russia, and Japan were honored at banquets. After Frank Miller died in 1935, the Mission Inn had a variety of owners until the Historic Mission Inn Corporation purchased the property.

For more than 130 years, the Mission Inn has been the center of social activity in the city and has attracted 10 presidents. Pat and Richard Nixon were married in the wedding chapel, while Nancy and Ronald Reagan honeymooned here. When President Taft, who weighed more than 330 pounds, came to visit, Frank Miller had a special chair built to hold his ample frame.

To guests and the people of Riverside, the Mission Inn has always meant more than simply bed, bath, and board. It is an assemblage of arcades and gardens, turrets and domes, flying buttresses and spiraling staircases, catacombs and carillon towers. It is also fine art and Spanish cannons, stained glass and ceramic tile, saints and dragons, bells and wrought iron. It is also an artful and architectural tribute to the vision of Frank Miller.

Mission Inn
3649 Mission Inn Avenue
Riverside, California 92501
(951) 784-0300

Seared Halibut with Potato Crust and Citrus Dill Sauce

MARINADE

½ ounce chopped shallots

1 ounce olive oil

½ cup orange juice

Salt and white pepper, to taste

SAUCE

½ ounce shallot, diced

¼ ounce ginger root, shaved

½ ounce white wine

½ ounce orange juice

1 teaspoon brown sugar

4 ounces heavy cream

¼ ounce dill butter

FISH

1 6-ounce halibut fillet

Olive oil, for pan-searing

1 ounce flour, for dusting

1 egg, broken for egg wash

3 ounces crumbled, fried potato hash or home fries

½ ounce shallot rings

Prepare marinade and allow halibut fillet to marinate for 30 minutes.

Meanwhile, prepare sauce. Sauté shallots and ginger, and then add white wine. In another pan, heat orange juice and brown sugar and reduce to half the original volume. Add orange reduction to white wine mixture and simmer for 5 minutes. Add the cream, reduce slightly, and then incorporate the dill butter.

Heat olive oil in a skillet until hot. Lightly flour the halibut fillet, dip in egg wash, and then roll in the potato hash. Sear the halibut until slightly golden in color.

Ladle sauce on plate, top with the seared halibut, and garnish with shallot rings.

YIELD
Serves 1

Penne Gorgonzola

Bring a large pot of salted water to a boil. Add the penne pasta and stir a few times to separate. Cook the pasta until it is tender to the bite (al dente) but still retains some texture. (Approximate cooking time is 6 minutes.)

Drain the pasta in a colander and set aside.

Heat the olive oil in sauté pan. Add the shallots and sauté for 3–4 minutes. Add the white wine and reduce by one quarter over medium heat. Add the chicken stock and simmer 4–7 minutes. Add the heavy cream and reduce until the sauce attains a balance of good flavor and smooth consistency.

Steam the shiitake mushrooms and the asparagus tips for approximately 2 minutes. Add the mushrooms, asparagus, and gorgonzola to the sauce. Season the sauce, add pasta until well coated and heated through, and serve.

YIELD
Serves 4

1 pound penne pasta

4 ounces olive oil

1 cup shallots

1 cup white wine

1 cup chicken stock

½ quart heavy cream

2 cups shiitake mushrooms, sliced

2 cups asparagus spears, cut into small pieces

8 ounces gorgonzola cheese

Salt and pepper. to taste

8 ounces mahi mahi

1 ounce olive oil

1 ounce pineapple juice

1 ounce soy sauce

¼ ounce sake

½ teaspoon brown sugar

¼ ounce garlic, minced

½ ounce lemon grass, minced

¼ ounce ginger root, grated

Salt and pepper, to taste

FRUIT SALSA

1 teaspoon brown sugar

½ ounce rice wine vinegar

1 ounce soy sauce

½ ounce pineapple, diced

¼ ounce bell pepper, diced

¼ ounce ginger, grated

¼ ounce red onion, diced

1 teaspoon cilantro, chopped

Tropical Mahi Mahi

Place the mahi fillet in a shallow pan and set aside. In a small bowl, whisk together the 4 liquid ingredients, then add the 4 dry ingredients, and whisk until thoroughly mixed. Add salt and pepper to taste. Pour the mixture over the mahi fillet and place in the refrigerator for 10–20 minutes.

To make the salsa, dissolve the brown sugar in the vinegar and soy sauce. Add the remaining salsa ingredients and set aside.

Sauté the mahi fillet over medium heat for approximately 10 minutes, or to the desired temperature.

Place the fish on a serving platter and garnish attractively with the fruit salsa.

YIELD
Serves 1

OJAI VALLEY INN & SPA

The first known residents of Ojai were the Chumash Indians, who still maintain an existence in the area. Their word for "moon" is *A'hwai*, and from this pronunciation, the valley—and later the community—got its name. Ojai is one of the smallest and oldest towns in Ventura County, settled in the 1800s and incorporated in 1921.

Edward D. Libbey, a wealthy glass manufacturer from back east, was responsible for the layout of the town. Previously, Libbey bought and operated the American Glass Company in East Cambridge, Massachusetts. When his workers struck, he responded by moving the company to Toledo, Ohio, in 1888. Today, that company is known as Libbey-Owens-Ford, one of the premier glassmakers in the world.

Early settlers such as Libbey and Robert Winfield guided the town's development. Winfield built the Arcade, which today houses various shops and eating places. Their early efforts were challenged by a raging fire that destroyed much of the town in 1917. Undaunted, Libbey set to work rebuilding key facilities in the Spanish-Revival architecture style.

In 1923, Libbey built a private country club and golf course designed to harmonize with the natural beauty of the valley. Over the next few years, it grew with additions. Like many of the nation's resorts, the Ojai Valley Inn was turned over to the Army in 1942 and was transformed into Camp Oak. A battalion of 1,000 Army troops used it for a training center until 1944 when it became an R&R facility for the Navy.

After the war, the government auctioned off the barracks and Quonset huts and the property was sold. The Ojai Valley Inn & Spa opened in 1947, playing host to Hollywood notables Clark Gable, Irene Dunne, Lana Turner, Loretta Young, Hoagy Carmichael, Walt Disney, Nancy and Ronald Reagan, Judy Garland, Paul Newman, and many others. Many well-known tennis stars frequent Ojai annually, attracted by the oldest amateur event of its kind in the country.

Ojai has long been known as a haven for artists, musicians, and health enthusiasts. It gained fame decades ago when the area was photographed to represent Shangri-La in the 1939 movie, *The Lost Horizon*. The Ojai Center for the Arts, the Summer Art Stroll, the Ojai Studio Artists Tour, and Art in the Park offer venues for an abundance of artistic expression.

The Ojai Valley Inn & Spa is listed as one of the top 25 golf resorts in North America. The Spa nearby soothes both golfers and non-golfers alike. Numerous galleries show the work of both local

artists and those from afar. For outdoor enthusiasts, the Ojai Valley Trail runs for more than 9 miles with a parallel path for horses. Bicyclists, walkers, joggers, and those exercising a variety of pets can be seen on the trail.

Ojai Valley Inn & Spa
905 Country Club Road
Ojai, California 93023
(805) 646-1111
(800) 422-6524

Molasses Brined Melting Beef Short Ribs

DAY 1: EARLY PREPARATIONS

Combine all brine ingredients, except meat, in a large nonreactive bowl and refrigerate for 1 hour.

Next, place beef into the liquid brine and submerge. Cover with plastic wrap touching beef so that it is completely covered with brine. Cover again with plastic and refrigerate overnight.

DAY 2: COOKING AND SERVING

Remove the short ribs from the brine. Let ribs rest on a paper towel or a wire resting rack to dry out. Season with salt and pepper. Preheat oven to 350 degrees.

In a medium roasting pan, sear short ribs on both sides until golden to dark brown. Remove ribs from pan and add onions, carrots, and celery. Cook until brown. Add veal stock and ½ cup molasses and stir to combine.

Return the short ribs to liquid and cover with aluminum foil. Cook ribs in oven for 2–3 hours. When done, they should be tender but not fall apart. Remove pan from oven, remove ribs from pan, and reduce liquid, skimming off any fat. Return ribs to sauce and keep hot on stovetop.

BRINE

1 cup molasses

½ cup kosher salt

3 tablespoons Worcestershire sauce

2 fresh bay leaves

1 tablespoon whole fresh thyme

2 tablespoons whole black peppercorns

1 tablespoon dry mustard

1 small white onion, rough chopped

6 cups warm water

4 pounds boneless beef short ribs, cut into 5–6 ounce portions

SHORT RIBS

1 large onion, rough chopped

1 carrot, rough chopped

2 ribs of celery, rough chopped

2 quarts of veal stock

½ cup molasses

(continued on next page)

FINAL DISH

3 tablespoons extra-virgin
  olive oil

6 garlic cloves, peeled,
  cleaned, and blanched

2 sweet potatoes, peeled, medium
  diced, and par-cooked

2 carrots, peeled, medium diced,
  and par-cooked

½ pound fingerling potatoes,
  sliced into rounds

3 celery ribs, peeled and medium
  diced

Salt and pepper

Celery leaves, for garnish

FINAL DISH

In sauté pan, add olive oil and bring up to medium heat. Add garlic and cook until golden brown.

Add rest of ingredients and sauté until golden brown. Add salt and pepper to taste.

PLATING

Remove 1 cup of root vegetable mixture and place in center of deep, 12-inch-wide bowl. Place one 5–6-ounce portion of short ribs on top of root vegetables. Spoon 3–4 tablespoons of braising liquid over rib (you can add more depending on what you like).

Garnish with fresh-picked celery leaves and finish with any flaky sea salt.

YIELD

Serves 6

"There is no love sincerer than the love of food."

—George Bernard Shaw

Fennel-Marinated Roast Duck Breast with Swiss Chard, Celery Root Puree, and Black Pepper Pinot Noir Redux

DAY 1: PREPARATIONS

Prepare duck breasts by using a small knife and scoring the skin side, making X patterns. In a bowl, whisk all brine ingredients until salt is dissolved. Add duck breasts, ensuring that they are submerged, and reserve in refrigerator for the next day.

DAY 2: COOKING AND SERVING

Preheat oven to 325 degrees.

Remove duck from brining container and rinse off excess brine. Dry with paper or linen towels. Season with salt and black pepper. In ovenproof sauté pan on low heat, place duck skin-side down and cook for 5–7 minutes, until skin is reduced by half and is golden brown.

When skin is correct, flip over and finish in oven for 5–7 minutes until medium rare. Remove pan from oven and set on top of oven, letting all the juice from the meat get reabsorbed.

3 6–8 ounce Sonoma Magret duck breasts

1 bulb fennel, shaved thin

1 teaspoon whole black peppercorns

1 teaspoon fennel seed, toasted

3 ounces fennel tops, chopped

½ cup white balsamic vinegar

4 cups cold water

2 teaspoons kosher salt

2 teaspoons honey

(continued on next page)

PUREE

4–5 medium sized celery roots, peeled and medium diced

1 russet potato, peeled and medium diced

1 quart cream

1 quart whole milk

1 teaspoon sea salt

2 cloves garlic, peeled and cleaned

CHARD

1 tablespoon chopped garlic

2 teaspoons olive oil

½ pound green chard leaves, cleaned and rough-chopped

SAUCE

1 tablespoon whole butter

1 white onion, peeled, cleaned, and sliced thin

4 tables of Ojai honey (or any local or organic honey)

1 cup of pinot noir wine (from Santa Barbara)

1 quart of duck stock or dark chicken stock

1 teaspoon black peppercorns

4 sprigs of fresh thyme

1 tomato, cut into quarters

Salt and pepper

PUREE

Add all puree ingredients to a medium pot and cook at low temp until celery root is soft, about 30 minutes.

Strain celery root and potatoes. Reserve liquid aside to adjust thickness. Place potato and celery root in food processor or blender. Blend at medium speed, slowly adding liquid until you get a smooth, loose consistency. Season with salt and ground white pepper.

Reserve and keep warm.

CHARD

In a medium sauté pan, over medium heat, add garlic and olive oil. Lightly brown.

Add chard and cook until it is wilted and most of the liquid is gone. Remove chard and set aside to plate.

SAUCE

In a medium sauce pot, brown the butter, add onions, and caramelize. Add honey and bring to a caramel consistency. Add wine and reduce until syrup. Add stock, peppercorns, thyme, and tomatoes. Reduce to medium sauce consistency. Strain and reserve in saucepot. Season with salt and pepper.

PLATING

On a large 12-inch plate or in a deep, wide bowl, place ½ cup of celery root puree and flatten out with spoon. Onto top of puree, place the sautéed chard in a ball.

Slice the duck at a bias into ¼-inch slices. Each breast should yield 2 portions, for a total of 6 servings; this is about 6 slices per plate. Place duck and fan across the chard. In a circular pattern, spoon sauce around the plate, not touching any of the product.

Garnish with fresh fennel tops and a drizzle of extra virgin olive oil.

YIELD

Serves 6

THE PALM

California is at the heart of the current debate about the economy and immigration (both legal and otherwise). It is fitting that the history of The Palm is based on the vision, hard work, and perseverance of immigrants. The deep history of The Palm begins in Italy and on the East Coast.

Toward the end of the nineteenth century, Italy's feudal land system offered little hope for personal improvement. If you were fortunate enough to own land, you could charge very high rent to farmers or pay very low wages to workers. As a result, many millions of Italians decided to move to the new land of America, where hard work and opportunity gave everyone the chance for a better life. Most of them came to New York through Ellis Island.

Two immigrants, John Ganzi and Pio Bozzi, who had arrived separately in the United States in the early 1920s from the Northern Italian town of Parma, met in New York City. Wanting to better their lives, they felt that they could serve New Yorkers, and particularly their fellow Italian immigrants, by opening a restaurant that featured the ethnic food of their homeland.

Although they had learned to speak English in their new country, their pronunciation of some words needed refinement. Applying for a business permit to open an eatery called *Parma* after their hometown, they were misunderstood. The license was granted, but the official heard *Palm*, and that's what he wrote on their newly issued license. An industry and a legend were born.

It wasn't long before famous and influential citizens were attracted to The Palm. Others came too, including artists from the King Features news syndicate who, short of cash, were willing to help decorate the walls with caricatures in exchange for food. Operating on a shoestring, and having no budget for decorations, John and Pio were only too happy to trade a meal for something to cover the bare walls.

Their fame grew, along with their families. Wally Ganzi and Bruce Bozzi, grandsons of the original proprietors, took over for their fathers in the early 1960s when The Palm was still a single restaurant. It was so popular, they found it necessary to expand. So, rather than incorporating the place next door, Wally and Bruce elected to open another restaurant across town. They called it Palm Too.

When George H. W. Bush was the U.S. Ambassador to the United Nations, he often frequented The Palm. Before he returned to Washington to become the head of the Republican National Committee, he suggested that they expand outside the City. Taking his suggestion to heart, they opened their first expansion restaurant, The Palm in Washington, D.C.

The expansions continued, as more offspring of John and Pio grew up and were assimilated into the business. They have since opened almost 30 locations, including their fourth restaurant, the celebrity magnet, The Palm in Los Angeles.

In LA, the place to see and be seen is The Palm. The likes of Mike Myers, Adam Sandler, Billy Crystal, and Brian Dennehy grace the walls as well as the tables. Because of the celebrity status of the well-known patrons that frequented The Palm, the caricatures offered in every Palm restaurant were often of them. These drawings soon took on a life of their own: Movie stars and pop idols were known to sometimes sign their own pictures. Fred Astaire literally tap-danced down the top of the bar in Los Angeles on his way to signing his likeness.

Originally, The Palm served only Italian food. But some customers would ask for a steak, so John or Pio would run down the street to a butcher shop, purchase fresh meat, and cook it to order. This happened so often that The Palm now runs its own wholesale meat company to ensure the quality of its steaks.

Seafood started with third-generation owners Wally Ganzi and Bruce Bozzi, who introduced gargantuan 4–8-pound lobsters in the 1970s, disproving the theory that larger lobsters are tough. The Palm soon went from selling 150 pounds of lobster per week to 25,000 pounds per week. Even with these additions to the old-style fare of the original restaurant, tradition at The Palm continues to honor its roots. Several of John Ganzi`s original Italian dishes are still on the menu today.

The Palm restaurant remains the oldest family-owned white tablecloth restaurant to expand across the United States and still maintain family ownership. Great grandchildren and great grand-children-in-law currently run the business. Celebrities frequent The Palm because of its fine food, casual setting, and accommodating service.

Reservations are recommended.

The Palm
9001 Santa Monica Boulevard
Los Angeles, California 90069
(310) 550-8811

2 parts brandy

2 parts gin

1 part orange Curacao

1 part apricot liqueur

The Famous McClure Cocktail

This is the invention of Senator John J. McClure of the Pennsylvania State Senate. The recipe for this 1930s drink was a secret, except to his sons, who were sworn to secrecy until his death in 1965. The senator never had a problem enticing his political friends over to the house, because they anticipated a McClure Cocktail after a session of political strategizing. No matter how many times they asked about the ingredients, he never told, so they kept coming back—exactly as he wanted. The recipe comes to The Palm courtesy of Walter McClure, grandson of its creator and senior vice president of operations for The Palm. The best-quality ingredients make the best cocktail, so feel free to upgrade the brandy to cognac.

This is not a cocktail for which you can "eyeball" the proportions; use a jigger or a large measuring device.

Prepare the mixture in a pitcher ahead of time and refrigerate until very, very cold.

Not for the weak of heart, this cocktail is neither diluted nor garnished. Serve "up" only, in a cocktail glass. It must never, ever touch ice.

 YIELD

Serves 1

Hearts of Palm Salad

Carlo Bruno used to be the executive chef at the Houston Palm, and he came up with this recipe because he thought The Palm needed a dish using hearts of palm. For a while, it was only available in Houston, but now it is on menus around the country. Hearts of palm vary in tenderness and quality. They can be woody or mushy—sometimes in the same can! Spanish hearts of palm are always good.

Cut the romaine leaves crosswise into thin strips. On four chilled salad plates, make a bed of lettuce and arrange the hearts of palm in parallel rows on top. Place a line of diced tomato at a crosswise angle, running from left to right on top of the hearts of palm. Place 6 olives in a pile at the bottom of the plate, and distribute the hardboiled egg quarters at the top.

Serve with the dressing of your choice on the side, such as vinaigrette or blue cheese.

YIELD
Serves 4

12 pale inner leaves from the
heart of a romaine lettuce

1¼ pounds best-quality canned
hearts of palm (preferably
from Spain), drained and
halved lengthwise

2 ripe medium-sized tomatoes,
cored and cut into ¼-inch
pieces

24 kalamata olives

4 hardboiled eggs, peeled and cut
into quarters

2 10-ounce boxes frozen chopped
spinach, completely thawed

2 tablespoons lightly salted butter

1½ cups heavy cream

1 teaspoon fine sea salt

½ teaspoon white pepper,
preferably freshly ground

½ teaspoon ground nutmeg,
preferably freshly ground

1 tablespoon cornstarch

1 tablespoon white wine

1 cup grated Parmigiano-
Reggiano

Creamed Spinach

Here is the definitive, time-tested, beloved recipe for all to enjoy. Even with a standard recipe, it's worth noting that the chef at each Palm location likes to put his own spin on the legendary creamed spinach. The differences may be subtle but they definitely exist.

Using your hands, squeeze as much water as possible from the thawed spinach. In a large saucepan, combine the butter and cream over medium heat. When the butter is melted, stir in the spinach, salt, white pepper, and nutmeg. Stirring occasionally, bring the mixture to a simmer, and cook for 3 minutes.

In a small bowl, blend the cornstarch and wine with your fingertips, so that you can feel when all of the starch is dissolved. Add to the spinach mixture, and continue stirring until thickened, about 2 minutes. Stir in the Parmigiano and taste for seasoning. Serve at once, or keep warm in the top of a covered double boiler over barely simmering water, for up to 30 minutes.

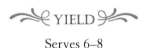
YIELD
Serves 6–8

"Everybody's worried about giving this recipe out. But I say, either you do it or you don't do it. If you use good butter, Parmigiano-Reggiano, and freshly ground nutmeg, you can make a great creamed spinach. I'm not saying it's going to be exactly like ours because there are, you know, variables at work in every kitchen."

—Tony Tammero, Executive Chef

THE PIERPONT INN & RACQUET CLUB

Back in 1910, enthusiasts were traveling up and down the California coast in that new fangled invention, the automobile. The Historic Pierpont Inn was built that year, in part to accommodate the growing number of people who were between destinations. Weary travelers required a comfortable place to rest and recharge their own personal batteries with a home-cooked meal. Josephine Pierpont saw the need and rose to the challenge. She commissioned the famous architect of the day, Sumner P. Hunt, to design a Craftsman-style bungalow inn. This form of construction was inspired by the Arts and Crafts Movement, which began in the 1880s. It celebrated handicrafts and encouraged the use of simple forms and natural materials. The name *craftsman* is actually taken from the magazine where the famous furniture designer, Gustav Stickley, offered floor plans in the early 1900s. It soon came to mean any dwelling that expressed arts and crafts ideals, most especially the simple, economical, and extremely popular bungalow.

The Pierpont Inn encompasses decades of rich architecture featuring two 1925 English Tudor Revival cottages, a 1935 Spanish-Revival banquet center, and a mid-century-modern retreat known as The 50's Flat. The romantic coastal charm of the property has made the Pierpont Inn a favorite location for weddings and receptions, family reunions, corporate retreats, and splendid overnight getaways for more than 95 years.

The Pierpont Inn & Racquet Club
550 Sanjon Road
Ventura, California 93001
(805) 643-6144
(800) 285-4667

Lemon Refrigerator Cookies

These cookies have welcomed guests to the historic inn for decades. This delectable cookie is a traditional signature trademark started by the Gleichmann Family, the owners of the Pierpont Inn for 70 years. The Gleichmann Family wanted to make their visitors feel at home upon their arrival at the Inn, so they greeted their guests with fresh-baked cookies to enjoy by the ever-faithful family hearth, which welcomed guests year-round. In the early days, the Gleichmanns often left the guests' room keys on the front desk counter for late-night arrivals. Although the key tradition has changed, the hospitality continues with the Gleichmanns' lemon cookies.

But why a lemon-flavored cookie? The Gleichmann family procured their produce from the local farming communities in Ventura County. Pierpont Executive Chef Louis Ludwig explains, "With bountiful orchards of lemons in the region, the Gleichmanns created this classic lemon cookie recipe, which remains the same today, and utilizes the rind, juice, and pulp of the lemon."

Admirers of the classic cookie often ask Chef Louis for the "secret" family recipe so they can take home a piece of The Pierpont tradition. The traditional Lemon Cookie recipe, as well as the popular Chocolate Chip Macadamia Nut Cookie recipe, are both available for visitors at the front desk upon request.

"This is one of our most sought-after recipes. We hope you enjoy a taste of The Pierpont! Bon appétit!"

—Chef Louis

Grate the rind of the lemon and set aside. Slice lemon in half, remove seeds, and ream juice and pulp. Cream the butter, sugar, eggs, and lemon rind with electric mixer until light and fluffy. Blend in vanilla and lemon extracts, along with juice and pulp.

In another bowl, sift flour, baking powder, and salt together. Add to lemon mixture. Form dough into 2-by-6-inch logs, seal in plastic wrap and refrigerate overnight.

Preheat oven to 285 degrees. Cut dough into ½-inch slices and space 2 inches apart on greased cookie sheets. Bake for 16–20 minutes; avoid over-baking. Allow to cool for 5 minutes before transferring to cooling racks. Dust with powdered sugar, if desired.

 YIELD

5 dozen

1 large lemon

1 cup butter, room temperature

1 cup sugar

2 eggs

1½ teaspoons vanilla extract

1½ teaspoons lemon extract

2½ cups sifted all-purpose flour

1½ teaspoons baking powder

½ teaspoon salt

Blue Hubbard Squash Soup with Walnut and Basil Pistou

SOUP

1 large blue Hubbard squash

1 tablespoon garlic, minced

2 tablespoons shallots, minced

2 quarts heavy cream

2 quarts whole milk

1 cup clover honey

½ pound butter

Italian sea salt

Fresh ground white pepper

PISTOU

1 cup roasted walnuts, ground

2 cups fresh basil, chopped

2 cups extra virgin olive oil, preferably Tuscan

½ teaspoon Italian sea salt

SOUP

Cut the squash into roughly 6 pieces. Roast in oven at 350 degrees for 30 minutes. Allow to cool for 10–15 minutes.

Scoop the seeds out and discard. Scoop the flesh out of the skin and rough-dice. Place in soup pot with all of the ingredients except the butter and seasonings. Simmer for 30 minutes. Blend until smooth. Strain through a fine sieve. Return to pot and bring to a simmer. Add the butter, a little at a time, until incorporated. Season to taste.

Serve with Walnut and Basil Pistou on top (recipe follows).

PISTOU

Roast the walnuts and then allow to cool. Add the oil and basil to a blender and liquefy. Add the walnuts a little at a time until incorporated. Add salt and more oil as needed. The finished product should be the consistency of vinaigrette. Enjoy!

Hummus

Combine garbanzo beans, liquid, and sesame oil in a food processor and pulse, scraping down sides until smooth. Add lemon juice, garlic, and cumin and blend, while slowly adding olive oil until very smooth in texture. Add salt to taste.

YIELD
4¼ cups

"I like a little more salt than most, especially when using a very natural sea salt that has not been overly processed."

—Chef Ludwig

2 cups garbanzo beans, canned

¾ cup liquid reserved from can

¼ cup sesame oil

¼ cup fresh lemon juice

3 tablespoons garlic, minced

2 tablespoons ground cumin

¾ cup extra virgin olive oil

Sea salt, to taste

THE QUEEN MARY

The story of Cunard's *Queen Mary* begins in North America. Samuel Cunard built and operated mail ships on the East Coast before securing the right to the transatlantic mail service between Great Britain and America in 1840. The new business allowed the company to add RMS (Royal Mail Ship) to the names of all their ships, but they soon changed to Cunard Steamship Ltd., after its founder.

The mail service route included Liverpool, where Cunard eventually built his headquarters in 1918. From this location, Cunard would dominate the transatlantic route for more than 150 years. One of her competitors was The White Star Line, who tried valiantly, some say recklessly, to capture the preeminent position Cunard held.

In December 1930, Cunard engaged the John Brown & Company Shipbuilding and Engineering shipyard at Clydebank, Scotland, to begin work on hull number 534. The Great Depression forced a halt in construction in 1931 and Cunard applied to the government for loan assistance. The loan was offered, along with enough money to build a companion ship (hull 552 would become the *Queen Elizabeth*), but there was a major condition that had to be met. Cunard must absorb The White Star Line, which was in severe financial difficulty following the sinking of its flagship, *Titanic*, in 1912 with a loss of 1,522 passengers and crew members.

The merger was completed, the loan given, and work resumed on hull 534 in 1934. The ship was launched later that year, and named after Queen Mary, the consort of King George V. At the time, a turbine steamer already carried the name Queen Mary, but Cunard convinced the other line to rename its ship TS *Queen Mary II*. Cunard called its newest ship the RMS *Queen Mary*.

When launched, the *Queen Mary*—at 80,774 tons—was about 1,000 tons larger than her French rival, the *Normandie*. But the French were not to be outdone. Modifications increased the size of the *Normandie* to make it 2,500 tons larger than the *Queen Mary*.

The ships continued to compete for superlatives and supremacy. The speed records for crossing the Atlantic from east to west and west to east changed hands several times between the two behemoths. The issue was not settled until 1952 when the SS *United States* surpassed them both.

When World War II broke out, the *Queen Mary* was in New York alongside the *Normandie*. They were soon joined by the Queen's sister ship, the *Queen Elizabeth*. Britain sent its ships to Sydney to carry Australian and New Zealand troops back to Great Britain for the war. These ships were prized targets for the Germans, with Hitler offering a $250,000 reward and the Iron Cross to any U-boat commander who could sink one.

As the fastest troop carriers afloat, they easily eluded the enemy, but their evasive maneuvers were also at high speed. The *Queen Mary* accidentally cut a light cruiser in half on October 2, 1942, leading to the death of 338 sailors. Fearful of enemy submarines, the *Queen* could not stop to search for survivors.

In December 1942, while carrying 15,000 American troops to England, she was hit broadside with a rogue wave estimated at 90 feet. Lifeboats were damaged and windows were broken on the bridge. The ship listed more than 50 degrees, and later study suggested that she very nearly capsized. This event prompted Paul Gallico to write *The Poseidon Adventure*, which was filmed in part on the *Queen Mary*.

When the war ended in 1945, the ship had to be rebuilt on the inside to undo the modifications made for troop carrying. It also needed painting. While in military service, it had served as Winston Churchill's headquarters at sea, and had been painted gray to camouflage it from the German submarines. "The Gray Ghost" had carried over 800,000 troops to battle areas, but now she was headed back to civilian service.

The *Queen Mary* sailed the transatlantic route until 1967, when transatlantic air travel by jet forced her to retire. Japanese scrap merchants bid for the iron and steel, but the City of Long Beach won with a bid of $3.45 million. The *Queen Elizabeth* was retired in 1968, to be replaced by the *Queen Elizabeth 2* in 1969. Still in service, the *QE2* was joined by the *Queen Mary 2* in 2004.

After the *Queen Mary* arrived in Long Beach, it had its insides modified once more to serve as a floating hotel, restaurant, shopping area, and museum. Engines, boilers, generators, the water softening plant, and all the other machinery inside have been taken out to make it more functional as a destination. The *Queen Mary* is located at the south end of the 710 Freeway, on the water in Long Beach.

The Queen Mary
1126 Queen's Highway
Long Beach, California 90802
(562) 435-3511

2½ pounds white beans

10 ounces fresh pork rind

7 ounces pork hock

1 onion stuck with a clove

1 mixed brunch of thyme
 and bay leaves

1 carrot, chopped

1 leek, chopped

1 stick of celery, chopped

2 garlic cloves

1½ ounces pork fat

2–3 tablespoons tomato paste

1½ pounds goose or duck
 conserve

14 ounces pork spare ribs

8 Toulouse sausages

Salt and pepper

Cassoulet

Soak the dry beans overnight in cold water.

Throw out that water. Put the beans in a saucepan of cold water and blanch them by bringing to a boil for 5 minutes. Throw out this water, too.

At the same time, prepare a stock with the pork rind cut into large strips, pork hock, onion stuck with a clove, thyme and bay leaves, carrot, leek, celery, and a mince of crushed garlic and salted pork fat. Filter the stock, taking out the rind.

You need to have about twice as much volume of stock as volume of beans. Cook the beans in the stock for 2 hours over low heat. The beans should be soft but still whole. During the cooking, add tomato paste.

In a frying pan, remove the fat from the pieces of duck or goose conserve; render the fat pieces. In the resulting fat, brown the pork spare ribs. Retrieve and drain them. Finally, in the same fat, brown the sausages.

With all these preparations finished, put all the ingredients in a deep earthenware dish. Line the bottom of the dish with the rind, all pork pieces, and one-third of the beans. Add duck, then cover with the remaining beans. On top, place the sausages in a spiral and embed them gently into the beans. Finish by pouring the warm stock and the juice from the frying pan. Pepper the surface generously.

Put the cassoulet in the oven at 300 degrees and let it cook for 2 to 3 hours. During the cooking, the top will develop a golden-brown crust that you should press down several times during the course of the cooking without squashing the beans. At that time, when compacting the top, check to see that the beans have not dried out, and if they do, add stock.

Serve very hot, in the casserole, of course.

Serves 8

"Dinner, a time when . . . one should eat wisely but not too well, and talk well but not too wisely."

—W. Somerset Maugham

4 cups corn, may be canned

½ cup roasted red bell pepper,
    diced

½ cup roasted green bell pepper,
    diced

½ cup roasted yellow bell pepper,
    diced

½ cup red onions, diced

2 limes, juiced

½ cup virgin olive oil

2 teaspoons garlic, crushed

¼ cup cilantro,
    very finely chopped

Cilantro Corn Salad

This recipe will taste better if prepared the day before. The corn will have time to marinate and take on all of the flavors.

For this simple salad, mix all ingredients in bowl and keep in refrigerator until you are ready to serve.

⚡ YIELD ⚡
Serves 4

Chicken Cordon Bleu

Preheat oven to 350 degrees. Pound each chicken breast to about ⅛-inch thick. Place cheese and ham on chicken breast and sprinkle lightly with salt, white pepper, and herb blend. Roll each breast with ham and cheese inside and fasten with toothpicks.

Dip each chicken in melted butter and roll in breadcrumbs.

Place each chicken in a greased baking dish and bake for 50 minutes until chicken is golden brown.

To make Cordon Bleu sauce, sauté mushrooms, add lemon juice, and reduce. Add chicken stock and reduce half of volume. Add cream and reduce by half again. Add salt and pepper to taste.

Serve hot over chicken. Best with mashed potatoes, peas, and carrots. Enjoy.

YIELD

Serves 4

4 skinless, boneless chicken breasts

4 slices cooked ham

4 slices Swiss cheese

Salt and white pepper to taste

1 teaspoon dried herbes de Provence

¼ cup butter, melted

1 cup fine breadcrumbs

1 cup mushrooms, sliced

1 teaspoon lemon juice

8 ounces chicken stock

1 cup cream

Salt and pepper

THE LANGHAM, HUNTINGTON HOTEL & SPA

Pasadena is perhaps best-known worldwide for the Tournament of Roses Parade, held every year on New Year's Day and culminating in the Rose Bowl football game. However, Pasadena's history is tied more to the people rather than to the land.

When the Spanish missionaries arrived in the area in their quest to establish Franciscan missions along the California coast, they encountered the Hahamogna Tribe, which had hunted and fished the land for centuries and had established several villages around the area. The missionaries were intent on converting these "heathens" to Christianity and convinced the tribe's head chief, Hahamovic, to be baptized.

After the chief followed their ritual, the missionaries renamed him "Pascual" and renamed the tribe after his new name. Their intent was to disrupt the tribal distinctions. Even then, they once again renamed the tribe the "Mission Indians" with the reference making the mission seem even more important. They further blurred the old tribal association by later renaming the Indians near the mission the "Gabrielinos" after the San Gabriel Mission. Finally, they called the mountain Indians "Serranos," meaning *highlanders*. If this sounds confusing, it's because the padres meant to confuse the Indians, thereby subjugating them.

As with all other missions along the King's Highway (El Camino Real), missions claimed huge tracks of surrounding land for ranching and agriculture in support of the mission. When Mexico achieved independence from Spain, the new government elected in 1833 to give the mission lands to private individuals, usually those wealthy and influential friends of the powerful in Mexico City or the local government of Alta (Upper) California.

Pasadena occupies part of a 14,000-acre land grant known as Rancho el Rincon de San Pascual, originally given to Doña Eulalia Pérez de Guillen in 1826. The new government of Mexico recognized this grant and the land passed through several hands before being divided and sold to Henry E. Huntington and the local Orange Grove Association.

Many members of the association were from the East Coast, and they referred to this land as the Indiana Colony. Later, the group changed the name to "Pasadena," which was a blend of Chippewa Indian words translated to "Crown of the Valley."

Henry Huntington was born in New York. As the nephew of Collis Huntington, one of the San Francisco "Big Four," Henry came to California for a job arranged by his influential uncle. Henry ventured on to Los Angeles to make his own fortune by creating the Pacific Electric Railway. As the forerunner of modern rapid transit systems, his "Red Cars" served more than fifty cities until it was dismantled in the 1950s.

Another wealthy settler new to the area was General Marshall Clark Wentworth. Having achieved his rank during the Civil War, the general found himself managing a hotel first in New Hampshire, then later in Pasadena, after being lured there by a friend. Wentworth was so impressed with the opportunities that hotels offered, he built his own in 1906.

The Hotel Wentworth boasted 275 rooms built in a concrete-reinforced structure designed to be fireproof and resistant to damage by earthquakes. Unfortunately, the hotel did not open on time, since most laborers were in San Francisco following the Great Earthquake there. It suffered from a leaking roof, forcing many guests to move elsewhere. Wentworth was forced into bankruptcy but his neighbor would benefit from his financial difficulties.

Henry Huntington eventually married his aunt, Collis's widow, and they set out to create an extraordinary estate on the land in Pasadena. He admired the Wentworth Hotel near his estate, and when it became available, he bought it. Renovating, redesigning, and adding new rooms, he reopened it as the Huntington Hotel in 1914.

Huntington hired D. M. Linnard to manage his new property, and Linnard eventually convinced his son-in-law, Stephen Royce, to take over. Royce would not only manage the hotel for the next forty-five years, he also owned it for much of that time.

Royce was responsible for installing the first Olympic-sized swimming pool in California at the Huntington. He also changed the schedule so that the hotel remained open year-round, rather than closing during the summer as all other hotels had done. During the Great Depression, reorganization of the hotel's financial structure left Royce the sole owner. He weathered the banking collapse of 1933 by issuing "scrip" to be used within the hotel in place of money, which was in short supply. Some of this "money" is on display in the Smithsonian.

The hotel has passed through several owners, a number of renovations, and a complete reconstruction of the main building. Each successive owner and manager has added something to the Huntington Hotel, but all have worked hard to deliver the quality of service first envisioned when it was conceived. Today, the Langham management carries on the hotel's long tradition of providing elegance and luxury in the heart of historic Pasadena.

The Langham, Huntington Hotel & Spa
1401 South Oak Knoll Avenue
Pasadena, California 91106
(626) 568-3900

Blueberry Tart with Lavender Bavarian Cream and Crème Fraiche

BAVARIAN CREAM

Butterfly vanilla beans and scrape seeds out of center; add to milk. In saucepan, boil milk, lavender, and vanilla. In mixing bowl, mix the sugar, cornstarch, and yolks. Slowly pour hot milk onto the yolks, sugar, and cornstarch, whisking all the while.

Return mixture to saucepan and continue to cook on medium-low heat for 10 minutes, stirring with a wooden spoon and constantly being sure to scrape all parts of the bottom of the pan. Add butter and gelatin. Stir in until incorporated. Strain and cool.

When cool, whisk the mixture to soften, then fold in whipped cream. Put into pastry bag and chill until ready to assembly tarts.

TART

In a mixing bowl, using your hands, mix the butter and kataifi. On a baking sheet, form kataifi into 4-inch circles and sprinkle liberally with powered sugar. Bake in preheated oven 10–12 minutes or until golden brown. Allow to cool to room temperature before assembly.

Pipe the cream onto baked kataifi, ½-inch thick. Arrange blueberries on top. Sprinkle with remaining powered sugar.

BAVARIAN CREAM

2 vanilla beans

2 cups milk

4 lavender sprigs

⅓ cup sugar

1 tablespoon cornstarch

6 egg yolks

2 tablespoons butter

1½ sheets gelatin, rehydrated in ice water for 10 minutes

¼ cup whipped cream

TART

8 ounces kataifi (see note below)

4 ounces clarified butter

½ cup powered sugar, plus more for garnish

2 pints blueberries

½ cup crème fraiche

Mint sprigs for garnish

Streak plate with spoonfull of crème fraiche. Place tart. Garnish with mint.

Note: Kataifi is shredded filo dough and is kept frozen until ready to use. For best results, remove kataifi dough from freezer 1 hour before using.

"Forbidden Halibut"

Halibut with forbidden rice (black rice), kumquats, and coconut milk sauce

Sweat the onion in oil. Add rice and stock. Bring to simmer and cover. Simmer on low heat for 45 minutes. Season with salt and pepper.

To prepare kumquats, boil water and sugar together until dissolved. Pour over kumquats and let stand until cool.

To make sauce, heat the oil in a saucepan, then sweat onion and ginger in oil. Add remaining ingredients and simmer 10 minutes. Strain through fine sieve.

Sauté fish in vegetable oil. When done, place on top of rice. Garnish with kumquat slices and pour sauce around.

YIELD
Serves 2

RICE

¼ cup diced onion

1 tablespoon vegetable oil

½ cup forbidden rice

2 cups chicken stock

Salt and pepper

KUMQUATS

1 cup water

4 tablespoons sugar

4 kumquats, sliced

SAUCE

1 tablespoon vegetable oil

½ cup onion, finely diced

1 tablespoon ginger, chopped

¼ cup fish stock

½ cup unsweetened coconut milk

¼ cup cream

FISH

2 6-ounce fillets of halibut

2–3 tablespoons vegetable oil

1½-pound lobster per person

Butter, few pats for boiling, few
pats melted for lobster

Salt and pepper

SAUCE

1 tablespoon butter

2 shallots, finely chopped

1 tablespoon ginger root,
finely chopped

½ teaspoon green curry

½ cup white wine

1 cup carrot juice

1 cup vegetable stock (chicken
stock can be used)

Juice of 2 limes

½ cup unsweetened coconut milk

½ cup heavy cream

1 bunch cilantro

Roasted Lobster with Fideuà, English Peas, Shiitake Mushrooms and Spicy Carrot Coconut Milk Sauce

Fideuà (toasted vermicelli) melds nicely with the vegetables and sauce to create a bed for the roasted lobster.

LOBSTERS

Bring a large pot of water to boil. Add butter. Place lobsters in and boil for 4 minutes. Remove and cool into ice water. Pull claws from body. Crack shell by tapping with the back of a heavy knife to release the meat within. Remove claw meat and reserve.

With a large knife, cut lobster tail in half to butterfly. Remove vein if in tail. Brush with butter and season with salt and pepper.

When ready to serve, heat skillet pan to medium-high heat and preheat oven to 400 degrees. Place lobster, meat side down, and cook in pan on stovetop until lightly brown. Turn onto other side (shell-side down), add claws, and place in oven for 5 minutes. Remove and serve.

SAUCE

In saucepan, melt butter on medium heat. Add shallots and ginger. Cook until tender. Add green curry and wine, simmer and reduce wine by half. Add remaining sauce ingredients and simmer for 1 hour. Strain.

FIDEUÀ

Break dry vermicelli into 1-to-2-inch pieces. On medium heat in a saucepan, add oil and dry pasta, stirring constantly with a wooden spoon until brown. Add chicken stock, continuing to stir until liquid is evaporated. Add shiitake mushrooms and peas. Finish pasta with butter, salt, and pepper.

Place Fideuà and sauce on plate and top with lobster.

FIDEUÀ

8 ounces vermicelli pasta

2 tablespoons vegetable oil

2 cups chicken stock

8 shiitake mushrooms, sliced

8 ounces English peas

3 ounces butter

Salt and pepper

SAN YSIDRO RANCH

When the Spanish explorers came to Santa Barbara and displaced the Native Americans, they took ownership and title to the property in the name of the king of Spain. It was common during those times for the king to reward the explorers and noblemen of his country with land grants, which put some of the property into private hands.

In some cases, various parts of the countryside were given to the church for its missionary work in trying to convert the Indians to Christianity. The first mission was built in San Diego in 1769. Over the next 54 years, the padres constructed 21 missions along the California coast, stretching from San Diego to San Francisco.

The Santa Barbara Mission was built in 1786, partially destroyed by a severe earthquake in 1925, and rebuilt to its present condition. Considered to be one of the most beautiful of all the remaining missions, the Santa Barbara Mission is the only one that has been continuously under the control of the Franciscans since its original construction. Many of the other missions were secularized by Mexican law after that country became independent of Spain in 1821.

The Franciscans traveled extensively throughout California territory while building their network of missions. The San Ysidro Ranch site, which was part of one of the original land grants, was first developed as a way station for the Franciscan padres in the late 1700s. Once the completed Santa Barbara Mission took in the traveling monks, the way station became a citrus ranch.

Known originally as the San Ysidro Citrus Ranch, and later as the Johnston Fruit Company, the ranch produced an average of 300,000 oranges and 100,000 lemons annually. A large sandstone packing house was built in 1889 to handle the citrus production. Today, that sandstone structure is the ranch's acclaimed Stonehouse Restaurant.

As agriculture turned to ranching, an adobe ranch house was built on the property in 1825. Still standing today, it is referred to as the "Old Adobe" and is one of the most unique private dining rooms in the state. Later, in 1892, a more substantial ranch house was built on the property. Only one year later, the ranch began to accept guests; the newer ranch house now serves as the guest check-in area and as a living room for guests to relax and socialize.

During the 1930s, British Oscar-winning actor Ronald Colman came to town. Having successfully made the transition from silent movies to "talkies" and an acclaimed role in *A Tale of Two Cities*, Colman, along with former Senator Alvin Carl Weingand, acquired the ranch and transformed it into an elegant retreat. The idyllic setting and personalized service attracted everyone, but their

extra effort to guard the privacy of guests made the ranch particularly attractive to celebrities and luminaries from around the world.

Famous guests over the years include Audrey Hepburn, Lucille Ball, Bing Crosby, Groucho Marx, Winston Churchill, Somerset Maugham, and Sinclair Lewis. Vivien Leigh and Laurence Olivier were married at the ranch, John and Jacqueline Kennedy honeymooned there, and John Huston completed the script for *African Queen* during a three-month stay.

The Santa Ysidro Ranch is located in the exclusive enclave of Montecito, just minutes from downtown Santa Barbara and 90 miles north of Los Angeles. Forty cottages offer fireplaces, private patios, sunken hot tubs, and elegant seclusion.

According to local legend, San Ysidro—Spanish for Saint Isadore, who was the patron saint of Madrid—was such a kind and caring shepherd that the Lord sent a guardian angel to watch over his flock while he tended to the sick and needy. It is this legendary example of selfless service that inspires the hospitality of the ranch today.

San Ysidro Ranch, A Rosewood Resort
900 San Ysidro Lane
Santa Barbara, California 93108
(805) 565-1700
(800) 368-6788

CRUST

3 ounces butter

6 ounces graham cracker crumbs

2 ounces sugar

FILLING

7½ ounces egg yolks

2¼ cups condensed milk

1 cup key lime juice

Key Lime Pie

Preheat oven to 350 degrees. Melt the butter and combine with the cracker crumbs and sugar for the crust. Press mixture down into an 8-inch pan and make it even on all the sides. Bake for about 8 minutes until golden brown.

Mix the yolks in a mixer for about 10 minutes until pale yellow. Add the condensed milk and key lime juice and mix until combined. Pour filling over crust and bake for about 10 minutes until it is set.

Let cool and set in refrigerator for 1 hour before slicing and serving.

Blackberry Clafoutis

Whisk the eggs and sugar in a bowl until pale yellow. Add milk, vanilla extract, and salt. Sift flour over the batter and fold in.

Cut blackberries in half. Using a melon baller, scoop a few scoops of batter into each ramekin. Then place cheese and berries on top, then pour remaining batter over cheese and berries. Bake at 350 degrees for 8–10 minutes until puffy and custard is set.

‿ YIELD ‿
Serves 6

6 eggs

⅔ cup sugar

2 cups milk

1 tablespoon vanilla extract

Pinch salt

1 cup all-purpose flour

1 pint blackberries

1 quart mascarpone cheese

11 ounces chocolate

4 ounces butter

8 ounces sugar

3 eggs

1½ teaspoons coffee extract

1½ teaspoons vanilla extract

3½ ounces all purpose flour

½ teaspoon baking powder

¼ salt

8 ounces white chocolate chips

Double Chocolate Chip Cookies

Melt the chocolate and butter together over a double boiler. Combine the sugar, eggs, and extracts in a mixing bowl. Once chocolate and butter are melted together, add sugar and egg mix.

Add all the dry ingredients and mix until combined. Add white chocolate chips. Scoop out on to a sheet pan. Bake at 350 degrees for about 8 minutes.

THE SKY ROOM

The Breakers Hotel first opened in 1926. Serving thousands of visitors as an exclusive waterfront resort, it was a favorite playground for many of the well-to-do. Long Beach was severely damaged by a very large earthquake in 1933, which destroyed buildings for miles around. The city slowly rebuilt itself over the next two decades, eventually attracting the motion picture industry.

In the process of building the Hilton hotel empire, Conrad Hilton acquired The Breakers in 1938, making it the eighth in the chain. The Sky Room restaurant had been the Penthouse, high atop The Breakers Hotel, when Hilton decided to convert it into a restaurant.

Hilton's prominence in the community caused many stars and celebrities to be attracted to The Sky Room: Charles Lindbergh, Babe Ruth, Clark Gable, Merle Oberon, Errol Flynn, Cary Grant, and many more. Elizabeth Taylor spent her first of eight honeymoons at the Breakers Hotel, when she married Nicky Hilton, the son of Conrad Hilton.

Long Beach was well known as the motion picture capital of the world—until after World War I when Hollywood supplanted it. Offering the world-famous balmy Southern California climate, Long Beach was the perfect setting for the industry. Eight film houses, two stock companies, and various amusements were located along the shore of downtown Long Beach. The most famous tenet was the Balboa Amusement Production Company, the world's most prolific silent-film studio. W. C. Fields and other stars occupied beautiful mansions in the Bluff Park neighborhood along Ocean Boulevard and First Street, and many of these homes remain in the families to this day.

A visit to The Sky Room restaurant, with its newly renovated Art Deco design, will bring you back to the Supper Club era of the 1920s and 1930s. This Spanish Baroque–style, sandstone-colored landmark offers a stunning 360-degree view of the harbor and city of Long Beach.

The Sky Room
40 South Locust Avenue
Long Beach, California 90802
(562) 983-2703

1 head iceberg lettuce, chopped

4 boiled eggs, quartered

1 hothouse cucumber, halved
  with skin

3 Roma tomatoes, quartered

1 ounce Italian parsley, chopped

6 each red radish, sliced

DRESSING

2 cups mayonnaise

3 tablespoons Dijon mustard

1 tablespoon fresh garlic, chopped

1 tablespoon fresh lemon juice

Salade Maman

To prepare this dish in a single bowl, make the salad dressing first, mixing thoroughly and seasoning to taste. Then add all salad ingredients and toss with dressing.

YIELD
Serves 2

Sautéed Jumbo Tiger Shrimp

Sautee shrimp in olive oil for about 2 minutes with fresh garlic. Add white wine and lemon juice. Cook down and reduce sauce. Add butter and salt and pepper to taste. Serve hot.

YIELD
Serves 2 or 3

6 jumbo tiger shrimp

1½ ounces olive oil

2 tablespoons fresh garlic, chopped

½ cup of white wine

2 tablespoons lemon juice

4 ounces unsalted butter

RICE MIXTURE

2 cups Valencia rice

4 ounces olive oil

1 each red and green bell pepper, chopped

1 yellow onion, chopped

4 ounces fresh garlic, chopped

1 pound chorizo

1 cup white wine

2 pounds tomato, pureed

4 cups chicken stock

Pinch saffron

SEAFOOD

1 pound of clams

½ pound black mussels

1 ounce garlic

4 ounces chorizo

10 ounces chicken breast, cubed

Pinch saffron

10 ounces shrimp (21–25)

4 ounces halibut, swordfish, or salmon

Salt and pepper, to taste

Seafood Paella

RICE MIXTURE

Cook rice with olive oil in large pot until golden brown. Add bell peppers, onion, and garlic; sauté until transparent.

In a separate pan, cook chorizo until done, then add to rice mixture.

Add white wine, stir and bring to a light boil. Stir in tomato puree and boil for 5 minutes. Add chicken stock and saffron. Keep warm.

Prepare seafood, as listed below, then add to rice mixture and serve.

SEAFOOD

Sauté clams and mussels until slightly open. Add garlic, chorizo, and chicken to sauté pan. Add saffron. Stir lightly, then add remaining shrimp and fish.

Mix seafood mixture with the rice. Add salt and pepper to taste before service.

YIELD

Serves 4

TAIX FRENCH RESTAURANT

In 1769, Gaspar de Portolá led a Spanish expedition to Alta California and discovered this quiet, beautiful valley full of Gabriellino Indians. He named the river El Río de Nuestra Señora La Reina de Los Angeles de Porciúncula, which translates to The River of Our Lady Queen of the Angels of Porciúncula. The shorter version of the river's name, Los Angeles, eventually led to the name of the city.

Spanish control over New Spain ended in 1821 with the declaration of independence by Mexico. This opened the way for settlers from other nations to come to the Americas to seek their fortunes. A large influx of French immigrants began to arrive in the Los Angeles area around 1828.

By 1832, the French settlers had planted the first vineyards in California using imported European grapevines. Various others had discovered local wild grapes earlier and planted vineyards using these varieties, but the French decided that it would be necessary to bring some samples of the best vines from their homeland to capitalize on the local weather. Little did they realize how much competition their efforts would eventually offer the French wine industry.

So many French immigrants came to California following the decline in Spain's influence that by 1853, there were an estimated 28,000 French inhabitants. By 1860, almost 10 percent of the Los Angeles population was French. In addition to working in wineries, they also worked in lumber mills and flour mills and as ranchers, militiamen, vegetable and orange grove farmers, gold miners, and butchers.

One of the early Los Angeles bakery shop owners was Jacques Taix, as were his five brothers. They had arrived in Los Angeles from southeastern France around 1870, having considerable experience as bakers and sheepherders.

The Taix family stayed prominent in food service. In 1912, Marius Taix Sr. built a hotel called the Champ d'Or in the French Quarter of downtown Los Angeles. The demands of their guests prompted his son Marius Taix Jr. to open Taix French Restaurant in the hotel in 1927. Chicken dinners were very popular at 50 cents each, both with guests and locals. Diners who preferred the privacy of a booth over their family-style tables could get the same meal for 75 cents.

The Taix family moved the restaurant to its present location in 1962. They have exchanged their family-style service for all private booths, but maintained their reputation for abundant portions of French country cuisine at affordable prices. Now run by Marius's son, Raymond Taix, and

through the influence of his son Michael, Taix French Restaurant offers excellent food and great wine selections.

The 321 Lounge, located within Taix French Restaurant, is named after the original location of the restaurant at 321 Commercial St. in downtown Los Angeles.

Taix French Restaurant
1911 Sunset Boulevard
Los Angeles, California 90026
(213) 484-1265

Braised Lamb Shanks

Use a very large skillet or Dutch oven, enough to hold 3–4 gallons of liquid. Heat pan over medium heat and add olive oil. Then dust the lamb shanks with flour and cook to sear until brown.

Remove the lamb shanks and add the sausage pieces until cooked, then all of the vegetables, garlic, then tomato paste. Add the shanks back to the pan, along with the red wine, stock, and herbs. Bring to a boil and cover. Cook in the oven for about 2 hours until tender. Season to taste and serve.

(Reduce ingredients 2 to 4 times for the home cook.)

1 cup olive oil

Flour, for dusting

24 pieces lamb shanks

3 ounces spicy sausages, sliced

4 fennel bulbs

6 carrots peeled and diced

2 stalks celery diced

6 onions diced

3 handfuls garlic cloves cleaned

2 tablespoons tomato paste

2 bottles red wine

2 gallons chicken stock

2 bay leaves

Thyme

Salt and pepper to taste

40 egg yolks

6 cups sugar

1 gallon heavy cream

4 vanilla beans

Crème Brulee

Break the egg yolks and stir with sugar until combined and pale yellow. Stir in heavy cream. Split the vanilla beans, scoop out the seeds, and let pods stay in mixture. Strain mixture in a chinois. Place into ramekins and bake in a bain-marie at 250 degrees for 2 hours.

YIELD

(Reduce ingredients 3 to 4 times for the home cook.)

½ ounce butter

4 ounces mashed potatoes

2 ounces blue cheese

¼ cup heavy cream

Blue Cheese Mashed Potatoes

In a saucepan, melt the butter, add the potatoes, and stir with a spatula until like a paste. Add the cream and the blue cheese. Season to taste.

THE US GRANT

As California moved toward statehood, the Spanish and Mexican settlers clashed with those who came from the Atlantic Coast. The Mexican-American War of 1846–1848 was particularly brutal on the Native Americans, who were forced to pick one side or the other—or be caught in the middle. Due to war, disease, and an influx of settlers with claims to the land, the Kumeyaay Indian population around San Diego Bay was reduced from 30,000 to around 3,000.

Formal statehood in 1850 saw treaties negotiated with the various Indian tribes of California, but they were not ratified by the U.S. Senate. Twenty-five years later, President Ulysses S. Grant set aside 640 acres for the use of the Kumeyaay Tribe. Interestingly, this would not be the last time the Grant family would have a hand in San Diego's history. Nor would this be the end of the Kumeyaay Indians' story.

As San Diego grew, a merchant from San Francisco, Alonzo Horton, arrived in 1867. He immediately fell in love with the place and purchased 960 acres of what is now the downtown area for the sum of $265. Following through on his dream, he laid out streets and sold lots to encourage development in his area of town. Horton deliberately made the blocks small, thus ensuring there were more valuable corners to sell. He built and opened the Horton House in 1870, the first luxury hotel in town. Horton had sealed his destiny as the Father of New Town San Diego.

In 1895, the hotel and surrounding property was purchased for $56,000 by Fannie Chaffee Grant, the wife of Ulysses S. Grant Jr. and the daughter-in-law of the eighteenth president. They had moved to California for the economic opportunity and they hoped the weather would improve her health.

California life was good for the Grants, and they decided that the Horton Hotel should be replaced with a much larger structure to be named after the former president and Civil War hero. They demolished the Horton in July 1905, with 91-year-old Horton participating in the event. Work was immediately begun on its replacement, but the Great Earthquake of 1906 caused all available workers and supplies in the state to go to San Francisco to help rebuild the city.

Work resumed in 1908 when financier Louis J. Wilde stepped in to help. Unfortunately, Fannie Grant died in 1909, but the US Grant Hotel opened with great fanfare in October of 1910 at a final cost of $1.9 million, a staggering sum at the time. Wilde went on to become one of the city's first mayors, and used his influence to make sure that the boulevard in front of the hotel was widened to ensure guests retained the uninterrupted view of the ocean.

The US Grant was full of modern amenities. Most of the rooms had a private bath. Italian marble was used for the Grand Staircase. A garden terrace above the lobby was eventually turned into the hotel's Grand Ballroom. Two saltwater swimming tanks were built on the lower level, with a direct waterline running to the bay. The hotel also offered shower baths, ladies' hair drying rooms and lockers, disrobing apartments, and billiards for the gentlemen. The Grant also included a lavish marble and onyx "Ladies Foyer," allowing these guests private access to the hotel.

Following the death of Fannie, Ulysses Grant Jr. secretly remarried a young San Diego widowed socialite named America Workman Will. In 1913, they moved into a 6th-floor suite at the hotel until 1919.

In 1915, the Pan-Pacific Exposition, designed to commemorate the Panama Canal, came to San Diego. While the exposition was built on barren land east of downtown, which later would become Balboa Park, the dignitaries stayed at the US Grant. Today, Balboa Park is host to the largest collection of museums in a single urban setting in the United States.

Charles Lindberg stayed at the Grant in April 1927 while his *Spirit of St. Louis* airplane was being built at the Ryan Aeronautical Company in San Diego. Lindberg made his historical flight from New York to Paris on May 21, 1927. Ulysses S. Grant Jr. passed away in 1929 while still in residence at the hotel. His widow, America Workman Will Grant remained in the hotel until her death in 1942.

The US Grant has passed through several owners over the decades, while several presidents passed through the Grant as guests. Woodrow Wilson came to visit in 1919. Franklin D. Roosevelt opened the California Pacific International Exposition in Balboa Park on October 2, 1935, and later addressed the national media from the 11th-floor radio station atop the US Grant. First Lady Mamie Eisenhower visited in 1960. Jimmy Carter attended his Naval Academy Class of 1947 reunion at the US Grant in the fall of 2000.

On December 3, 2003, the Sycuan Band of the Kumeyaay Indians purchased the hotel for $45 million: The land had come full circle with ownership returning to its original ancestors. Even though the hotel has been listed on the National Registry of Historic Places since 1979, a major

renovation and management by Starwood has recently returned the US Grant to its position as one of the preeminent hotels in San Diego.

The US Grant
326 Broadway
San Diego, California 92101
(619) 232-3121

2 ounces mirepoix (onions, celery, leeks, medium diced)

½ ounce olive oil

2½ cobs white corn, fresh

½ ounce white wine

2 bay leaves

2 sprigs thyme

½ quart vegetable stock

1 sprig chervil

½ teaspoon micro cilantro

1 coriander seed oil

White Corn Soup

Sauté the onions, celery, and leeks in olive oil until soft. Cut the kernels from the corncobs, and add the corn. Continue to cook on low heat for 20 minutes.

Add white wine and let the mixture reduce by half. Add bay and thyme for flavoring. Add vegetable stock and continue cooking for another 10 minutes.

Puree soup until creamy and smooth. Strain soup and garnish with chervil, micro cilantro, and coriander oil. Serve.

YIELD
Serves 1

"I feel a recipe is only a theme, which an intelligent cook can play each time with a variation."

—Madame Benoit

Dayboat Diver Scallops

Crust scallops on one side with porcini powder and set aside.

Place apple juice on low heat and reduce until syrup consistency. Set aside for later.

In sauté pan, add olive oil, and sauté shallots, garlic, saffron, and tomatoes together, and allow it to cook on low heat for 10 minutes. Add fish stock and season with salt and pepper and set aside. This is your sauce.

In another sauté pan, heat olive oil and sear scallops on side with porcini powder until golden brown. Turn over and sear other side until golden brown. Let this cook until scallops are medium rare. Add leeks at last moment to pan for 1 minute.

To plate dish, place scallops on leeks, then place tomato saffron sauce over scallops. Drizzle apple reduction over scallops as a finishing touch.

YIELD

Serves 1

4 U-8 scallops

1 teaspoon porcini powder

16 ounces apple juice

1 teaspoon olive oil

1 ounce shallot

1 ounce garlic

6 strands saffron

3 tomatoes for chutney

4 ounces fish stock

2 teaspoons salt

Pepper

½ cup julienned leeks

2 medium-sized heirloom
tomatoes (such as zebra
or brandy)

3 ounces Burrata mozzarella

1 teaspoon olive oil

Pinch of black pepper

¼ teaspoon sea salt

¼ once truffle oil

2 ounces 50-year-old balsamic
vinegar

1 teaspoon basil oil

Heirloom Tomato Salad

Cut tomatoes into wedges and place in circle on plate.
Place the Burrata cheese in the middle of the tomatoes. Drizzle olive oil and sprinkle salt and pepper
on tomatoes and cheese. Drizzle truffle oil, balsamic
vinegar, and basil oil over tomatoes and serve at room
temperature.

YIELD
Serves 1

RESTAURANT INDEX

RECIPE INDEX